INTO THE WORLD

How Waldorf Graduates Fare After High School

Written by
Ilan Safit, Ph.D. and Douglas Gerwin, Ph.D.

with
Connie Stokes, M.S. and Andrew Starzynski, M.S.

A Survey by the
RESEARCH INSTITUTE FOR WALDORF EDUCATION
2019

Into the World: How Waldorf Graduates Fare After High School

This research was made possible by the generous funding of
the Waldorf Educational Foundation, the Waldorf Curriculum Fund,
the Grace Charitable Foundation, and Charlton Campbell Hughes

Authors: Ilan Saft, Ph.D. and Douglas Gerwin, Ph.D.
Research and Management: Connie Stokes, M.S. and Andrew Starzywski, M.S.
Research Survey: Research Institute for Waldorf Education
Layout Design: Maris Van de Roer
Cover Design: Maris Van de Roer
Tables/Graphics: Andrew Starzywski, M.S.
Proofreader: Ruth Riegel, M.S.

In collaborations with the Association of Waldorf Schools of North America (AWSNA)
and the National Association of Independent Schools (NAIS)

Waldorf Publications
ISBN 978-1-943582-36-5

Contents

Into The World:
How Waldorf Graduates Fare After High School

INTRODUCTION

I look into the world
In which the sun is shining,
In which the stars are sparkling,
In which the stones repose;
Where living plants are growing,
Where sentient beasts are living,
Where human souls on earth
Give dwelling to the Spirit.

With these or similar words of translation, a growing number of children and adolescents in Waldorf schools around the world begin each day. The verse, originally written by Rudolf Steiner at the founding of the first Waldorf school in Stuttgart one hundred years ago, summons students to look into the world and notice its various marvels, then look into their own being as they invoke strength and blessing "for learning and for work."

By now, this verse, recited from fifth grade through the high-school grades, is spoken around the world in well over a thousand schools in some 65 countries. One can say that at virtually every hour of the day, somewhere on the globe, groups of students are beginning their Waldorf school day with this verse.

Less than a decade after its founding in Germany, Waldorf education was introduced into North America. Since the summer of 1943, Waldorf high-school graduates on this continent have been stepping into the world equipped with the skills and unique formative experiences designed—in the words of Steiner's wife, Marie von Sivers—"to develop free human beings who are able of themselves to impart purpose and direction to their lives."

For the past 15 years, the Research Institute for Waldorf Education (RIWE) has tracked North American independent Waldorf graduates in their studies as well as their professional and personal lives post high school. The current survey, focusing on the most recent quarter-century of graduates from the Class of 1990 through the Class of 2017, has employed several methods of collecting information, impressions, and testimonials from Waldorf alumni[1] and some of their teachers. Online questionnaires, face-to-face interviews, published statements, and written testimonials have been processed through statistical analysis to draw a general portrait of a Waldorf graduate.

For the first time, we can compare Waldorf graduates to alumni from other U.S. independent schools, thanks to collaborative research with the National Association of Independent Schools (NAIS). Specifically, NAIS shared with us its own questionnaire of independent school graduates as well as the results of their most recent survey of this population. In addition, we offer a few statistical comparisons with the general U.S. population, drawing upon official government data. (Canada, we discovered, does not collect comparable statistics.)

Based on responses to our latest survey, our own data tell us that 98% of Waldorf alumni attend college and that a growing number—especially among the younger graduates—major in Social Science and in the so-called STEM (Science, Technology, Engineering, and Math) subjects. We also see that the most popular fields in which alumni develop a professional career include education, followed by medicine and the health services.

Beyond the statistical results, we record narrative comments, face-to-face interviews, and some personal essays and speeches intended to add detail and nuance to the statistical data. We quote at length from these comments, including in Chapters VII and VIII sample transcripts of interviews and some personal narratives. We encourage readers to pay close attention to the descriptions, reflections, and views of alumni in their own words.

From the outset, it needs to be stated that our aim is not to evaluate Waldorf education—and certainly not to assess the efficacy of specific schools from which survey respondents and interviewees have graduated. Instead, our intention is to collect descriptions, describe data, analyze aggregated information, detect trends, and deliver the words of alumni as they said or wrote them. In short, our aim is to explore

---

1   Throughout this work, we will be using the Latin and gendered word "alumni" as if it was an English word, therefore ungendered, to signify the plural form of high-school graduates of any gender whatsoever.

the long-term impact of Waldorf education rather than sing its praise. Another aim is to listen to and communicate voices of criticism and complaint in order to present a fuller picture of what students perceived—both during their time in Waldorf high school and in retrospect—as shortcomings in need of improvement.

Since this latest survey was designed specifically to focus on graduates from the last decade of the 20th century and the first 17 years of this century, we need to note the advent of at least two dramatic and all-pervasive transformations during this period of time. The first is the high-tech revolution, from the introduction of personal computers and the rise of the internet to the ubiquitous use of smartphones and the explosion of social media. The second involves what might be called the mainstreaming of progressive ethics, in which long-lasting social hierarchies are challenged and rejected in favor of diversity as a blanket term for advancing social equality. The story of the Waldorf graduate who has stepped into the world in the midst of this dramatic period, and whose early adult experiences have been shaped by such technological and cultural shifts, cannot be told in isolation from these current trends. We will have to remember that we are not describing here any group of Waldorf alumni but specifically North American, millennial graduates whose progressive elementary and secondary education has often led them to progressive colleges and lifestyles.

The study that follows is divided into 11 chapters, starting with an historical perspective and description of methods used in the survey and proceeding to separate analyses of responses first from college-aged, then post-college students. Summaries and excerpts of face-to-face interviews and correspondence with alumni and their teachers flesh out these responses in their own words. We devote a separate chapter to the graduates' responses to their ongoing relationship to their schools as alumni, as these stand in stark contrast to responses of alumni from other independent schools polled by NAIS. A closing section of overarching conclusions, as well as a list of acknowledgements, suggestions for further reading, and a series of appendices, completes this document.

I Historical Background of this Project

In the first year after its inauguration in Stuttgart as a grades 1–8 school in September 1919, the original *"Freie Waldorf Schule"* was enlarged to include the beginnings of a high school with the addition of a ninth grade. This means the Class of 1924 constituted the world's first Waldorf high-school alumni. Rudolf Steiner, the founder of Waldorf education and mentor to the school, traveled to Stuttgart at Easter of that year to bestow on the graduates a school leave-taking verse that to this day is given to Waldorf Seniors around the world.

The initial growth in the number of Waldorf schools was slow, but the increase in the number of Waldorf high schools was even slower, especially in North America. The Rudolf Steiner School in New York City, the first Waldorf school of North America, was founded in 1928 but did not graduate a high-school senior class until 1959, some thirty years later. In fact, the first Waldorf high school on this continent was not the Steiner School in Manhattan but rather a rural boarding and day high school in the southeast New Hampshire town of Wilton. High Mowing School opened its doors—and its dormitories—in September 1942, during the depths of World War II, and graduated its first senior class the following spring in June of 1943.

For the next three decades, the growth of Waldorf high schools on this continent was modest yet steady. What is now called the Waldorf School of Garden City, located on the campus of Adelphi University on Long Island, inaugurated its high school in 1956, with its first seniors graduating in the summer of 1960. Two more high schools— including the first one for handicapped children—were added in Kimberton, PA, just west of Philadelphia, during the mid-1960s, and Highland Hall, the first Waldorf school on the West Coast, opened a high school in Los Angeles in the fall of 1968. Three more high schools—including the first in Canada—opened during the 1970s and a further four during the 1980s. (A few other Waldorf schools, not included in this tally, briefly initiated a high school but then dropped back to having just elementary grades.)

It was only in the 1990s that the number of Waldorf high schools began to take off, with a burst of 13 new high schools that are still running strong today (in addition to a couple of schools that lasted just a few years). In effect, the number of Waldorf high schools on the North American continent doubled in a single decade from 13 to 26. This growth spurt slowed during the first decade of the current millennium—10 new high schools plus a few more short-lived attempts—and an additional six high schools during the present decade, including two brand-new ventures launched in the fall of 2018.

During the 2018-19 school year, there were 42 Waldorf high schools in English-speaking North America—four in Canada, and 38 in the United States. In addition, we can count 13 schools that opened high-school grades but closed them after graduating only a few senior classes, or in some cases even before reaching a 12th grade.

Over the years, there have been various informal surveys of these schools, but the first formal study was conducted between 2005-2007 in three phases by Douglas Gerwin and David Mitchell, who at the time were the co-directors of the Research Institute for Waldorf Education (RIWE). *Survey of Waldorf Graduates, Phase I*, though published by RIWE in book form, was little more than a listing of universities where Waldorf graduates had applied and been accepted. The most striking result of this first phase was the very broad range of colleges and universities that accepted Waldorf graduates. Of the 20 categories of college enumerated by the Carnegie Foundation, 18 were present in this list; colleges accepting exclusively Native Americans or specialized undergraduate training institutions were the only two categories not represented on this list.

Survey of Waldorf Graduates, Phase II, which came out two years later (2007), was conducted in conjunction with a survey of German Waldorf graduates that included many questions, some of them of Teutonic length and complexity, concerning the graduates' *college life, professional life,* and *personal life.* In all, some 550 Waldorf alumni from 26 high schools and spanning more than 60 years (from that first High Mowing Class of 1943 to graduates from the youngest high schools of 2005) responded via an online survey. The results of that survey were supplemented by comments from two sources: college professors who had taught Waldorf students as undergraduates, as well as employers who had hired Waldorf graduates.

From the data provided by the graduates, we created an overall statistical "profile" of a typical Waldorf graduate, based on the responses submitted by individual respondents:

94% attended college, and **88**% graduated or were about to graduate with a degree

47% majored in the arts or humanities, while 42% majored in the sciences or math

96% highly valued inter-personal relationships

94% described themselves as being self-reliant and valuing self-confidence

93% valued verbal expression and 92% valued critical thinking

91% reported practicing life-long learning

90% highly valued tolerance and viewpoints other than their own

89% were highly satisfied in their choice of occupation

82% cared most about ethical principles in the workplace and greatly valued helping others

Some of these statistics, when compared to the general U.S. population, demonstrated that Waldorf alumni were up to twice as likely to have majored in science as undergrads, whereas students from the general population, when compared to Waldorf alumni, were about four times more likely to major in business and management. While considerably fewer Waldorf alumni majored in education as undergraduates, compared to the national average, these same alumni elected the teaching profession over all other professional fields (14%) later in life. This suggested to us that Waldorf alumni use their undergraduate education as a time for learning and expanding their horizons rather than as training for a specific profession.

A professional life in the arts accounted for one in five of the younger alumni, one in six among the older graduates—lower than might be expected of graduates of a school that stressed the arts to such a high degree in its curriculum. Overall, the five most popular professions—education, fine and studio arts, administration, performing arts, and health or medicine—all suggested the possession of strong social skills among these Waldorf educated professionals.

When it came to assess their professional lives, participants were asked to rank the aspects of their current or most recent employment from 1 to 5 on a scale of greatest importance (from "totally unimportant" to "extremely important"). Highest scores went to "good work atmosphere," which was rated as very important or extremely important by 94% of the respondents, while not a single respondent rated this aspect as being totally unimportant or unimportant. Next highest aspects included "ethical principles of the profession," "chance to help others," "chance to introduce one's own ideas," and "self-reliance at work," all of which were rated as very or extremely important by more than 80% of the respondents. Barely 2% of respondents rated these aspects as being unimportant.

By contrast, only 26% of the respondents rated "high income" as being very or extremely important, whereas an almost equal 24% rated this aspect of their job as being totally unimportant or unimportant. Similarly, just 25% rated "life-long security" as being very or extremely important, while 35% characterized this aspect of their work as being either totally unimportant or unimportant. Taken together, the topmost rankings representing what Waldorf graduates valued most highly about their jobs underscored the theme of social awareness and concern, whereas the least-valued rankings all had to do with self-interest and personal security.

In a separate question, Waldorf graduates were asked to choose three life skills to which they attached most importance. *Communication*, *truthfulness*, *problem solving*, and *ethical values* were held in the highest regard. The respondents also placed a much higher value on *initiative* than on leadership, sociability, or reputation. Wealth and control received the lowest rankings in importance.

Regarding their personal values, the survey showed that Waldorf graduates highly value human relationships, and they work actively to cultivate them. In all, 96% placed an extremely or very high value on friendships, and 78% found their friendships to be very or extremely satisfactory. By contrast, not a single respondent spoke of friendships as having no or only slight value, and just 2% felt either somewhat or extremely dissatisfied with their friendships. In response to the question, "What has been your greatest gift this far in life?," respondents cited most often their immediate family. They also cited as gifts or joys—but also sometimes as major challenges—friends and relationships, secondary education, artistic practice, helping others, health and illness, and the cultivation of a balanced private and professional life. Several respondents noted that their greatest gifts were also their greatest challenges—for instance, their children, marriages, relationship with parents, or state of physical well-being.

Finally, in statistical and narrative responses assessing their Waldorf education, the Waldorf graduates taking part in this Phase II survey overwhelmingly endorsed their experience, even if they voiced some concerns about the treatment of science and math, especially during the high-school years. While a few felt they were not sufficiently well prepared for college, a great majority reported they entered college ready to take on its challenges. In the words of one respondent, "I didn't know it at the time, but my academic preparation in high school was more than adequate for the rest of my academic career, and my artistic and spiritual preparation put me on more comfortable footing in life than some of my peers."

In the final questions about their education, Waldorf graduates by an overwhelming ratio of 10 to 1 said they would send their own children to a Waldorf school if they could, though a third of these respondents qualified their answer to say that it would depend on proximity and cost.

Survey of Waldorf Graduates, Phase III, published a year later in 2008, recapitulated the main findings of Phase II and offered some further analysis and critique of these findings, along with comparisons to surveys of Waldorf students conducted in Europe. Specific attention was paid in this final phase to the graduates' concerns about their education, including the lack of resources in many schools, the small size of some classes, and the shortcomings of what were perceived to be inadequately trained teachers. Some students complained, as one of them put it, that "Waldorf education awoke my interest in too many areas and now I find it difficult to select one specific career choice." Others remarked that their schools did not keep up contact with them once they had graduated, while others felt the school needed stronger organization both in terms of student discipline and school governance and administration. A few felt the school could have done more to prepare them in terms of sex education and computer technology. Asked whether Waldorf education prepares one for life beyond high school, one student responded: "No! I am totally lacking in competitiveness." Another remarked, "I had a problem sticking with rules. At Waldorf if you wrote a paper over the maximum assigned, the teacher would not care. In college I received an "F" for exceeding the maximum by one page."

Many of these comments and critiques now resurface a decade later in the current study. A more detailed comparison of the previous and current survey can be found in Chapter X of this report.

II Research Methods and Resources

The Research Institute for Waldorf Education (RIWE) formally contacted all 39 North American Waldorf high schools with 12th grades in October of 2017, inviting them to take part in a survey of Waldorf alumni who had graduated between 1990 and 2017. Building on the RIWE's previous survey of Waldorf graduates a decade earlier, schools were informed that the goals of this latest poll were:

> To inform school communities of how our graduates are doing in the world after their formal high-school education.

> To highlight aspects of Waldorf education that work well and examine aspects that need review and revision.

> To publish an updated version of "The Results of Waldorf Education," which summarized the results of the 2007 survey of Waldorf graduates, in time for the celebration worldwide of the 100th anniversary of Waldorf education.

High schools were asked to update their lists of students who graduated between 1990 and 2017, including current college-age students. "Graduates" were defined as students completing the 12th grade, regardless of the year they enrolled in a Waldorf school.

Each school completed its own demographic survey that included the year its high school was founded, the year of the first graduating class, total number of graduates since that first graduating class, total number of 12th-grade graduates from 1990-2017, percentage of 8th graders continuing on into the high school, percentage of graduates going on to college, junior college, or taking a gap year. The schools were also asked to describe their alumni programs and state how many, if any, Waldorf graduates are now Waldorf faculty or staff members.

Through our partnership with the Association of Waldorf Schools of North America (AWSNA), we contacted the National Association of Independent Schools (NAIS) and asked them to co-administer this project. NAIS agreed to manage the survey on our behalf as part of an experiment in which NAIS conducted a poll of multiple schools that associated together under the umbrella of a single organization (AWSNA). AWSNA and many of our schools are members of NAIS. The survey included all 39 Waldorf high schools in North America with graduating seniors—36 in the U.S. and three in Canada.

RIWE used the NAIS template in order to be able to compare—for the first time ever—responses of Waldorf graduates with alumni from other independent schools. While using the NAIS questionnaires as the basis for our survey format, we added quite a few questions to both college-age and post-college questionnaires in order to get at the more specific aspects of Waldorf education. Statistical charts compiled by NAIS were supplemented with graphs and charts of our own. In this way we were able to build a more granulated picture of Waldorf graduates than the NAIS questionnaires would otherwise have made possible. In the end, our college-age questionnaire included 51 questions, whereas the post-college questionnaire stretched to a total of 104 questions—a number that at least some respondents found rather daunting—including a large number of "free narrative" (rather than standard multiple choice) questions. The results of these surveys are summarized in Chapter III, and then examined in more detail in Chapter IV (college age) and Chapters V and VI (post-college age).

Online links to questionnaires were sent by e-mail to alumni via the Waldorf high schools they had attended to preserve the privacy of students' addresses. Because of staffing issues at the schools, other means of distribution were also used by the project organizers, RIWE, and AWSNA, including social media (specifically Facebook). Given that the surveys were anonymous, it was not possible to contact respondents for any questions of clarification or to correct cases in which respondents appeared to have completed the wrong survey.

For certain questions, we were also able to weigh the Waldorf and NAIS statistics against the general U.S. population of comparable ages. We should note, however, that NAIS limits its membership to U.S. schools, whereas our survey included graduates of our Canadian high schools, who constituted about 10% of our response pool. It should be noted that Canada does not currently collect comparable statistics on the education of its general population.

By focusing on the last 27 years of Waldorf graduates, our survey was deliberately pitched towards capturing the voice of recent Waldorf alumni. However, as the following graph shows, a strong majority of respondents came from the more youthful end of this targeted population.

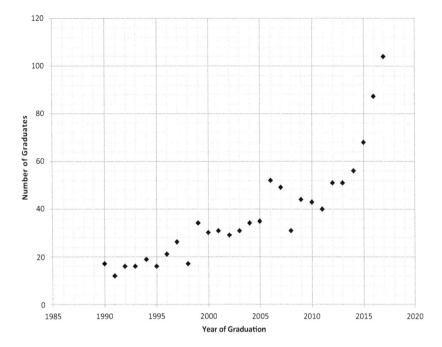

Of the 1,066 respondents, 424 (or 40%) were of college age, and a further 298 (or about 30%) were still in their twenties. This was due in some measure to the fact that Waldorf schools were more successful at locating their more recent alumni, compared to those who may have graduated as far back as 1990. This fact points to a weakness among at least some Waldorf schools, which have not developed a comprehensive program for tracking and staying in touch with their alumni.

Beyond the online surveys, we conducted face-to-face interviews with 22 Waldorf graduates, representing a cross-section of the country (East, West, and Midwest) and age groups (19 to 45). The interviewees were either approached by their schools or by the survey team, which relied on professional and personal contacts in reaching out to alumni willing to be interviewed. These interviews are summarized in Chapter VII of this report, as are the complete transcripts of two sample interviews. A quartet of alumni speeches is collected in Chapter VIII.

Finally, we invited some 75 experienced Waldorf high-school teachers to reflect back on the generations of students that had passed through their classroom. A selection of these teacher responses makes up the content of Chapter IX.

A separate section is included examining the differences between Waldorf and NAIS graduates concerning their relationships with their former schools, including the degree to which they do—or do not—offer financial support to their *alma mater* (Chapter X). In the last chapters of this report, we offer some extended comparisons of this survey with the poll of Waldorf graduates conducted a decade ago, including a selection of student critiques from both eras. Conclusions and recommendations, based on these student comments and suggestions, round out our survey (Chapter XI).

Acknowledgements and a suggested bibliography of resources and suggestions for further reading complete this report. A set of appendices lists details of the Waldorf high schools included in this survey, a sampling of colleges attended by Waldorf graduates, names of alumni who were interviewed, and samples of the questionnaires used for this survey.

In addition to these written materials, slides for a PowerPoint presentation have been created for free download from the website of the Research Institute: www.waldorfresearchinstitute.org/research-on-waldorf-graduates-into-the-world-how-waldorf-graduates-fare-after-high-school/

III | Profile of a Waldorf Graduate

Generalizations about the nature of Waldorf graduates run the risk of being either vague to the point of obscurity or specific to the point of exclusionary, requiring all manner of caveats and exceptions. This dilemma should be no surprise, however, given that a professed aim of Waldorf education is to help each student find her or his individual and self-chosen destiny. Indeed, it has been suggested that Waldorf students are likely to experience the full benefit of their education only as fully mature adults; in the words of one seasoned teacher, "Waldorf education prepares you best for the second half of life."

That said, the latest survey of Waldorf alumni—covering only the most recent quarter century of high-school graduates—does point up some common traits, accomplishments, and attitudes articulated by a large majority of the respondents. It is their responses that generated the composite profile offered in this chapter. The percentages (listed in descending order of frequency) are derived from multiple-choice responses that graduates made to questions posed in this latest survey. General statements without accompanying percentages represent summaries of the graduates' most frequent narrative responses to open-ended questions in the latter part of the survey.

As it happens, a great number of these shared traits surfaced in the Research Institute's previous survey, which was published in 2007 and spanned some 60 years of Waldorf alumni. This earlier survey, titled *Survey of Waldorf Graduates, Phase II*, also included a single-page profile of a Waldorf graduate; a comparison of these two profiles is offered at the end of this chapter.

Since the current survey contains additional questions as well as data from the National Association of Independent Schools (NAIS), a lengthier list of profiled highlights is possible this time, including some direct comparisons of Waldorf graduates to alumni from other independent schools. More detailed explications and comparisons of these highlights can be found in the final chapters of this survey.

The chief data points of this portrait not only depict common traits of Waldorf graduates but may also help put to rest some long-standing concerns and even misperceptions about Waldorf schools, specifically in regard to their graduates' college/ university majors, career choices, and life-long values. To be sure, a small minority of respondents to this survey painted quite other pictures of their Waldorf experience than the general snapshot offered here; these other pictures, albeit a minority view, are reported in the body of the chapters that follow.

This profile is intended to show how a majority of alumni fare after graduating from a Waldorf high school. It makes no claim to bestow sole credit for these traits and accomplishments upon their Waldorf education. Many factors contribute to the achievements of these students—not least of all their home life, as well as the inborn talents and intentions with which they entered life on earth.

Profile of a Waldorf Graduate (2017)

After high school, attends college/university (98%)

Feels prepared for college/university (95%)

Completes initial college degree (92%)

Gets into top three choices for college/university (90%)

Would recommend Waldorf education (87%)

Strongly feel Waldorf education prepared them to:

Be creative and innovative (96%)

Be open-minded (95%)

Empathize with others (92%)

Think in whole pictures (88%)

Take leadership roles (86%)

41% have a career helping others [education (23%), medicine (13%),
or social work (5%)] compared with 32% NAIS and 23% general U.S. population

A majority would send their children to a Waldorf school

Comparing Profiles of a Waldorf Graduate	2007	2017
After graduating from a Waldorf high school, attends college	94%	98%
Majors in arts/humanities as an undergraduate	47%	34%
Majors in a science/math as an undergraduate (including social science)	42%	45%
Majors in a STEM subject as an undergraduate	12%	19%
Graduates or is about to graduate from college	88%	91%
Ranks greatest gifts as:	1. Family 2. Education 3. Friends/ relationships 4. Social interactions 5. Artistic practice	1. Family 2. Friends 3. Waldorf education 4. Ongoing education 5. A fulfilling career
Values as most important:	1. Communication 2. Truthfulness 3. Problem solving 4. Ethical standards 5. Initiative	1. Communication 2. Problem solving 3. Ethical standards 4. Truthfulness 5. Initiative

IV College-Age Alumni

INTRODUCTION

The following information and analysis are based on an online survey completed by 424 Waldorf alumni, most of whom graduated from high school in the six-year period immediately prior to taking the survey (2011-2017). This group is therefore considered here college-age Waldorf alumni. This means that the vast majority of respondents are either still in college or are recent college graduates; their responses are at times compared to those provided by their contemporaries who have attended other independent high schools throughout the United States, and who have responded to a similar survey conducted by the National Association of Independent Schools (NAIS). We will be referring here to this, much larger comparison group, consisting of 8,622 respondents, as college-age NAIS graduates. In Chapters V and VI we will be reviewing information collected from an older cohort of Waldorf alumni, who, for the most part, graduated from high school prior to 2011.

OVERVIEW

Waldorf graduates go to college. In most cases they attend the college of their first or second choice, and they are pleased with their college experience. They do well, often earning grades of A- and above, and they often report that what they like most about their college experience is what they liked best about their Waldorf schools: the intimacy of academic and social communities and the individualized attention of their teachers and mentors. About a quarter of Waldorf graduates precede their college education with a well-structured gap year to undertake meaningful work, travel, and volunteering activities.

Their choice of college is based on academic program, culture, social activities, and financial support. They report feeling well prepared for the performative elements of college—public speaking, leadership and collaborative roles, writing—but at times complain that they could have been better prepared for test-taking and study skills. Quite a few mention that they could have been better prepared in science, math, and technology, but often these same students were inspired to pursue higher education and even professional careers in these very same fields.

Like Waldorf alumni who have graduated from high school more than a decade or two ago, more recent Waldorf alumni's top choices for a college major fall within the wide scope of the Arts & Humanities. However, very closely behind come subjects that fall into the wide categories of the Social & Behavioral Sciences or of the pure science and technological fields known as STEM (Science, Technology, Engineering, and Math). In fact, a far greater number of Waldorf alumni major in the sciences—when these two wide categories are combined—than in the Arts & Humanities. This means that Waldorf alumni proceed to study visual and performance arts, languages and literature, cultural studies and communications, but also psychology, international relations, political science, environmental studies, environmental science, chemistry, physics, kinesiology, and many other subjects. Very few of them, however, take on business, accounting, and management subjects as their undergraduate major.

When they look ahead to the future, almost a quarter of these current undergraduates plan to proceed to a post-graduate or professional degree, while about a third are planning professional careers equally distributed among non-profit, for-profit, and self-employed pursuits. These pursuits, they now believe, will be in the following areas (listed in descending order of interest): Arts, Science, Business, Community Services, Education, Medicine, Engineering, Technology, Communications, and Law. Most of them, however, will pursue the category listed as "Other," testifying to the wide variety of interests that Waldorf graduates are likely to pursue beyond college.

Finally, when reflecting as college undergraduates on their time in high school, these alums emphasize time and again the intimacy of setting and the quality of interpersonal relationships with teachers, peers, and staff in their Waldorf high schools.

THE GAP YEAR EXPERIENCE
Almost a quarter of current Waldorf college-aged respondents report taking a gap year between high school and further studies. In most cases (82% of those who took this break), a "gap year" lasted a full year. Others (14%) waited more than a year to enroll in college, while an even smaller group (4%) entered college less than a year after high-school graduation.

Of those who reported taking such a break, almost all spent at least a portion of their time working, traveling, or doing both.

More specific responses tell a varied story of the interests, pursuits, and inclinations of Waldorf graduates coming directly out of school. "I went to Alaska to work. I then traveled to Ghana and India, where I volunteered at schools and at Camphill," writes one graduate. Another reports working at the Waldorf farm-to-table summer camp Glen Brook in Marlborough, NH, before continuing to volunteer on an organic farm in Lebanon, Maine, in what has become known as WWOOF ("World Wide Opportunities on Organic Farms"). This organization, mentioned several times in the survey's open responses, appears to be especially popular among students and graduates of rural Waldorf schools. A third graduate tells of working as a kindergarten and first-grade teaching assistant at the Rudolf Steiner School of Ann Arbor, while a fourth states simply, "I started my own business, and traveled."

Perhaps the most detailed response combines environmental, educational, and volunteering experiences with adventurous traveling in Europe, South America, and the Far East:

> I worked at Kroka Expeditions [a non-profit, wilderness expedition school in New Hampshire, which has been collaborating with various Waldorf schools for more than 20 years] for two summers as an apprentice and assistant teacher. I also traveled around Europe (Germany, Czech Republic, France, Italy, U.K., Denmark, Switzerland, Norway, Sweden), Thailand, Peru, and Ecuador. In Europe I spent time visiting friends, family, and the sites. [I]n Thailand I worked at the Dulyapat Waldorf School in Khon Kaen. In Peru I visited friends of mine from exchange. And in Ecuador I volunteered on the coast building houses as well as going to a farm of friends of mine and just helping out there[.]

Many elements of the experiences mentioned in this rich description—the association with Waldorf schools in other countries, work and volunteering, travel, and the mention of friends and friendships—recur throughout the survey responses reproduced below. In addition to these quoted here, many briefer responses simply stated spending the year working (11), traveling (14), or working and traveling (30).

> I spent 6 months in Italy (Tuscany) going to a language school, and then another year working as a production assistant for a couple of TV shows

> I took a class in college, but mostly traveled and spent time with family. Then I joined the Navy and took college classes while enlisted

> I completed a program called LeapNow based out of Northern California, and spent time in India and Peru. [LeapNow is an organized gap year program that includes

group travel to the Far East and Central America, individual internships, personal workshops, and retreats aimed at acquiring "life skills" and exploring career options]

Working in a Camphill community in Cape Town and traveling India for two months

In Germany working at a school

Traveling with a program, working on a farm, interning, and living in a different city

I worked full-time as a nanny, volunteered as a youth mentor, and attended some professional trainings and conferences in the field I intend to work in (clinical mental health counseling)

Volunteering in Peru

I had an internship at the University of Valparaiso in IN working for the department of Integrated Marketing and Communications

I worked a lot on an organic farm near me to save up money, and also did some traveling: Montreal, Canada, for a weekend trip; West Virginia for a week on a mission trip rebuilding homes after a flood; Alaska for around 9 days visiting friends of my parents, and they took us around in an RV to see a lot of different areas; Galapagos Islands, Ecuador, for 3 weeks volunteering on a reserve to help remove invasive plants and reintroduce endemic ones, with various other tasks, and traveling around/ exploring 3 of the islands on weekends

Traveled to Nepal, Qatar, Oman, and London for about 2 months total, then I went to Brazil for another two months. Then I came home and worked and prepared for college

In Germany and Italy all year

Figuring out if cinematography was the way to go for me

National Security Language Initiative for Youth Turkish academic year program in Izmir, Turkey

Traveling in Europe as an au pair

I had a bit of a whirlwind gap year. I spent a month on a service trip in Kenya, another month on a solo road trip, and a couple months backpacking in New Zealand. During the periods when I was home, I worked at a family company and served as an alumni rep to Maine Coast's Board of Trustees. Finally, for the summer after my gap year I started my own small business, an ice cream boat

Working on pianos and teaching violin

I worked and applied early-decision to Champlain College. I also participated in a couple dramas with a local theatre

During this year I cooked at a Waldorf farm camp, WWOOFED [volunteered on an organic farm] in Southern California, traveled on the West Coast, then drove back to Vermont, where I worked for the rest of the year to save money

Hiked the Camino de Santiago in France and Spain (6 weeks), worked, went on a cross-country drive (5 weeks)

I worked for the summer and fall, then traveled for three months in Central America. During the next summer I became a raft guide and worked for the summer in Leavenworth

I spent my gap year in Israel, volunteering, working, and just living

Two internships abroad

Traveling and interning with artists, permaculture farmers, working on personal projects and assessing all schooling options

Ski training and racing

I did a year long volunteer stint with AmeriCorps – NCCC [National Civilian Community Corps]

Kroka Expeditions' Semester in Ecuador

I worked at the Camphill Dorfgemeinschaft Lehenhof

I spent 3 months traveling Europe with my friend from high school, and now I am working to save money for another trip to Europe this summer

I moved out of state and became financially independent from my family and recognized my want to attend college, not just go because I had finished high school

I worked in an orphanage in Peru and on a farm and traveled for a total of six months abroad

As an Au-Pair, worked for a family in Germany while studying German

I worked as an au-pair (live-in childcare) in Vienna [...] and in the Netherlands [...]. I took Ontario Education Ministry grade 12 biology and advanced functions (math) for university entrance because I didn't have space in my schedule in grade 12

Medical treatment

I did a gap year program in Jordan for the fall semester, worked as a middle school ski coach for the winter, and traveled in Turkey for the spring

I biked across the country with one of my LCWS classmates (since kindergarten) from Portland, ME, to Portland, OR, and wrote a daily blog of our progress and stories from the road. I then spent the winter teaching ski lessons and assistant coaching my high-school basketball team, and in the spring I worked as an intern at a wildlife rehabilitation center specializing in birds of prey in California

These reports, short as they are, bustle with youthful energy and curiosity about travel and exploration to remote destinations and cultures, with an ethical sense for work and volunteered work, with a gravitation towards nature and organic practices, and with the wish to explore new paths towards further education.

These descriptions, we should remember, represent only a portion of the 26% who indicated they took a gap year before entering college. We should also remember that the remaining 74% of respondents to this survey continued straight to college.

COLLEGE CHOICES

More than 68% of college-age respondents are attending the college of their first choice and 83% of either their first or second choice. By comparison, 61% of NAIS graduates report that they are attending the school of their first choice and 81% are attending either their first or second choice school. (For a list of universities and colleges attended by Waldorf graduates, see Appendix B of this report.)

What, though, are the most important common factors that high-school graduates list in deciding which college to attend?

Survey responses explicitly addressing this topic suggest that Waldorf students rank the perceived academic qualities of their college choices and the imagined social and cultural experience as being most important factors. At the same time, the survey responses on which we base this conclusion are somewhat complex and require more careful explication.

Table 4.1: How important were the following factors in your choice to attend this college/university?

(Highest percentage and score average in each row are highlighted.)

	Very Important (5)	Important (4)	Somewhat Important (3)	Of Little Importance (2)	Un-Important (1)	N/A	Score Average
Academic Program	**177 (58.6%)**	93 (30.8%)	20 (6.6%)	7 (2.3%)	3 (1.0%)	2 (0.7%)	**4.45**
Location of School	**114 (37.5%)**	98 (32.2%)	55 (18.1%)	23 (7.6%)	13 (4.3%)	1 (0.3%)	**3.91**
Financial Assistance Offered	**124 (40.8%)**	56 (18.4%)	51 (16.8%)	28 (9.2%)	24 (7.9%)	21 (6.9%)	**3.81**
Cost of School	**109 (36.0%)**	78 (25.7%)	65 (21.5%)	28 (9.2%)	18 (5.9%)	5 (1.7%)	**3.78**
Size of School	87 (28.6%)	**93 (30.6%)**	63 (20.7%)	38 (12.5%)	21 (6.9%)	2 (0.7%)	**3.62**
Reputation of School	61 (20.1%)	**116 (38.3%)**	82 (27.1%)	28 (9.2%)	15 (5.0%)	1 (0.3%)	**3.60**

Respondents were initially asked to rank six factors that influenced their choice of a specific college or university, ranging from "very important" (5 points) to "unimportant" (1 point). A clear majority of 58.6% of respondents indicated that the college's *academic program* was most important. Lesser factors, listed in order of importance, were *financial assistance offered* (40.8%), *location of school* (37.5%), *cost of school* (36%), *size of school* (28.6%), and *reputation of school* (20.1%).

A nearly identical ranking order arose when we calculated the average ranking of all respondents to this question, where 5 = very important and 1 = unimportant. In this calculation, *academic program* received an average of 4.45 points, *location of school* 3.91, *financial assistance offered* 3.81, *cost* 3.78, *size* 3.62, and *reputation* 3.60. This ranking order confirms not only that the perceived quality of a college's academic program appears to come first, but also that the reputation of the school comes last. However, a different picture emerges when we move from factors voted "very important" to those voted "important." Here the school's reputation leads the pack with the largest number of respondents determining it an important factor (nearly 38.3%), followed by *location* (32.2%), *academic program* (30.8%), *size* (30.6%), *cost* (25.7%), and *financial assistance offered* (18.4%). And we should also note that only about 5% of respondents claim the school's reputation is of no importance at all. In other words, while the highest importance in choosing a college is given to its academic program, culture, and social activities, the initial impression that a school's reputation is a superficial factor holding little importance among Waldorf students needs to be modified if factors of "importance" are added to the picture.

Still, "substance over style" comes out on top also in the responses to the follow-up question, in which respondents are offered additional factors to explain their college choice. Here, the school's culture and social activities lead both categories of "very important" and "important," while other factors—whether a high-school teacher or college counselor recommended the school, or whether a friend attended the school, or whether a college was attended by a parent—are all decisively marked as being of little to no importance at all. By comparison, NAIS graduates also grade academic program as the most important factor in choosing a college, with 65.4% of respondents voting "very important" and an additional 26% voting "important" and earning the highest score of 4.56 points. However, *reputation* is the second most important factor, both in the "very important" (36.5%) and "important" (36.2%) columns, earning a score of 4.00. Note also that the lowest scores of importance are given to the cost factors – *cost of school* 3.14, *financial assistance offered* 3.02. And, similar to the Waldorf graduates, NAIS graduates score the culture and social activities of the school above and beyond other factors in importance, giving it a score of 4.05 while the next in line, that the school was recommended by a college counselor or high-school teacher, receive only 2.77 and 2.63, respectively.

Table 4.2: How important were the following factors in your choice to attend this college/university?

	Very Important (5)	Important (4)	Somewhat Important (3)	Of Little Importance (2)	Un-Important (1)	N/A	Score Average
Culture Of/Social Activities at School	90 (29.8%)	**104 (34.4%)**	54 (17.9%)	33 (10.9%)	18 (6.0%)	3 (1.0%)	**3.72**
High School College Counselor Recommended It	8 (2.6%)	40 (13.3%)	63 (20.9%)	61 (20.2%)	63 (20.9%)	**67 (22.2%)**	**2.44**
High School Teacher Recommended It	9 (3.0%)	30 (10.0%)	56 (18.7%)	62 (20.7%)	56 (18.7%)	**87 (29.0%)**	**2.41**
Friends Attend School	2 (0.7%)	16 (5.3%)	40 (13.3%)	51 (16.9%)	93 (30.9%)	**99 (32.9%)**	**1.93**
Parent/Relative Attended School	6 (2.0%)	13 (4.3%)	23 (7.6%)	42 (14.0%)	82 (27.2%)	**135 (44.9%)**	**1.91**

Table 4.3: Comparative ranking of factors in choice of college:

	Waldorf Graduates	NAIS Graduates
Academic Program	4.45	**4.56**
Location of School	**3.91**	3.86
Financial Assistance Offered	**3.81**	3.02
Cost of School	**3.78**	3.14
Size of School	3.62	**3.77**
Reputation of School	3.60	**4.00**
Culture of/Social Activities at School	3.72	**4.05**
High School College Counselor Recommended It	2.44	**2.77**
High School Teacher Recommended It	2.41	**2.63**
Friends Attend School	1.93	**2.16**
Parent/Relative Attended School	1.91	**2.33**

The insignificance of "heritage attendance" for Waldorf graduates is evident in that fewer than 10% of Waldorf respondents attend a school which their mother attended, fewer than 7% a school their father attended, and fewer than 5% a school that a sibling attended. Indeed, close to 70% report that no family member attended the school where they are currently enrolled. The situation is very similar among NAIS graduates, with more than 72% of respondents reporting that no family member attended their current school, while just 11% report they are attending their father's college and 9% their mother's college, with a similar figure reporting they are enrolled in a college attended by a sibling.

To conclude: Waldorf college-age graduates are largely pleased with their choice of college, which they appear to have chosen on the basis of its academic program, its culture, and its social activities, all of which can be seen as the most substantial aspects of a college experience. The clearest difference between Waldorf graduates and graduates of other private schools in the United States is that members of the latter group do give higher importance to the reputation of a college, while they are less concerned about cost and financial aid than their Waldorf peers.

COLLEGE MAJORS AND OTHER ACTIVITIES

Waldorf graduates report a very wide variety of major courses of study. Respondents were asked to identify their major from a list of 23 leading subjects, from Architecture to World Languages, or, alternatively, to list their major as "other." The largest group of responses showed dissatisfaction with readymade subjects such as "Biological, Environmental, or Physical Sciences," "International Studies," "Technology/Computer Programming," or "Sociology," and designated their major instead as "other" (32% of responses). However, a follow-up question, requesting to specify these "other" majors, allowed us to discern further what contemporary Waldorf graduates are choosing to study in college. We were then able to fit these subjects into specific categories, such as Arts & Humanities, and Social & Behavioral Sciences, as seen in the comparative table below, thereby reducing the list of "other" majors to 8% of responses. Note that the figures here refer to the *subjects* studied as a major rather than to the number of students who study them, since some students take on two majors at a time (double-majors). The figures presented here show the percentage of the subject in relation to the totality of subjects that the survey respondents major in – a figure which is very close but slightly smaller than the percentage of individual respondents majoring in the subject. For example, we will say that Psychology makes for 6% of the different subjects in which respondents major, rather than that 6% of respondents major in Psychology. (To illustrate the difference: 7.2% of respondents major in Psychology.)

Table 4.4: Waldorf and NAIS majors:

	Waldorf			NAIS
	Post-College Majors	College Currently or Expecting to Pursue		College Currently or Expecting to Pursue
Arts & Humanities	38%	**28**%		19.2%
Social & Behavioral Sciences	28%	**23.5**%		22.6%
STEM – Natural Sciences + Engineering + Math	17%	22.2%		**23**%
Total Sciences (*above two rows*)	45%	**45.7**%		45.6%
Business & Accounting	3.5%	4.6%		**10.3**%
Health-related	4%	**6.8**%		5.2%
Education	3.3%	**3.3**%		2.3%
Other	6%	8%		**14.7**%

Grouping these majors into categories offers a clearer picture of the choices made by Waldorf graduates currently attending college or having graduated in recent years. We found that 28% of them choose subjects that fall within the Arts & Humanities, including the Visual and Performing Arts, Languages and Literature, History, Philosophy, and variations of Cultural and Liberal Studies. This figure represents a major drop when compared to older Waldorf alumni who attended college between 1990 and 2010, for whom Arts & Humanities make up 38% of major subjects. At the same time, the subjects in this category are clearly more popular among recent Waldorf alumni than among their contemporaries from other independent schools, for whom Arts & Humanities make only 19.2% of majors.

A little less than a quarter of recent Waldorf alumni major in the Social and Behavioral Sciences, which include subjects such as Psychology, Sociology, Economics, and Political Science, and almost the same number of students major in STEM subjects that include the Natural Sciences, Engineering and Technology (including Computer Science and Programming), and Math. These numbers are almost identical to the majors selected by contemporaries from other independent schools, with less than one percentage point differences up or down: Social & Behavioral Sciences comprise 23.5% of majors among Waldorf alumni, while they are 22.6% among NAIS graduates; STEM subjects comprise 22.2% of majors among Waldorf alumni and 23% among NAIS graduates; and the combined figure of all the sciences stands at 45.7% among Waldorf alumni and 45.6% among NAIS graduates. These figures indicate a certain drop in the study of Social & Behavioral Science among contemporary Waldorf graduates in relation to those who graduated high school during the two previous decades, from 28% to 23.5%, but also a proportionate rise in the study of STEM subjects as a major, from 17% to 22.2%.

Finally, we note a significant difference between contemporary Waldorf graduates and their NAIS peers in that for the latter group, Business & Accounting fields make for more than 10% of the majors studied, while it makes for less than 5% among Waldorf graduates. We interpret the considerably smaller numbers of students choosing to major in Education and in Health-related fields—which is the case for contemporary Waldorf graduates as for their comparison groups—by the fact that these fields are usually taken up in professional studies and training programs, such as teaching certifications or medical degrees, that succeed undergraduate studies. This explanation is substantiated by responses to questions regarding plans for future studies or employment, described later in this chapter, where 12% of respondents say their future lies in medical studies or other health-related fields, and 10% in education.

What else do Waldorf alumni do while in college? Half of them say they also work for wages, either part-time or full-time. Half say that they are members in a specialized club, group, or center. A quarter say they volunteer at school or within the community, and a quarter say they intern in a field they would wish to explore as a career. A fifth say they are members of an athletic team, and a slightly smaller group of students say they are members of a music group. Five percent of students state they have volunteered for a political campaign.

SELF EVALUATION OF COLLEGE SKILLS

It is a testimony to their sense of self-confidence that a generation of students educated in private schools throughout the country, *including* Waldorf schools, can so decisively and consistently evaluate their capacities as being above the perceived average of their peer group.

The two survey questions teasing out this sense of confidence asked, "When considering other students at your current college/university classes, how would you rank your abilities in comparison?" Each one of the questions then asked respondents to rank a set of academic skills, from overall academic ability to writing skills, leadership, and collaboration, in relation to their fellow college students. About three-quarters of respondents ranked their skills as being either "above average" or "well above average." Whatever their actual performance in college seminars and study halls, in term papers or other learning assessments, only a small fraction of graduates from Waldorf and other independent schools actually ranked their skills as being below average.

In comparing the responses of Waldorf alumni to graduates of other independent schools documented in the NAIS survey, we notice that more Waldorf graduates are willing to rank their academic abilities as "average" than are NAIS graduates. Between a quarter and a third of Waldorf graduates rank their abilities as average, compared to their college peers. By contrast, only a fifth of NAIS graduates assess their own skills as being average. A smaller percentage of Waldorf graduates evaluate their skills as above average—taking into account both the "above average" and "well above average" categories offered in both Waldorf and NAIS questionnaires. Whereas 73% of Waldorf graduates see themselves as above average in their *overall academic abilities*, 77% of NAIS respondents feel the same about their own abilities. Whereas 58% of Waldorf graduates see themselves above average in their *study and organizational skills*, 72% of NAIS graduates rank themselves as such. Whereas 63% of Waldorf graduates see their *analytical skills* as above average, more than 77% of NAIS students regard their skills as such. And while close to 70% of Waldorf graduates give themselves above-average ranking for their *writing skills*, close to 77% of NAIS graduates believe they surpass the average level of their undergraduate cohort.

Waldorf graduates are also less inclined than NAIS graduates to rank themselves *"well* above average" in various areas of academic skills. For example, 29% of NAIS graduates rank themselves as "well above average" in their overall academic ability, while only 19% of Waldorf graduates evaluate themselves similarly. For analytical skills, 33% of NAIS graduates feel they are well above average in their command of these skills, while only 24% of Waldorf graduates feel the same about their own. And while 38% of NAIS graduates give themselves the ultimate rank as regards their writing ability, only 28% of Waldorf graduates rank themselves at this top level.

Since these rankings are self-reported, they raise the question whether they reflect greater modesty or lesser academic aptitude on the part of Waldorf college students. We observe that, while a great majority of Waldorf graduates are confident about most of their academic skills and the degree to which their own college-preparedness compares favorably to their peers', they seem less inclined to assess their abilities as exceeding those of their peers, especially when we compare this self-assessment to that of graduates of other independent schools.

An interesting insight into the question of confidence is offered by the second of the two survey questions, which requests them to evaluate their capacity in comparison to their peers. Four categories of evaluation are specified: public speaking, leadership, collaborative/team skills, and self-confidence. When responding to the general question about their level of self-confidence, NAIS graduates again appear more confident, with 68.5% ranking themselves above average against 61% of Waldorf graduates who see themselves as such. But when the categories are more specific, in the sense that they can be self-checked against actual experiences—such as public speaking, leadership abilities, and collaboration/team skills—Waldorf graduates' self-evaluations of being "above average" surpass those of their NAIS peers:

Table 4.5: Waldorf and NAIS self-evaluations:

	Waldorf Graduates	NAIS Graduates
Public Speaking	66%	62.3%
Leadership Ability	75%	73%
Collaboration/Team Skills	80%	77%

Only in these specific and experience-based categories do Waldorf graduates reflect greater confidence than NAIS graduates. This finding suggests *not* that Waldorf graduates are lacking in confidence; after all, only 3% of these respondents rank their overall academic ability below average, while 73% rank it as being above average. Instead, this data suggests that Waldorf graduates award themselves the highest evaluation in regard only to specific skills that could be measured by reference to concrete cases, rather than in terms of a more general sense of overall self-confidence.

Finally, we should note some striking contrasts concerning technological skills included in this section of the survey. While 51% of Waldorf respondents deem their technology skills to be "average" in comparison to their peers, about a quarter conceded these skills to be "below average" (25.5%), with just another quarter thinking of them as being "above average" (23%). Clearly, Waldorf graduates feel the least confident about their technology skills. But so do graduates from other independent schools. Compared to the other categories in this section of self-evaluation in the NAIS survey, this question has the highest number of respondents that grade their skills as average (35%). And while more than half of NAIS respondents evaluate their skills as above average in this domain, the number of respondents who feel this way is the smallest of any skill category: 59%. By comparison, 77% of NAIS respondents feel they are above average in their overall academic ability.

To summarize: Both Waldorf and NAIS graduates are very confident about their various academic skills in comparison to their peers, though Waldorf graduates are less inclined to rank themselves higher than their peers in a general way. The trust that Waldorf graduates place in their abilities surpasses that of NAIS graduates when self-evaluation refers to skills that can be measured by specific experiences, such as public speaking or team work. Waldorf graduates feel least secure about their technology skills, but so do NAIS graduates.

PREPARATION FOR COLLEGE

It is interesting to note that in those categories where Waldorf graduates evaluate their skills on a higher level compared to NAIS graduates, they also give greater credit to the school for preparing them in these areas of expertise. Specifically: 66% of Waldorf graduates respondents self-evaluate their public speaking ability as above average, while 81.5% of them state that their high school prepared them well in this area. 75% of respondents see their leadership abilities as above average, while 85.5% of them credit their school with preparing them well in this area. 80% of respondents evaluate their skills of collaboration and teamwork as above average, while almost 90% give credit to their Waldorf school for preparing them well to be such team-players.

And while 69.5% of Waldorf respondents are confident that their writing skills are above average, more than 86.5% of respondents credit their Waldorf school for preparing them to reach this level.

In all other categories of self-evaluation that have a parallel question about school—such as overall academic ability, study skills, and technology skills—respondents give practically the same high-level evaluation to their perceived abilities and to the school they believe has prepared them well to achieve this skill.

In scoring how well their secondary education prepared them in a set of subjects, it is clear that Waldorf graduates believe they were better prepared in some areas (Humanities and the Arts) than in others (Math, Science, and Sports). Based on a scale of 1 to 5, where 5 designates being "very well prepared" in a subject and 1 "not well at all," the differences are clear:

Performing Arts	4.46
Visual Arts	4.45
English: Literature	4.33
English: Reading and Composition	4.30
Compare to:	
World Languages	3.76
History	3.73
Physical Education	3.69
Sports/Athletics	3.60
Geography	3.43
Religion	3.36
Science	3.26
Math	3.19

Surprisingly, the stark distinction in the scores of the humanities compared to the scores of the sciences is blurred by a relatively low score for History, which received a score of 3.73, and World Language (French, Spanish, Mandarin, etc.), which scored 3.76. In addition, Religion is also scored at the low end by Waldorf graduates, receiving a score of 3.36. The fact that this subject also has the highest number of respondents marking it as "not applicable" explains this low score for a subject that schools in the United States, except for parochial schools, tend to avoid altogether. Indeed, NAIS graduates give Religion their lowest score (3.15), with nearly a quarter of respondents marking this subject "not applicable."

If we take a second look at the subject area evaluations offered by Waldorf graduates, this time placing them next to the evaluations provided by NAIS graduates, we discover some telling elements:

Table 4.6: Waldorf and NAIS evaluations of their school subjects:

	Waldorf	NAIS
Performing Arts	**4.46**	3.71
Visual Arts	**4.45**	3.71
English: Literature	**4.33**	4.27
English: Reading & Composition	4.30	**4.32**
World Languages (French, Spanish, Mandarin)	3.76	**3.94**
History	3.73	**4.06**
Physical Education	3.69	**3.88**
Geography	**3.43**	3.30
Science	3.26	**3.96**
Math	3.19	**3.99**

While there is a marked difference in size between the two surveys (the NAIS sample contains more than 6,600 respondents, while the number of Waldorf respondents in this section number slightly over 300), we can note here some similarities in the rankings. Both NAIS and Waldorf graduates evaluate the Humanities significantly higher than Math and the Sciences, though the score *gap* between the two academic subjects is larger in the evaluations offered by Waldorf graduates. We also note that NAIS graduates evaluate their preparation in History and World Languages somewhat higher, while Waldorf graduates evaluate their preparation in the Visual and Performing Arts *significantly higher*. (Both groups seem to share a tepid and nearly equal response to their preparation in Geography and Physical Education.)

The level of insecurity regarding preparation in Science and Math, which Waldorf graduates express to a greater degree, is contextualized by this comparison, since these numbers show that insecurity concerning the study of math and science is shared by graduates of non-Waldorf independent schools across the country. Still, we cannot ignore the difference in the degree of insecurity expressed, for example, by Waldorf graduates, who give an average 3.19 score to their high school preparation in Math, whereas NAIS students score their preparation at an average of 3.99.

There is a second lesson that comparisons with NAIS graduates teach us about Waldorf graduates: If the latter appear less secure at times about the level to which their Waldorf school has prepared them academically, this uncertainty disappears when academic *skills* are assessed with greater specificity and when questions of adequate preparation shift from academics to other areas of competence.

When asked about skills in general terms—such as *studying, conducting research,* or *interpreting mathematical concepts*—more Waldorf respondents evaluate their preparedness as "well" rather than "very well." However, when the skills asked about are more specified, and their evaluation can be carried out by matching them with specific products (for example, the skill of writing measured against grades in Composition/English courses), or with specific experiences (for example, the skill of public speaking measured against specific oral presentations), evaluations decisively shift to the "very well" column.

Thus, we see preparation in *writing* evaluated as "very well" by 56% of respondents, compared to 30.6% who evaluate it as "well," *public speaking* evaluated as "very well" by 54.4% compared to 27% who evaluate it as "well," *contributing to class discussions* 69% "very well" compared to 23.1% "well," *working collaboratively on a team* 58.8% "very well" while 30.7% vote "well," and *taking a leadership role* evaluated "very well" by 49.3% compared to 36.2% who evaluate it "well."

These specific and measurable skills also receive a significantly higher general score than the less defined ones, as we see in the table below:

Contributing to Class Discussions	4.60
Working Collaboratively on a Team	4.45
Writing	4.38
Public Speaking	4.30
Taking a Leadership Role	4.30

Compare to:

Studying	3.66
Conducting Research	3.42
Interpreting mathematical/scientific concepts	3.21
Using technology	2.61

First, we should note two outliers to the pattern of evaluating specific skills at a higher level. One is the skill of *using technology*, which receives the lowest score of all the skills (2.61). However, the same percentage of respondents (16.9%) views preparation in technological skills as either "well" or "not well at all" (16.9%), and the same percentage (29.3%) evaluate the same preparation as being "somewhat well" or "not too well." The low score here is fully aligned with the *perception* that Waldorf education is lagging behind with the incorporation of advanced technology into the classroom. The balance of positive and negative views regarding preparation for the use of technology is more difficult to explain; perhaps it is saying something about the ambiguity of the question that refers to unspecified "technology" and the variety of views and expectations this might generate.

The second outlier is the evaluation of *balancing workload*, a skill that can be viewed as either a general or a specific capacity. With a score of 3.93, *balancing workload* is located more or less in the middle point between the high end of the specific skills scores (4.60) and the low end of the more generally defined ones (3.21); the gap between being "very well" prepared and "well" prepared is almost invisible – 35.6% and 34.3%, respectively.

With these caveats in mind, we note further that the pattern of giving a higher evaluation to skills that can be measured by specific outcomes (e.g., the essays one has written) and experiences (the public speeches one has given) is not only visible here, but also when we compare these responses to the ones offered by NAIS graduates. The latter give their secondary schools (and themselves) higher scores than Waldorf graduates do for the general, unqualified skills, but they significantly check themselves when they come to evaluate the skills that are more specifically measurable. These receive lower scores than the general skills, and they are lower than the scores Waldorf graduates give themselves:

Table 4.7: Comparison of NAIS & Waldorf grads on how well their school prepared them for college (on a scale of 1-5)

	Waldorf	NAIS
Contributing to Class Discussions	**4.60**	4.32
Working Collaboratively on a Team	**4.45**	4.23
Writing	4.38	**4.40**
Public Speaking	**4.30**	3.85
Taking a Leadership Role	**4.30**	4.21
Studying	3.66	**4.06**
Conducting Research	3.42	3.70
Interpreting mathematical/scientific concepts	3.21	3.89

One way of accounting for the differences we see in this comparison is that Waldorf graduates are more careful, perhaps more modest, than their NAIS peers in evaluating their overall academic skills and the preparation they received for them. This element of caution or modesty seems to disappear when the survey question directs the respondents to check their specific achievements rather than offer a general evaluation.

But something very interesting happens when we move from the self-evaluation of academic skills to the self-evaluation of other skills and qualities.

When the survey turns to questions about sensitivity and creativity of thinking and feeling—hallmarks of the language used by Waldorf educators to describe their approach to teaching—the numbers reflect a surge of confidence among Waldorf graduates. Here the scores evaluating preparation are the highest, and the numbers in the "very well prepared" column are multiples of those in the merely "well prepared" column:

Table 4.8: Waldorf and NAIS grads on specific areas of preparation for college

How well did your [Waldorf] school prepare you in the following areas?	
Being creative and innovative	4.75 (*77.85% - Very Well, 18.57% - Well*)
Being open-minded	4.73 (*78.50% - Very Well, 15.96% - Well*)
Empathizing with others	4.59 (*69.38% - Very Well, 22.80% - Well*)
Appreciating and/ or participating in the arts	4.77 (*79.74% - Very Well, 15.69% - Well*)
Thinking in whole pictures	4.45 (*57.33% - Very Well, 30.94% - Well*)

The scores in the comparable section of the NAIS survey—"thinking in whole pictures" is not included in the NAIS questionnaire—are consistently lower (see below). In addition, the highest percentage of respondents evaluating their preparation on any of these qualities as "very well" is never higher than 47% ("being open-minded") but can be as low as 36.4% ("being creative and innovative").

Table 4.9

How well did your [NAIS] school prepare you in the following areas?	
Being creative and innovative	4.03 (36.4% - Very Well, 38.1% - Well)
Being open-minded	4.15 (47.3% - Very Well, 30.9% - Well)
Empathizing with others	4.15 (44.6% - Very Well, 33.4% - Well)
Appreciating and/ or participating in the arts	4.10 (45.2% - Very Well, 29.1% - Well)

We learn here that Waldorf graduates—displaying caution in other parts of the survey and generally responding more modestly in their self-evaluations than their NAIS peers unless there is a verifiable basis for such evaluation—exude much greater confidence when asked about their social, aesthetic, and cognitive sensibilities and sensitivities and how well they were nurtured by their pre-college Waldorf education.

We can perhaps explain this difference by the fact that the qualities being assessed in this section of the survey—creativity, open-mindedness, empathy, artistic sensitivity, coherence of thought, and visual thinking—are core features of Waldorf education throughout the grades. Indeed, these aspects of a student—*being* open-minded, *empathizing* with others—are less learned skills than they are dispositions and qualities that form a person's identity. In other words, the survey here is not asking "How well did your school train you to do something?" as much as it is asking "To what extent did your school guide you to become a certain kind of person?" The outstandingly positive response of Waldorf graduates to this question suggests that they recognize the broader aims and achievements of their education and that these qualities are not simply academic.

SATISFACTION WITH COLLEGE

There is no question that Waldorf graduates are satisfied with their college experiences. Just under 5% of current Waldorf college-age respondents report that they are not satisfied. The other 95% report they are either very satisfied (40% of total respondents), satisfied (42%), or somewhat satisfied (12.8%). The figures are almost identical for NAIS graduates, with 95.4% reporting satisfaction and about 4% claiming dissatisfaction. Those Waldorf alumni still in college largely express confidence that they will complete the course at their current institution – 89% of respondents confirm this expectation, with 5% saying they plan to transfer to a different school and 6% admitting that they are not sure where they will conclude their current course of study.

In terms of their self-reported grades, it seems that Waldorf current college students have good reason to be satisfied, with nearly half of respondents reporting grades that qualify them for High Honors (GPA of 3.68 or above), a little over a quarter of respondents qualifying for Honors (GPA between 3.34 and 3.67), and a total of close to 90% of respondents holding a GPA that is higher than 3.0.

Table 4.10: What is your current grade point average?

Answer Choice	Response Percent	Response Count
4.01 or higher	4.7%	14
3.68 to 4.0	43.7%	131
3.34 to 3.67	27.3%	82
3.01 to 3.33	14.0%	42
2.68 to 3.0	6.3%	19
2.34 to 2.67	2.7%	8
2.01 to 2.33	0.7%	2
1.68 to 2.0	0.3%	1
1.34 to 1.67	0%	0
1.33 or below	0.3%	1

When invited in a follow-up question to explain the grounds for their satisfaction (or lack thereof) with their college experience, two-thirds of those who responded to the first question chose to elaborate. These elaborations are very telling. A clear majority draw glowing pictures of delight in their social and educational experiences. Here is a short sample representing the most common response to the follow-up question "Why?" to the query: "How satisfied are you that the college/university in which you are currently enrolled is the right match for you?"

Small class sizes, good academics, great people, beautiful campus, good opportunities

Small, individualized, has my major, strong sciences, accessible

I'm doing exactly what I want to do at an institution that gives me loads of opportunities and is in a great location

Middlebury is a beautiful, welcoming, and academically challenging campus, with small class sizes, devoted professors, and extremely nice people. I think a liberal arts education complements my Waldorf background extremely well

The elements mentioned positively in these responses recur again and again in many of the other comments: small size of class and/or college, personal attention, the culture, the people, the (not always specified) "opportunities" and abundance of "choices," the college location, campus atmosphere, the personal "good fit," and the touching assessment that it "feels like home." (By the same token, a significantly smaller pool of negative comments about the college experience tend to name the opposite aspects: "The class sizes are generally larger than I'd want and the huge student population makes student-teacher interaction uncommon and not encouraged in the way I would like.") Other aspects mentioned positively are the ability to work closely with professors, to participate in arts or athletics programs, and to experience diversity on campus.

Of the handful of negative or critical descriptions of the college experience, the terser ones state that "the atmosphere turned out not to be the right fit for me," or that their college is "unfriendly and too easy," or "not challenging." The more detailed complaints appear to express disappointment that college life did not live up to the personal, dialogical, and creative aspects of learning they experienced during their Waldorf high-school years. "I don't like the lecture setting. It is very impersonal and very "teach at you." They try to be more interactive, but the object of the game is still just to memorize how to do things to get a good grade on the exams."

If a comparison with high-school experience appears to be implicit in this response, a recurring theme in this section of the survey is the spontaneous comparison of a respondent's current college experience to his or her previous experience of Waldorf education. In fact, 35 of the 212 responses to this section include comparisons or references to Waldorf education. Many of these explicitly express satisfaction with the college experience *because* it feels like a continuation of the Waldorf experience. For example, one respondent, naming many of the positive elements already mentioned above, writes:

It is like the college version of a Waldorf School! I love the small class sizes, project-based work, individualized curriculum, opportunities to work closely with professors, and the ability to study a wide range of specific subjects.

Another writes, "I like it very much, owing in large part to its similarities to Waldorf education, its emphasis on liberal arts and ensuring well-rounded graduates." Similarly, others write, "feels like the Waldorf environment but expanded," or "I like it for many of the same reasons I liked Waldorf." And another starts by enthusiastically describing a current graduate school experience: "studying a topic I'm passionate about and having success publishing and presenting my work," before commenting: "I don't believe I would have been as successful without my education at the Denver Waldorf School."

Very rarely, a hint of critique of one's previous education seems to flicker in some comments. One states, "Faculty/students are more scientific minded, unlike the Waldorf high school I attended," though this comment comes across as a matter of perceived fact rather than as a value judgment. Another writes that the "tools of math and physics I picked up here are leagues above what I ever thought I could accomplish," which seems to resonate with the dissatisfaction, observed in other parts of this study, with the kind of attention that math and the exact sciences receive in the Waldorf high-school curriculum. At the same time, even if this statement describes the perceived limitations of a graduate's capabilities in math and physics, it also suggests the student was generally *prepared to learn* math and science even if her or his previous education in this area appeared to be limited.

Explicit praise of Waldorf education by comparison to a less-than-optimal, even negative, college experience suggests, repeatedly, that the positive nature and the standards set by the Waldorf school lead some students to feel disappointed in their college experience. We read this in statements like, "The people here are not as genuine as the people I was surrounded by in Waldorf school," or "I chose a small liberal arts college and because of [my] background in Waldorf education it put me above the levels of so many of my classmates in class discussion." And "I miss the community that I loved so much at Waldorf. The classes are big where I attend and half the time it seems like people don't care at all to be here. It's quite frustrating."

The sentiment expressed here is summarized in a single, straightforward and slightly melancholic comment by this respondent: "I sometimes worry that high school was such a positive experience that no college would ever match up."

A more distanced view on the impact that a strong Waldorf experience can have on subsequent steps in life is offered by an advanced graduate student:

> *Following completion of dual bachelor degrees in the U.S., I continued graduate education in Switzerland at a research university. While I am proud of my achievements thus far, I am also not 100% satisfied. I often feel that academia doesn't allow me to make the most of or integrate my varied interests that I learned while at Waldorf.*

The comparisons of college learning to the Waldorf experience volunteered by these in-college respondents, many of them just a year or two into their university studies, suggest how many of them still view themselves from within the identities they formed during high school, a place that is warmly remembered as an intimate and supportive learning environment. It is interesting to compare these perspectives to the ones offered in the comments made by older graduates, who have traveled further away from their high-school years and into the experiences of adulthood. We will be reviewing such post-college graduates in the next two chapters.

LOOKING BACK

Respondents were invited to reflect on their time in high school using two measures: (1) ranking their top five aspects of the school out of a list of 16, and (2) offering a free-form response to the following question: *As you look back on your years at your school, what other courses of study or extracurricular activities could have been offered that would have enhanced your experience or better prepared you for college/university?*

A striking element in this ranked list (see below) of "most valuable aspects" of the school experience is the extent to which it elevates *relationships*, *setting*, and *experiences* over academic content. This picture clearly suggests that, at least in hindsight, high-school students most value the people *from* whom and *with* whom they have learned and the interpersonal elements of their learning experience.

It is true that of the 16 aspects named in the questionnaire, only three are specifically content-centered—"core academic courses," "elective courses," and "AP courses"—while the rest focus on activities, events, settings, and community. But it is also telling that the first of these three aspects (core academic courses) makes an appearance only half way down the list at number 8; elective courses are listed 13th and AP courses (which are rarely offered in Waldorf schools) are last. Academic content does not make it into the top five most valuable aspects of high school.

By contrast, the top spot on the list is shared by "interaction with teachers" and "small class size," followed by "individualized attention" in a shared third place. It is clear that the quality of direct human interaction is the most highly valued feature of the high-school experience. In other words, it is the *how* of learning more than the *what* that is most positively remembered, and this *how* is specifically qualified by the intimate, individualized interactions with teachers and peers. We further see evidence of the importance of the social element in the high ranking of "other students at your school" and the "culture of your school."

This ultimate valuation of interpersonal learning and socialization does not appear to be unique to Waldorf education: the list of top five (or so) aspects of school experience ranked by graduates of other independent schools in the United States is practically identical to the list ranked by Waldorf graduates. The difference at the top of the lists is limited to "academic overnight field trips," which is ranked third by Waldorf graduates but was not offered in the menu of options in the NAIS questionnaire and is therefore absent from the list.

The two lists begin to deviate when we come to the "culture of your school" aspect, which shares the fifth spot on the NAIS list with AP courses. AP courses are last on the Waldorf list, which is not surprising, given that most Waldorf schools simply do not offer them—a fact addressed in the free-form following question, in which about 13% of respondents feel they would have benefited from AP course offerings at their school.

In addition, appreciation for high-school AP courses among current college students appears to be motivated by the fact that these courses reduce the number of required college courses. This is suggested by several free-form responses from Waldorf graduates who lament the unavailability of these courses in their high school.

Table 4.11: Most valuable aspects of your high school

Waldorf Graduates	NAIS Graduates
1. Interaction with Teachers	1. Interaction with Teachers
1. Small Class Size*	2. Small Class Size
2. Academic Overnight Field Trips	N/A
3. Individualized Attention	3. Individualized Attention
3. Other Students at Your School*	4. Other Students at Your School
4. Culture of Your School	5. Culture of Your School
5. Foreign Exchange	5. AP Courses*
6. Core Academic Courses	6. Participation in Athletic Team
7. Interaction with Staff	7. Interaction with Staff

same number of votes as above category

Only about half of the Waldorf college-aged alumni surveyed chose to respond to the follow-up question, which offered the chance to specify missing elements in their high-school experience. Of this group, a third mentioned either basic or advanced science and technology courses, a fifth said they wished for better and broader preparation in math, and 14% stated specifically that computer skills, from basic programming to training in commonly used software such as Excel and Adobe, would have been advantageous.

There is no question, then, that for those opting to look back on their Waldorf high school, the most commonly perceived shortfall is concentrated in the "STEM" (Science, Technology, Engineering, and Math) subjects and skills. At the same time, this perception, at least among recent high-school graduates, is not widespread. Given the limited response to this free-form question, we should note that if some 30% of respondents complain of insufficient preparation in these subjects, they represent only about 14% of the total group surveyed.

Secondly, we should look closer at what is expressed in these comments. The sample below of three of the more detailed remarks on the subject captures a certain nuance in the attitudes expressed:

As a physics and math major I can firmly say that the potential to teach students physics in the way they did [at the Waldorf school,] (conceptually over mathematically) can be a very big boon for those going into college and wanting to study further in physics BUT it needs to happen in a more coherent way.

Development of a core scientific curriculum to teach foundation topics [is] necessary for further study in science (e.g. Chemistry, Biology, Physics courses rather than Botany, Astronomy).

[A]s someone who went into engineering it would have been very helpful to have been at least introduced to most of the scientific concepts taught in my [college] introduction courses.

The first comment acknowledges the great value of the Waldorf approach to teaching science, in that it de-emphasizes the procedures and skills needed to test theories and results already established within the fields of physics and math in favor of discovering them through a phenomenological approach. At the same time, in mentioning the need for clarity and coherence in such an approach, this comment gives the impression that math and science courses in Waldorf schools may lack organization.

The second comment seems to levy the harshest criticism. It implies that Waldorf education fails to prepare students for college level studies because it lacks a "core scientific curriculum" focused on the foundations of the empirical sciences. The third comment repeats this criticism while mitigating the implied complaint ("it would have been very helpful"). But what is of great significance in the latter comment is that it comes from "someone who went into engineering." In other words, it is quite possible to graduate from a Waldorf school and still develop both interest and aptitude in the STEM fields. This is also demonstrated by the first commentator, who is identified as a "physics and math major." Both comments, in fact, represent a pattern detected in different sections of the survey, in which suggestions of deficiency in teaching STEM on the secondary school level come precisely from those students who were inspired nevertheless to pursue higher education and even a career in STEM fields.

A further set of comments on elements perceived to be missing from the respondents' school experience focuses on both life and study skills. These include references to "real world" skills: basic economic functions, health (including specific mentions of mental health and sex education), and college-related skills such as critical thinking, notetaking, test-taking, and how to study. Finally, several comments were very much in tune with contemporary frustrations concerning a perceived neglect of non-European cultures and non-normative identities in the curriculum, as expressed by this Waldorf graduate:

[C]ourses on sexuality and gender studies, and race relations—these topics were often completely ignored during my time at Steiner and it would benefit students greatly to learn about them before college, and would make Waldorf education much more accessible to people who are non-white and are not heteronormative or cisgender.

LOOKING AHEAD

Finally, looking to their next steps in life, almost half of current Waldorf college-aged students (44.5%) stated they plan to continue their education towards higher degrees, such as a Master's or a Ph.D., or professional degrees such as J.D. or M.D. A quarter of respondents reported that their future goals involve entering the for-profit business world, 20% said they plan to start their own business, and another 20% stated they plan to pursue a career in the non-profit sectors.

Many wrote in response to follow-up questions regarding future plans that they are already working in areas such as Government, Collegiate Recreation, Law Enforcement, Medical Services, or running their own business.

Here are the general fields marked out by responses, in descending order of frequency:

Table 4.12: Waldorf fields of employment:

	Number of Responses	% of responses to question
Fine/Performing Arts or Design	70	17%
Medicine or Health Services	49	12%
Business/Finance	44	11%
Sciences	43	11%
Education (K – University)	40	10%
Social Services	40	10%
Engineering/Agriculture	27	7%
Media/Publishing/Communications	22	5%
Computer Science/Technology	19	5%
Law & Legal Services	18	4%
Hospitality/Travel	8	2%
Don't Know	8	2%

Several respondents write that their future is "uncertain," "undecided," or "unknown," an uncertainty that is also expressed in responses such as "I am open to what is to come" and "This is a very complicated question for me."

Other undecided respondents suggest a general direction where they believe their future lies. Some of these include:

Combination of business and engineering

Work with people and the environment, having a holistic approach of integrating both

I'm hoping to have a wide-ranging career that encompasses far more than the "select one" option. Ideally spanning business, community service, education and law

Science (probably conservation biology) and community service

And one respondent circumscribed her or his outlook by writing: "My talents are the arts, my skills are scientific, my passion is for a lifestyle full of meaning and quality centering around family."

Sixty percent of those surveyed included a resounding "Yes" in their response to the question "Did your experience at your school influence your thinking about a career choice?" But they also took a lot of space and time to elaborate on this question (40% of respondents contributed 176 written elaborations). This is what some of them had to say:

We received a good (and inspiring) base in the biological sciences, which included an appreciation for all things living and the world around us. We also were taught to accept all walks of life and help others in need. I think the combination of this knowledge and these concepts, along with my passion for human movement and connecting with people, has led me to being a physical therapist.

I started doing the Audio and Mixing for the High-School Musicals while I was attending high school. This led to my initial interest in audio engineering.

Every year from first to twelfth grade we did a play. It was my favorite time of year; the rehearsals, the lines, the characters, and when looking for a career path that suited my interests the rest was easy. I was also quite good at mathematics so I pursued computer science. Not terribly Waldorf, but the math background and the creative problem solving and even the spatial awareness given to me by all those years of eurythmy helped.

It comes down to one lecture in one science class – electromagnetics. It struck a bone and made clear my calling out of many interests.

Everything I do now professionally is oriented around the visual arts, and it is Waldorf where I discovered my love for them. Everything from drawing to drama, eurythmy to stone carving, veil painting to main lesson books, I owe my entire career to the education I received during my [time] at Waldorf. Waldorf informs so much of work I create today, if not aesthetically, then very much in spirit.

Being at WWS shaped my love for the environment as well as my ability to critically think and debate, which led me to love politics, shaping my interest in my current major, Environmental Science and Policy, which I hope will lead to a relevant career in that field.

I think my Waldorf education played a big part in my decision to study and conserve the environment since my education was deeply integrated in the outdoors from a young age.

I had the best physics teacher in high school. She kindled the passion for physics in me.

I learned an appreciation for local land management through our trips to farms around the Denver area, and ultimately this informed my choice of graduate study. While I didn't receive much scientific training per se, I use the skills I learned at the Waldorf school every day in graduate school.

My school provided me the perfect balance between dreams and logic in terms of career path.

I was exposed to a lot of hands on work, art, creativity, critical thinking, systems understanding. And ultimately what I would say was a largely design thinking approach to education, as I was constantly supported to redesign and recreate my life, projects, ideas, surroundings, etc. I felt right at home when going on to study architecture, and feel this will be a lifelong passion.

I wanted to be more tech-capable person because I was so tired of Waldorf teachers disliking the use of technology and treating it as something that harms development of children – and I disagree with that.

From my experiences in school and extracurricular activities, I was fairly certain I wanted to pursue engineering.

I knew when I graduated high school I would be a teacher.

The structured flexibility to pursue my artistic or scientific passions allowed me to discover who I wanted to be.

I learned how to be caring and compassionate towards others through my Waldorf education, which heavily influenced my decision to pursue nursing so that I can care for and give back to patients.

I'm interested in computer coding and digital arts. These are two things that [my Waldorf school] never really provided in my studies but completely gave me the tools to be able to teach myself and how to use the resources around me to pursue those passions.

Waldorf helped me become a well-rounded individual and taught me one lesson of utmost importance: how to love learning.

Part of my decision in becoming a Classics major stemmed from my exposure to the classics at my Waldorf school.

There was not a strong focus on "career choice" but more pursuing my own goals and how to make a living doing that.

I felt confident in being able to learn anything, to teach myself, and to ask for help and guidance. My education gave me a global view and a sense of responsibility to leave the world better than when I arrived. This sense led me to pursue global studies and international affairs for my respective degrees.

I struggled with math and science. The teachers at Waldorf helped give me an incredible foundation and worked with me to build confidence and skill, as well as engaging me in subjects I would not have anticipated enjoying as much as I did. This enjoyment grew into interest and new possibilities I would not have otherwise explored.

I also had a great experience in my science classes throughout high school (Zoology being my favorite), so I would like to do research as well.

I was the "local IT" guy for my school. Having discovered that I was good with computers and enjoyed working with them, I decided to pursue a college degree in Computer Science and later got a job as a Software Engineer.

It made me want to change the world.

V Post-College Alumni (1)

WHO ARE THEY NOW? PROFESSIONS, EDUCATION, LIFE EXPERIENCES

OVERVIEW

The population studied in this and the next chapter consists of Waldorf alumni who graduated from high school between the years 1990-2010.[2] This means that at the time of responding to the survey these alumni could be of any age between 26 and 47, representing several stages of life beyond college. Almost half of respondents, though, report to being under 30 years old.[3] Indeed, we often refer to this group as "post-college alumni" as a marker of both age and minimal level of post-secondary education. This title is mostly supported by the survey, in that 90% of respondents in this group said they had acquired an academic education of an Associate degree or higher, 86% had completed education on the level of a Bachelor's degree or higher, and more than a third had obtained graduate and advanced professional degrees, while many more were either in the process of doing so or planning to obtain such an advanced degree in the future.

---

2   Information for this chapter was gathered through an online questionnaire, prepared and administered in early 2018 by the National Association of Independent Schools (NAIS), and adapted by the Research Institute for Waldorf Education (RIWE) to address issues specific to Waldorf education. Respondents remained anonymous but were asked for demographic information, including race, gender, and financial history. A total of 643 post-college alumni completed the survey, representing about 15 percent of an estimated 4,000 individuals who graduated from a Waldorf high school between 1990 and 2010.

3   Due to a clerical error by a participating school, about 16% of this survey's post-college questionnaires were filled out by a younger cohort of alumni who had graduated between 2011-2017. Although taking these respondents into account might slightly affect the numerical accuracies of the data presented in the following pages, it should not alter the broadly representative picture of the life and times of the post-college Waldorf alumni.

In college, these graduates studied a wide variety of subjects, with the largest group of alumni (38%) majoring in a subject that falls within the Arts & Humanities, followed by the Social & Behavioral Sciences (28%), and STEM (Science, Technology, Engineering, and Math) subjects (17%). They felt very well prepared by their Waldorf high schools to meet the intellectual, social, and organizational challenges of college life, even if they discovered that they needed at times to work hard to acquire advanced skills in math, science, and technology. They further found they arrived in college well prepared for public speaking, collaborative work, leadership roles, and active participation in the social and cultural life on campus. And while—contrary to common opinion—Waldorf schools do not produce legions of artists (though many do end up working in creative professions), their graduates believe that the systematic weaving of the arts into their pre-college education has instilled in them a strong confidence that they can meet challenges and succeed in whatever they set their mind on doing.

While in college, these graduates realized they were more comfortable thinking in wholes, rather than breaking these down to their constitutive components; they tried to see the big picture, allow for association and creativity, and seek essential meanings. They also felt they were prepared to work in teams, collaborate, and elevate the needs of the group or community over their own individual goals. In this sense, they did not feel very well prepared—nor were they particularly attracted—to engage in competition.

The latter qualifications also seem to direct their moral compass, which clearly points in the direction of responsibility towards the community at large, respect towards all "others," rejection of privilege, and inclination toward causes that are not limited to their own personal needs and desires.

After college, and one or more graduate degree or professional certification, they find themselves working in a variety of fields and taking on a wide variety of roles. Still, the largest number of alumni (23%) are to be found in the wide field of education ranging from early childhood to academia, followed by the various medical and health professions (10.3%).

They are very happy with their lives and extract the greatest satisfaction from their family and friends. For the most part, though, they don't become great earners. In fact, they might well end up earning less than their parents have, and close to 16% of them say their greatest challenge in life is financial.

When they think back on their Waldorf schools, a decisive majority (82%) say they have a "positive" or "very positive" view. They are proud of their affiliation with their former school and agree that it has become part of who they are today. No less than 87% of alumni say they would recommend their former school to a friend or family member.

However, collaborative, community-oriented inclinations that they practiced while at school, and the progressive climate of the millennial age to which they belong and with which they are in tune, have made them very much concerned about *diversity* as the measurable marker of equality, inclusiveness, pluralism, and the dismantling of an outdated and unjust social hierarchy. And even if the origins of this worldview could be traced back to their time spent in a Waldorf school, it often also leads them to cast a critical eye over this very same school, where they often experienced a predominantly white, affluent community and a Euro-centric curriculum. This, many of them say, may deter them from sending their own children to a Waldorf school, even if an impresive majority of them remember their time there with great fondness.

Finally, many of them are not familiar with the anthroposophical foundations of their Waldorf education. Close to half (43%) of alumni report they know very little or nothing at all about anthroposophy, and 14% express a dismissive to outright hostile view of anthroposophy, which they see as "cultish," "outdated and racist," "bunk," and a "liability" to Waldorf schools. (And, yes, these alumni do not hold back when they have a negative opinion.) At the same time, 43% have been exposed to or have actively sought to learn more about anthroposophy and Waldorf education—some of them becoming Waldorf teachers. Most of these alumni profess to having an appreciative general familiarity with anthroposophy, though very few identify themselves as "card-carrying anthroposophists."

SOME DEMOGRAPHICS

An outstanding characteristic of this cohort of Waldorf alumni who graduated prior to 2010 is that they clearly come from well-educated families, with 75% of respondents saying at least one parent has earned an undergraduate degree or more, and 42% coming from a household with a parent who has earned either a graduate (e.g., M.A., Ph.D.) or advanced professional degree (J.D., M.D.). (For comparison: the U.S. Census of 1990 showed that only 20% of the adult population, 25 or older at the time, had obtained a bachelor's degree.)

A second striking characteristic of this group is its lack of racial diversity. Of the survey respondents, 97% identify as White, though some of these also checked other racial boxes, with 5% identifying as or *also as* Hispanic, 5% as or *also as* Asian, and less than 3% as or *also as* African-American. One third of the respondents are male, almost two thirds are female, and 1.3% of respondents identify as transgender or gender non-conforming.

In terms of income we found that a little less than a third of respondents, roughly 29%, report household earnings of under $40,000 a year (though we should remember that with close to half the population being under 30, it could be expected that many of these households consist of singles and/or single earners). A little more than half (53%) located their annual household earnings between $40,000 and $150,000, and 17% earned more than $150K a year. In general, these alumni earn less than their parents do. (About a third of parents enjoy an annual income greater than $150K a year, and only 15% earn under $40K.)

Reporting their employment status prior to the national employment peak of 2019, the vast majority of alumni, nearly 70%, have full-time jobs, while 7% report part-time employment and 6% are full-time students (mostly in graduate or professional school); 10% are employed in multiple jobs, a contemporary trend[4] that might be saying more about what the job market has to offer than about voluntary choices made by these individuals. A little less than 2% report that they are unemployed but seeking work. Of those who are employed:

37% work in for-profit companies

23% work in non-profit companies and non-governmental-organizations

19% are self-employed or business owners

15% work in a governmental or public agency

PROFESSIONS AND EMPLOYMENT

Waldorf alumni work in academic institutions such as Ohio State, Utah State, and Florida State Universities, as well as the Universities of Maryland, Washington, Michigan, Texas, and Chicago. They work at NYU and Tulane University and Bryn Mawr College and Bard College and also at Switzerland's University of Geneva or Ontario's York University.

Others work in public school systems, both primary and secondary, such as the Tacoma Public Schools, the North Vancouver School District, the Berkeley Unified School District, and in the NYC Department of Education. Many others teach in a host of Waldorf schools across the United States and Canada, as well as in Europe.

Waldorf graduates further report working in law offices, small businesses, and mega-corporations such as Nestlé, PepsiCo, Viacom, and General Motors. They are to be found in well-known private financial institutions such as Citigroup, The Canadian Imperial Bank of Commerce (CIBC), and Goldman Sachs, but also in the Federal Reserve Bank of New York and in the World Bank. Others provide financial analysis in organizations such as the Economist Intelligence Unit and Los Angeles Business Journal.

They serve in governmental offices such as the U.S. Department of State, the Department of Veterans Affairs, the Environmental Protection Agency, and in the U.S. courts, but also in non-governmental organizations and think-tanks such as the Council on Foreign Relations and the Tony Blair Institute for Global Change, and in intergovernmental organizations such as the World Trade Organization and the United Nations.

---

4   See Census Bureau online publication, About 13M U.S. Workers Have More Than One Job (June 18, 2019).

Waldorf alumni also serve in the Coast Guard, the United States Marine Corps, the Air Force, and Army, as well as in the Peace Corps, in the National Park Service, and in AmeriCorps.

They are found in software and tech companies such as Adobe Systems, Google, Apple, and Facebook; they work for entertainment giants such as Warner Brothers and Netflix, and in the tourism industry, occupying jobs in companies such as Marriott International and Royal Caribbean international cruise liner.

They are creative artists that run their own independent studios or are employed in established performing-arts groups, such as Ballet Idaho or the American Players Theatre in Wisconsin. Others work in leading cultural organizations such as National Public Radio and New York's Whitney Museum of American Art and the Museum of Modern Art.

Many Waldorf alumni are employed in healthcare fields. They hold different positions in health centers, senior living housings, and hospitals such as Stony Brook Southampton Hospital, the Good Samaritan Hospital, Cincinnati Children's Hospital, and at the NYC Department of Health & Mental Hygiene. They are also found in health insurance companies such as Cigna, and work in animal hospitals and veterinary clinics.

The single field of work attracting the greatest number of Waldorf alumni is clearly **Education**, with 23% of respondents identifying either primary, secondary, or higher education as the field of their occupation, and more than 15% identifying their specific profession as "educator" on any level (see comparative table below). Second in line are the **Health Professions** or **Medicine**, with 10.3% of respondents identifying their professions as that of a health professional in the wide field that includes nurses and therapists as well as surgeons and specialists. And while a good 12% report their principal occupation as being artist, entertainer, or other creative professional, a smaller percentage, 5%, identify their creative field as being the Fine and Performing Arts. The same number of respondents work in Computer Science/Technology, while a slightly larger group, 5.4%, report working in the Social Sciences. Very closely behind follow the fields of Media/Journalism/Publishing (4.34%), Law/Legal Services (4.16%), and Financial Services (4.16%).

As in many other sections of the survey, one of the largest group of respondents consists of those who did not find their profession or field represented on the menu and selected the category "Other"—no less than 16%, in this case. This data point suggests that Waldorf alumni are often not satisfied with ready-made categories and that their interests, including professional ones, range over a wide variety of fields. (Were we to exclude the category "Other" and those who have opted for it from our response count, we would have reached a higher percentage of respondents in the top categories of Education [27.4%] and Medicine [12.3%] but with a difference of only 1 percentage point or less in the other categories.)

COMPARISON OF WALDORF GRADUATES WITH ALUMNI
OF OTHER INDEPENDENT SCHOOLS

We compared the top industries or fields of work in which Waldorf alumni are employed to those in which NAIS alumni find their employment. The data regarding NAIS graduates are drawn from a parallel survey conducted by the National Association of Independent Schools in 2017, with responses collected from a smaller number of subjects (562 individuals responded to the NAIS survey and 643 to the Waldorf poll) representing, though, a much larger group of nationwide independent schools alumni. One unfortunate asymmetry in the two surveys is that one third of the NAIS respondents had graduated from their high school in the years and even decades prior to our focus time range of 1990-2010. This does not necessarily mean that we are comparing apples to oranges, but some of these apples might have been on the shelf quite a bit longer than others.

With this caveat in mind, we note that in both groups, Education is the top field of employment, though a greater percentage of Waldorf alumni, 23%, are employed in this field than NAIS's 17.5% (see comparative table below). The two cohorts also share the same field in the second place, Medicine, where 10.3% of Waldorf alumni and 9.3% of NAIS alumni are employed. Decisive differences are apparent, though, in Higher Education professions, and in the Fine or Performing Arts, where twice as many Waldorf alumni work compared to the NAIS alumni group. This relationship is flipped when we look at the fields of Law and Legal Services and of Financial Services, which appear to be twice as attractive to NAIS alumni than to Waldorf. The figures are almost identical in the fields of Computer Science/Technology and Hospitality, Tourism, and Travel. And slightly more Waldorf alumni turn to professions in the Social Services, while more NAIS alumni turn to retail.

Here are the top industries or fields of work in which Waldorf alumni are employed, paired with their peers from NAIS schools:

Table 5.1

Fields of Employment	Waldorf Alumni	NAIS Alumni
Education – All levels	**23.0%**	17.5%
Education – Elementary, Secondary, or Adult	**15.2%**	13.5%
Medicine	**10.3%**	9.3%
Higher Education – College/University	**7.8%**	4.0%
Social Services	**5.4%**	3.3%
Computer Science/Technology	**5.0%**	4.9%
Fine/Performing Arts	**5.0%**	2.2%
Media/Journalism/Publishing	**4.3%**	3.3%
Law/Legal Services	4.2%	**7.3%**
Financial Services	4.2%	**8.2%**
Hospitality/Tourism/Travel	**2.5%**	2.4%
Retail	2.0%	**3.8%**
Other	16.0%	**16.6%**

PROFESSIONS

When we zoom in on their specific professions, rather than on the field to which their employing organization or company belongs, we find that Waldorf alumni work in a variety of professions from social media marketing to toxicology to fire fighting and yoga instruction. Many report they are self-employed or own their own businesses.

Educators are featured, again, at the top of the list of specific professions, followed by medical providers. Artistic, creative, and entertainment professions rise to third place, and scientists receive a clearer representation on the fourth spot. The category "Other" expands here to include almost a quarter of respondents.

The focus on the alumni's specific professions reveals more differences between Waldorf and NAIS alumni. Here we see that the portion of Waldorf alumni who identify their professions as artist, entertainer, or other creative professional is two-and-a-half times the portion of NAIS alumni who do so, and more than twice as many Waldorf alumni write or edit for a living as NAIS alumni do. Also, in the computer professions—which include programmer, computer scientist, and system analyst—we find twice as many Waldorf alumni as NAIS graduates. On the other hand, the percentage of

NAIS alumni working in sales, advertisement, or public relations is almost triple that of Waldorf alumni, and it is more than double for those working as lawyers or other providers of legal services.

Table 5.2

Profession	Waldorf Alumni	NAIS Alumni
Educator – all levels	15.5%	10.5%
Medical/Mental/Other Health Provider	12.3%	10.4%
Artist/Entertainer/Other Creative	12.0%	4.8%
Scientist – including Life, Physical, & Social Sciences and Math/Statistics	5.2%	4.0%
Salesperson/Advertising/PR	5.0%	13.9%
Administrator	5.0%	6.8%
Lawyer/Other Legal Services	3.7%	8.2%
Writer/Editor/Journalist	3.4%	1.5%
Computers – Programmer, Scientist, Analyst	3.2%	1.7%
Engineer	2.7%	3.0%
Other	22.3%	16.9%

The job titles of the Waldorf alumni responding to the survey cover a very wide range demonstrated by, though by no means limited to, the list below, culled from the many responses offered in the survey:

Actor and Freelance Writer

Artist, Designer, Researcher, Social Entrepreneur, Consultant

Assistant Athletic Director/ Head Boys Lacrosse Coach

Associate Producer/Marketing Specialist

Associate Professor of Art History

Attorney

Author & Founder

Automation/Software Engineer

Ballet Dancer

Blacksmith

Cancer Data Analyst

CEO

Chef

Chemist

Chief Financial Officer

Chief Technology Officer and Post-Harvest Coordinator

Clinical Psychologist

Clinical Research Associate

Commercial Diver

Content Provider and Copywriter

Creative Director

Credit and Portfolio Sr. Risk Manager

Crisis Counselor Coach

Data Scientist

Designer

Director of Engineering

Director, Integrated Marketing

Educational Consultant,
and Theater Director

Engineer

Engineering and Sales Manager

Environment Artist

Executive Coach and Consultant

Executive Producer

Executive/Administrative Assistant

Farmer

Film Director/Editor

Financial Advisor

Foreign Service Officer

Freelance Filmmaker
and Film Instructor

Freelance Journalist

General Counsel, Director of
Compliance & Accountability

Goldsmith

Graphic and Web Designer,
Festival Director

Head Basketball Coach

Insurance Underwriter

Justice Services Coordinator

Landscape Architect

Managing Editor

Massage Therapist

Midwife

Office Manager

Photographer

Photojournalist

Physical Therapist

Priest

Physician

Registered Nurse

Reiki Master & End of Life Doula

Research Scientist/
Public Health Epidemiologist

Residence Director/Title IX Coordinator

Sales Manager

Senior Creative Director

Senior Firefighter

Senior Sustainability Manager

Social Media Manager

Software Engineer

Speech-Language Pathologist

Surveillance Agent

Teacher

Television Development Executive

Town Planner

Writer, Director, and Executive Producer

EMPLOYMENT SECTORS AND THE CURRENT U.S. POPULATION

We were able to access employment data for the U.S. population for the year 2018, provided by Bureau of Labor Statistics. These data allow us to make a very general comparison among professional positions held by Waldorf alumni who are eight years or more out of high school, their peers who have attended other independent schools in the United States, and the general U.S. population (see table below). What makes this comparison "general," first and foremost, are the employment categories according to which the Bureau of Labor Statistics organizes its data. We do have to question the merits of grouping Education, Health, and Social Services all in one category, or of including the Fine and Performing Arts in the category of Leisure & Hospitality. We would also note that the category Professional & Business Services could cover such a wide range of professions that it calls into question the coherence of this grouping. With these reservations in mind, we note the following outstanding elements of this comparison:

> When grouping together Education, Health, and Social Services, we find a decisively larger percentage of Waldorf alumni employed in such fields than of the general U.S. population (39.13% vs. 22.5%) or of their NAIS peers (31.77%).

> Conversely, compared to the general U.S. population, we find a substantially smaller percentage of Waldorf alumni in Wholesale & Retail Trade (2.36% vs. 13.01%), as well as in Manufacturing (2.36% vs. 9.99%) and Construction (1.27% vs. 7.18%).

> As previously observed, the percentage of NAIS alumni engaged in Financial Activities is practically double the percentage of Waldorf alumni professing to engage in similar activities (8.28% vs. 4.17%), while the figure for the general population is set neatly in between the two (6.84%). Similarly, there is a decisive gap between NAIS alumni engaged in Professional & Business Services (17.23%) and Waldorf alumni in this wide field (12.32%).

Table 5.3: Waldorf and NAIS employment sectors

Sectors	Waldorf Alumni	NAIS Alumni	US Population (2018)
Education & Health (including Social) Services	**39.13**%	31.77%	22.50%
Professional & Business Services	12.32%	**17.23**%	12.17%
Transportation & Utilities (including Science/Engineering)	8.33%	**8.72**%	5.49%
Leisure & Hospitality (including Fine and Performing Arts)	7.61%	4.70%	**9.16**%
Financial Activities	4.17%	**8.28**%	6.84%
Public Administration	3.80%	2.01%	**4.76**%
Wholesale & Retail Trade	2.36%	3.58%	**13.01**%
Manufacturing	2.36%	2.68%	**9.99**%
Construction	1.27%	1.57%	**7.18**%
Information	1.27%	**2.24**%	1.87%
Agriculture and related	1.27%	0.45%	**1.56**%
Other Services	16.12%	**16.78**%	4.97%

It is worth noting that only in the fields of education and health are a greater percentage of Waldorf graduates represented, compared to NAIS alumni and the general U.S. population.

These relationships are also represented by the following graph:

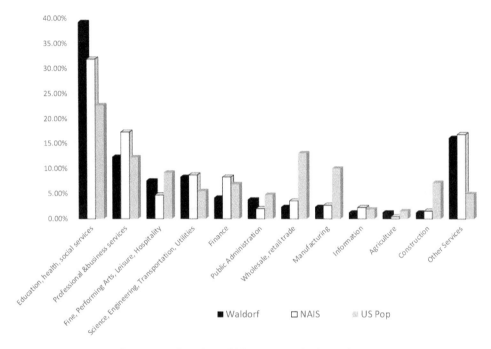

Color Version of Graph Available at www.waldorfresearchinstitute.org

EDUCATION

Before reporting some details regarding Waldorf alumni's college experience, we note that one-third of respondents have embraced the opportunity afforded by their high schools to study a semester abroad, mostly (88%) at another Waldorf school. The top five countries traveled to for this opportunity were:

Germany (39%)	Switzerland (12%)	U.K. (3%)
France (17%)	Austria (5%)	

Three of these top five destinations are German-speaking countries. They attracted a total of 56% of those who studied abroad, while only a total of 13% attended schools in Spanish-speaking countries including Spain, Mexico, Guatemala, Peru, and Argentina.

GAP YEAR ACTIVITIES

A quarter of respondents reports having taken a gap year or even a longer pause after high school before pursuing further studies. Many describe a period of national and international travels, working to raise money for college, taking on volunteer work—including many who volunteered in Camphill communities in the U.S. and abroad—childcare jobs abroad, and taking time to figure out their next steps. Here is a sample of such gap-year experiences in the alumni's own words:

Pursued music photography at live concerts.

Worked as a nanny in France.

Volunteered at a Camphill in England.

Interned on a farm in France to learn cheesemaking. Also worked with a contractor in PA doing weather sealing and a wilderness program in Canada leading canoe trips.

Undertook biodynamic farming, political activism. Worked as a barista, moved to Taos, NM, worked as a dye assistant, traveled in Peru.

Lived and worked in Berlin for 6 months to work on my German, and then went to Scotland for 4 months to work and spend time with family there. Then I spent a summer in Brazil, during which time I attended a youth conference and did volunteer work. I then moved back to Switzerland where I worked several different jobs before starting university.

Joined the Canadian Armed Forces and served as a Medical Technician. I served two tours of duty with the United Nations and participated in Op Assist and Regard.

Moved to San Francisco with a group of fellow students to play music.

Worked at a homeless shelter through AmeriCorps.

Traveled, built a boat, worked as a deckhand on an educational sailing vessel, worked in a boatyard, worked as the mate on a sailing catamaran.

Worked as a model, stone mason, biodynamic farmer, Waldorf kindergarten assistant, barista, Spanish translator, and artist before attending college many years later when I found what I wanted to study.

Spent 1-year apprenticeship on an organic farm in New Zealand.

Had children.

Studied to be a private investigator and worked at that for a year.

Worked 4 part-time jobs for 6 months, then went to Peru and Ecuador with a friend from a Waldorf school in Germany. We took Spanish classes, backpacked, and volunteered.

Worked at the Khujand, Tajikistan Waldorf School.

Worked on a biodynamic farm in Namibia in the fall, and worked at an Olympic horse stable in Germany in the spring/summer.

Spent time as ski bum in Lake Tahoe.

Attended and worked in an Ashram in India helping to guide students through workshops, took a two-months cross country trip across the US with two of my best Waldorf friends. Worked at a bird rehabilitation sanctuary in Greece, traveled around Europe, went to a Rainbow gathering in Hungary. Worked in a Camphill in Germany, and took a Naturopathic course in Northern Ireland.

Worked on a Marine Conservation Project in Thailand.

Traveled as a musician.

Joined non-profit film collective and began working in the film industry while studying experimental and non-narrative film formats.

Worked on a fishing boat traveled around the world.

Moved to Japan to perform and study Taiko [Japanese percussions] and Japanese language.

Worked for about a year at ConEd. as a meter reader.

Shoestring backpacked in Asia; studied Chinese, Tibetan Buddhist meditation, volunteered. Spent 4 months in a Camphill in Switzerland.

First year: volunteered at the Community Association of Monte Azul (an anthroposophical NGO). Second year: Traveled around Europe and lived in Norway. Third year: intensive 12 month primitive skills training in the forest on the Oregon coast. Fourth year: lived and traveled around the Middle East. Fifth year: lived in Copenhagen and NYC before moving to California to start university.

COLLEGE MAJORS AND HIGHER DEGREES

Virtually all alumni of the generation surveyed in this chapter have proceeded to post-secondary studies at one level or another (only 2% did not). 86% of them earned a Bachelor's degree or higher; by comparison, according to the U.S. Census Bureau's estimate, in 2018 only 30.9% of the adult population in the U.S., age 25 or older, had completed a bachelor's degree.[5] Another 4.2% of Waldorf alumni earned an associate's degree, and 7.8% attended but did not complete their college studies.

These Waldorf alumni majored in a wide variety of fields and subjects, with especially strong attraction to the study of Literatures & Languages, Visual & Performing Arts, Psychology and other Social Sciences such as International Relations/Political Science. The general distribution of undergraduate majors for this cohort is as follows:

Arts & Humanities	38%
Social & Behavioral Sciences	28%
STEM Subjects	17%
Health-related Subjects and Professions	4%
Business & Accounting	4%
Education	3%
Other	6%

More than a third of these alumni, or 35%, have already proceeded to obtain professional or higher degrees beyond their undergraduate studies, while another 15% state that they are currently pursuing a higher degree or professional certification beyond the undergraduate level, and another 41% say they intend to pursue either a professional or postgraduate degree in the future. If all of these individual plans come to fruition it will mean that more than 90% of Waldorf alumni will have sought education or professional training beyond the undergraduate level.

Even with the additional time and resources spent on further education and training before fully embarking on a professional career, alumni, for the most part, claim to be satisfied with the way their Waldorf school prepared them for their careers. That is to say, 78% say they are either very satisfied (43.3%) or satisfied (34.75%) with their preparation in secondary school, while 4% say they are dissatisfied and 2.2% very dissatisfied; 15.7% are neutral on this subject.

The variety of professional certifications and postgraduate degrees obtained by Waldorf alumni are represented by the following selective list, redacted from the survey responses:

Welding Certificate	Esthetician Degree
Massage and Healing Vocational License	Waldorf Teacher Training

---

5   Census Bureau statistics and other data are taken from the United States Census Bureau's website: www.census.gov

J.D. (Doctor Joris/Professional Degree in Law)

Master's in Accounting (M.S.)

Master of Architecture (M.Arch.)

Master's in Math Education

Master's in Social Work (M.S.W.)

Master's in Music (M.M.)

Master of Nursing Science (M.S.N.)

Master of Public Health (M.P.H.)

Master's in Social Sciences (M.S.Sc.)

Master of Science in Civil Engineering (M.Sc.)

M.Sc. in Global Health Policy

Master's in Geography specializing in Hydrology

Master of Science in Sustainable Management

Master of Environmental Engineering Science

Master's in Business Management (M.B.A.)

Master's in Nonprofit Management

Master of Fine Arts (M.F.A.) in Contemporary Performance

M.F.A. in Music Production and Sound Design for Visual Media

M.A. in Graphic Design

M.A. in International Economic History

M.A. in International Affairs

M.A. in Museum Studies

Master's in Waldorf Education

Master's in Dance/Movement Therapy and Counseling

Master's in Chinese Medicine

DUAL MASTER DEGREES:

Literary Studies + Counseling

Landscape Architecture + Horticulture

M.Sc. in Bioengineering + Business Administration (M.B.A.)

M.Sc. in Geophysics + M.A. in Science Education

Ph.D. in Anthropology

Ph.D. in Biology

Ph.D. in Paleobiology

Ph.D. in Chemistry

Ph.D. Clinical Psychology

Ph.D. in Germanic Languages and Literatures

Ph.D. in English

Ph.D. in Sociology

Doctorate in Education (Ed.D.)

Doctor of Medicine (M.D.)

Doctor of Dental Surgery (D.D.S.)

Doctor of Veterinary Medicine (D.V.M.)

Doctor of Chiropractic (D.C.) and Licensed Acupuncturist

Doctor of Osteopathy and Master of Public Health (M.P.H.)

When we focus on the highest degree obtained by respondents, regardless if it is an undergraduate, graduate, or professional degree, the top-ten subjects studied are ranked in the following order of popularity:

1. Social & Behavioral Sciences
2. Arts—Fine & Performing
3. Humanities
4. Health & Medicine
5. Business & Management
6. Education
7. Life Sciences
8. Physical Sciences, Engineering & Math
9. Law & Legal Services
10. Computer & Information Sciences

In comparing this ranked list to the highest degrees obtained by NAIS alumni who have graduated high school prior to 2010 (see table below), we observe some striking differences alongside a handful of similarities. While the Social & Behavioral Sciences clearly make the top choice among Waldorf alumni, it is Business & Management that tops the list with NAIS alumni. In fact, more than twice as many NAIS alumni obtained their highest degree in this field as those who earned their degree in the second field on the NAIS list, the Humanities. And while the Fine & Performing Arts feature second on the Waldorf alumni list, they are to be found almost all the way to the bottom of the NAIS list, in eighth place. The third major difference is observed in the field of Law & Legal Services, which holds the one-before-last spot on the Waldorf top-ten list, while it occupies the third rank on the NAIS list, very closely behind the Humanities. All the other fields—Health Professions, Education, Life Sciences, STEM, and Computer/Information Sciences—have either the same or very close spots in the two top-ten rankings lists.

Table 5.4: Waldorf and NAIS rankings of highest degree

	Waldorf Alumni Ranking	NAIS Alumni Ranking
Social & Behavioral Sciences	1	4
Arts - Fine and Performing	2	8
Humanities	3	2
Health	4	5
Business & Management	5	1
Education	6	6
Life Sciences	7	9
Physical Sciences, Engineering & Math	8	7
Law & Legal Services	9	3
Computer & Information Sciences	10	10

CURRENT LIFE EXPERIENCE: GIFTS, CHALLENGES, JOYS, SKILLS

A very strong majority of Waldorf alumni—90%—report feeling satisfaction with their lives. That is to say, 48% state that they are "*very* satisfied" with their lives while 42% say they are "satisfied." (Note, though, that an even greater number of NAIS alumni report a high level of life-satisfaction, with close to 55% stating they are "very satisfied" and nearly 40% saying they are "satisfied.") Only 6.5% of respondents are neutral about the full picture of their lives, while 3% say they are not satisfied. (Among NAIS alumni, 5% report to be neutral on this question while less than 1% say they are not satisfied with their lives.)

There is no doubt that Waldorf alumni draw the greatest satisfaction and joy in life from their immediate families—an answer offered by 46.3% of respondents—and from their friends (15.4%). On the other hand, when asked about life *challenges*, respondents most often mention finances (15.8%), followed by health issues of oneself or family members (10%), and troubles in that very same life-sector that is regarded the source of greatest joy, namely family (9%).

Here are the most frequent themes named in response to the questions of life's greatest gifts, sources of joy, and challenges:

What has been your greatest gift thus far in life?
Family (mentioned by 46.3% of respondents)
Relationships/friends (15.4%)
My Waldorf education (8.9%)
Ongoing learning/education generally (8.5%)
A fulfilling career (7.3%)
Travel (5.0%)
Practicing the arts (3.2%)

What brings you the greatest joy in life?
Family (37.8%)
Friends & Community (30.0%)
Practicing the arts (14.5%)
Helping others (12.5%)
Being in nature (12.5%)
Being creative (3.7%)

What is your greatest challenge thus far in life?
Finances (15.8%)
Health issues (10.0%)
Family troubles (9.0%)
Lack of direction (8.2%)

Deciding on a career-path and work-related difficulties (7.0%)
Finding balance in one's personal/professional life (6.3%)
Self-doubt/lack of self-confidence (5.3%)
Dealing with anxiety or depression (4.9%)
Dealing with death of family-member/loved one (4.4%)
Communication in relationships/lack of social skills (3.0%)

GIFTS AND CHALLENGES

While a clear majority of comments referred to immediate family members—specifically children and partners—as their greatest gifts in life so far, other responses shed more light on the variety of their lives and experiences. These include:

Freedom to do literally anything

The ability to share what I'm passionate about through education

My powers of imagination, conceptualization, visualization, and introspection

Doing things with my hands

Meeting many mentors and kind people who helped me through different stages of my life

Being able to do what I love for a living!

Being adaptable in my thinking and open to new ways of being in the world

Deep incessant curiosity – it has fueled everything I have done from career to hobbies to friendships to travel

My adaptability and ethics

Creative and Emotional thinking skills

My capacity for awe and wonder and empathy

The ability to have a job that both inspires me creatively and also seeks to make the world a better place, using community as a way to nourish change

My life as an artist

I am a renaissance man

Learning how to heal myself and change directions in life

The love I've felt for other human beings

Life itself

Several respondents show particular awareness of the privilege that comes with the circumstances of their birth, as expressed in comments such as, "I was born with every possible advantage – skin color, socio-economic status, education, etc."

In terms of life's challenges, many of the respondents appear to refer to difficulties in reconciling an idealistic image of humanity with their actual experiences as well as to challenges in finding their place in the world. This is expressed in comments such as:

Staying grounded, focused, and attuned to what my path in life is

Not getting stuck in the difficulty and pain of navigating and reducing the immense suffering in the world

Working in a very stressed society that does not value the well being of individuals

Not being able to help people in need; every day I have to bypass homeless people on the street

Understanding my privilege as a white male and learning how to live a life dedicated to anti-oppression

Self-acceptance and disappointment in humanity

Focusing in a single direction long enough to truly succeed

Being disillusioned with how completely broken our entire system is

Knowing when to quit something that isn't working

Seeing the suffering of others

Coming to terms with human flaws

Having trouble committing to one path because it might mean sacrificing other possibilities

"Work ethic," "Boredom," "Disorganization," "Perfectionism"

Life

WALDORF REFERENCES

Quite a few respondents chose to name their Waldorf education as a major life gift, with comments such as the following:

My Waldorf education, truly a gift from my parents to my brothers and me.

Having received Waldorf Education! The strength to live a life with little security comes a lot from that.

Waldorf education and the dedicated master teachers I grew up with and get to still cultivate deep relationships with.

The confidence Waldorf gave me to chase dreams and make them my reality. I'm able to tackle any new situation with enthusiasm and see that everything is an opportunity.

I can honestly say that my Waldorf education has been one of my greatest gifts thus far, and one that I'll be forever grateful to my single mom for her commitment to. I feel it set me up in the best possible way for the kind of life I want to pursue, and every time I speak with someone who had a dissatisfying public education I feel more grateful for my own experience; while of course not without its challenges, as a whole it nurtured me and pushed me in the ways I needed to be nurtured and pushed, and instilled in me a subtle sense of culture, of harmony, and of beauty that I still find affects me in both small and enormous ways today.

Attending a Waldorf School has been a great gift. The nurturing and patient teachers at Waldorf prepared me for life's challenges and instilled a life-long love of learning in me. I am a well-rounded, compassionate person and my friends from Waldorf are my "forever" friends.

I am very proactive and driven to see my inspirations and pursuits come to life. There is much that I attribute to my Waldorf education. I feel that much of my perspective, creativity, and optimism was shaped by my early education.

SKILLS

Another reflection of the values that matter collectively to Waldorf alumni is suggested in their response to a prompt inviting them to choose the three "skills" most important to them from a menu of ten items, plus "other." While several options on this menu are not really skills (a fact commented upon by multiple respondents), the selection is telling. The items receiving the least number of votes are "control" and "wealth"— each selected by less than 5% of respondents—followed by "reputation" (selected less than 9%). The top five items selected are:

Communication (selected by 68% of respondents)

Problem solving (57%)

Ethical Standards (46%)

Truthfulness (41%)

Initiative (28%)

To this list, which also included "leadership" (25%) and "sociability" (15%), several respondents added "compassion," "creativity," and "empathy." And the following comment appears to represent the critical view, as well as the set of values, that is expressed in many of the other free-form comments: "Many of the options on this list are not skills—is the question "which of the following do you value most"? If so, leadership, communication, ethical standards."

By now we have learned much about the general contours of the course of life of Waldorf alumni who have graduated from high school either during the last decade of the 20th century or the first decade of the 21st. We have observed gap year activities—for those who chose to pursue one—courses of study in college and beyond, chosen professions and fields of work, and general self-evaluations of their gifts and challenges in life. In the next chapter, we will study closely this cohort's assessment of the long-term impacts of their Waldorf education—from the preparation for college to the preparation for life.

VI Post-College Alumni (2)

REFLECTING ON THEIR WALDORF EDUCATION:
SATISFACTION & CRITICISM

OVERVIEW

In the final analysis, Waldorf alumni are clearly appreciative of their secondary education. Asked time and again how satisfied they are with different aspects of their Waldorf education and the effects it had on their lives after graduation, alumni consistently express high levels of appreciation. Their evaluations of various aspects of faculty engagement show 85%-91% of respondents stating they are either satisfied or very satisfied; 82% of respondents say the same about their preparation for further education (college and beyond), and 78% are either satisfied or very satisfied with the way their high schools have prepared them for their eventual careers. Presented with a long and varied list of skills—academic, social, and work-related—respondents repeatedly offer a high score for their preparation in each, resulting in a collective score of being "well prepared" (4 out of 5 points) for most of these skills.

Of course, satisfaction comes in many shades and with various reservations, and the positive responses should not overshadow the finer details of the Waldorf experience as reported by its graduates. In the following pages, we aim to represent the valuations and reflections of this experience as captured by words and numbers. These take the form, on the one hand, of responses to several free-form questions that allowed alumni to express themselves in detail, and, on the other, tabulated scores that summarize their feelings about their education. Even in these numerical valuations, which might appear foreign to the spirit of Waldorf education, we were able to discern trends and extract insights that draw a fine-grained picture of the Waldorf experience and its later consequences.

FACULTY AND SCHOOL IMPACT

There is no question that the vast majority of alumni view their former faculty positively. Graduates score highly their appreciation for the personal interest faculty members showed in their students and their readiness to support growth beyond purely academic achievement. Alumni strongly agree that their teachers and the school culture have had significant impact on their personal and intellectual development.

In this regard, Waldorf alumni are not much different from graduates of other independent schools in North America. In fact, Waldorf and non-Waldorf alumni respond with nearly identical high scores when asked to evaluate their general satisfaction with their former schools and teachers. However, the responses tellingly begin to diverge in relation to two questions. The first inquiries about the impact school and its teachers had on one's "ethical reasoning," to which 76% of Waldorf alumni reply that school was significantly influential, whereas 71.5% of NAIS alumni say the same.

The second question concerns the influence that high-school experience had on later career goals. In a survey section that otherwise records acknowledgment of a very high level of influence, only 51% of NAIS alumni agree that their school experience has been significantly influential on their careers. Even fewer Waldorf alums— barely 40%—say the same. These relatively low evaluations by both alumni groups suggest that career choices and goals are not necessarily formed in high school. Such decisions, the responses indicate, are better informed by the various academic and social experiences taking place in college or other post-secondary settings.

High school, these alumni—and especially Waldorf alumni—seem to be saying, does not prepare you for a specific job or career path. Instead, Waldorf education, in the words of one alumnus, "prepares you for *life*!"

PREPARATION FOR PROFESSIONAL LIFE: ALUMNI COMMENTS

From the hundreds of comments on the various impacts of Waldorf education on professional life, the selection listed below represents a sampling of issues and voices reflected in the survey. While we let these comments speak for themselves, we have added italics to draw attention to the specific skills and qualities cited in the graduates' responses.

Appreciative Overviews

Among the more elaborate responses, we find appreciative overviews such as:

Waldorf education cultivated my creativity, my drive, and my willingness to persevere to get work done.

Critical problem-solving ability (i.e. finding the root issue quickly) and an ability to work harmoniously with others have helped me succeed. I learned this at Waldorf.

Manual dexterity and three-dimensional thinking are critical to my line of work, and I can't imagine an education that could have better prepared me.

Empathy, imagination, creativity, passion for learning new things: I have all the skills that are the most essential, rare, and useful. And the drive to learn everything else!

I credit my Waldorf education with a degree of critical thinking and mental elasticity that has been very useful in my professional life.

My Waldorf education has been the perfect preparation for the work I do which is creative, innovative, and requires a 360-degree perspective. In this industry there is never one right path or direction. The flexibility in thinking and confidence in my intuition that came from my Waldorf education has stood me in good stead.

My education supported me in my audacity to question. Without this I would never be doing what it is I do, namely working on the forefront of global and local solutions for an abundant and sustainable life.

Software development is a creative process and I do think the Waldorf approach encourages a creative mind.

Just as my college education followed very naturally from my time in Waldorf school, my career has followed naturally from my college education. I am happily employed in the field I trained for, and I use skills learned in Waldorf school every day.

Waldorf education instilled the freedom and independence to pursue what is meaningful to me, and to find creative ways to make alternative professional choices work. I am a big-picture systems thinker and I think this is largely due to my Waldorf education. Over the course of my professional life, I have been hired largely due to the confidence I display in my thinking, as I am able to articulate and express complex ideas clearly and respond to questions creatively. However, because of this, I don't make a great employee, as I don't easily accept top-down management and I have quit several jobs because I couldn't "pull a blind eye" to upper-level incongruity. I've basically come to the conclusion that I need to work for myself so I can be congruent with my own values.

It prepares you for life!

Arts and Humanities Professions

Some respondents specifically emphasize how their education has led them to a profession in the Arts and Humanities:

> *I wanted to be an actor and a writer. Aside from musician or professional juggler, there could hardly be two careers that Waldorf BETTER prepared me for!*

> *My love of literature and how I approach teaching literature is directly related to how and what I was taught.*

Effects of a Holistic Approach

Others underline the holistic worldview that their education fostered and the value of a liberal arts emphasis, even when they have chosen a career path in the fields of science or business:

> *It's all about creativity at this point, and a thorough understanding of what you want out of life. If you've got those two points, you're set up to be a solid entrepreneur. I feel I got a good head start on those, although not a direct education in entrepreneurship.*

> *There was not enough computer training, but Waldorf gave me the ability to connect with a person and close a sale.*

> *The creative skills and holistic world view provided by Waldorf Education have served me well. Most of the more practical and pragmatic skills have come from elsewhere.*

> *Waldorf's holistic approach definitely shaped who I am and helped to inspire me to pursue my work in the arts. At the time I graduated, it did not necessarily give all the computer/tech skills, but I don't see it being an issue.*

> *The hands-on learning that I received from my school was my inspiration to be a physical scientist in the first place, and hence led me to my current job.*

> *Waldorf education and osteopathic medicine share some important qualities – primarily a social-emotional orientation rather than a focus on grades and achievements. I think my K-12 education prepared me to be a humanistic physician.*

> *The liberal arts curriculum gave me an excellent foundation for the practice of medicine. I am able to converse with patients on a wide range of subjects, and learning moral philosophy, world religions, and accepting different lifestyles and world views at a young age has had a very positive impact on my practice. At Waldorf I learned*

many "soft skills" that are important when working with patients, especially people who are sick.

Criticism: Technology and Science

Critical and even negative comments focused on a sense of under-preparedness in technology and science:

Chemistry was something that I needed for university, which was a challenge to adjust to different requirements, given the alternative approach to teaching chemistry at my Waldorf school.

Money and the financial industry were not discussed during my Waldorf education. Perhaps they should have been, along with how to manage personal finances. I believe students would benefit from such information.

We wasted so much time on fun yet USELESS things like Eurythmy, ceramics, or orchestra. We should have been focused on useful topics like, oh I don't know, psychology, sociology, computer science, advanced economics, actual sex ed. and/or other important topics that prepare us for the world we live in.

Science and math were woefully lacking. I always thought I was bad at math until I realized it was the teaching method. I turned out to be good at it, apparently!

Inadequate Preparation for Work Experience

Others fault a pleasurable school experience for not serving as adequate preparation for the humdrum nature of professional life:

Waldorf did not do a good job preparing me for the grind of working a corporate job. In grade and high school (and college), learning was fun and exciting and satisfying. I expected to be as engaged in my working career. That has not been the case.

Very little at Waldorf trains for the sales interactions that every person in every business has to deal with.

The level of competition in corporate America was a big surprise to me.

Dazed and Confused

Another recurring complaint is the feeling that students come out of Waldorf education indecisive and confused:

The hindrance in a Waldorf education is that it can be difficult to narrow interests down to fully commit to a single career trajectory – I still often feel like I'm trying to decide what I want to be when I grow up!

Waldorf fails to create confident and successful individuals. Most of my classmates are 30-years-old children that have barely made it out of the nest. Most struggle with depression and mental health issues.

Positive vs. Negative

Several comments balance the aspects in which their education served as a good preparation against those in which they felt it was lacking:

Waldorf school prepared me to be in the helping professions by teaching empathy and social justice but did not adequately prepare me for the science required in the medical field.

Waldorf prepared me well to learn in new situations and to write and communicate. Technically, I was not well prepared for my current career (in engineering) coming out of Waldorf.

I was very well prepared to carry out qualitative research, but very poorly prepared to enter quantitative fields.

I was prepared in my social skills and critical and creative thinking, but I had to learn post-Waldorf about diversity, inclusion, cultural understanding, and the history of race relations in the U.S.

Waldorf education eschews film & video as a medium. In this instance, there's no way around it – Waldorf approaches video from a luddite perspective, attaching to it all sorts of antiquated and outdated notions about its "negative effects." This only hurts Waldorf. I am thankful that its students, like myself, are taught to think for themselves and generally see video in a modern sense, and therefore a more informed and realistic sense. In a slightly bizarre way, I think I profited from Waldorf's prohibition of video, because I come to the medium in a very different way than most of my peers. Happily, being different from your peers is often rewarded in creative fields.

PREPARATION FOR COLLEGE AND BEYOND

The responses of alumni cited above reflect their views on the effect of Waldorf education as it related to their experience as working professionals. In other sections of the survey, alumni were invited to reflect on various aspects of their preparation for undergraduate studies. Responses were gathered through numerical evaluations of a long list of college-relevant skills as well as through free-form comments.

Overall, alumni are decisively positive about how their Waldorf education prepared them for college. Given a scoring scale of 1 to 5, from "not well at all" (1) to "very well" (5), alumni collectively scored most aspects of their high-school preparation above 4 ("well" prepared). The combined positive votes ("well prepared" + "very well prepared") consistently represent the largest percentage of votes for each item, and, with one telling exception, no item receives a collective score under the middle mark of 3 points.

Within this overall positive assessment, we were able to discern finer details and distinctions by looking closely at the scoring differences within each skill set, and, most tellingly, by comparing the Waldorf alumni responses to the ones NAIS alumni provided to similar questions. Based on these close and comparative analyses, we reached two major conclusions.

First, Waldorf alumni feel they have been best prepared for creative, holistic thinking that focuses on whole pictures and on contexts, relations, cycles, and general meanings; this kind of thinking is also seen to facilitate new ideas and innovative solutions. Holistic thinking is usually characterized in contrast to analytic thinking, which breaks down wholes into their constituent parts and seeks meaning and explanation in these parts by means of drawing logical and causal connections among them.

Second, Waldorf alumni perceive their education as having prepared them to be more attentive to collective needs, to work in collaboration with others, and to take multiple perspectives into account. They appear to have been guided away from a worldview that places one's self in the center and instead have been encouraged to adopt a community-oriented one. This orientation towards social wholes seems in many ways like the social correlative to the cognitive tendency towards holistic thinking. It becomes a clear feature of Waldorf education when compared to the responses of NAIS alumni, who echo a more strongly individualistic approach in response to these same questions.

Finally, there is no need for close analysis to conclude that Waldorf alumni view the weakest elements of their high-school education in their training in mathematical skills and use of advanced technology. Alumni give the lowest scores of this entire section, averaging 2.53, to their preparation in the use of media technology, and the second lowest scores, averaging 3.30, to their training in Quantitative Literacy/ Mathematical Skills.

SKILLS AND PERSPECTIVES: ANALYSIS AND COMPARISONS

In this section of the questionnaire, alumni were presented with seven clusters of cognitive, social, and practical skills and attitudes, preceded by the instruction: "For each of the areas listed below, please rate how well the Waldorf school from which you graduated prepared you." The first of these clusters offered generally titled items such "Critical Thinking" or "Communications," while subsequent options probed these general categories in greater detail. The specific responses presented below are shown in the descending order of their overall score. Highest percentile score in each row is highlighted.

Table 6.1: General skills and capacities

	Very well (5)	Well (4)	Somewhat well (3)	Not too well (2)	Not well at all (1)	Score average
Creativity	84.5%	12%	3%	0.3%	0%	4.81
Critical Thinking	65%	23%	9%	1.9%	0.8%	4.50
Collaboration	64%	23.8%	8.4%	2.5%	1.1%	4.47
Communication	59%	28%	9.5%	2%	1.3%	4.41
Reading Comprehension	58%	26%	11%	2.8%	1.3%	4.38
Information Literacy	41.6%	32.5%	17%	5%	2.7%	4.07
Quantitative Literacy/Mathematical Skills	18%	29%	27%	16%	9.5%	3.30

Even though all items on this menu of general skills receive an overall positive score, i.e., above the middle choice of being "somewhat well" prepared (a 3-point value), the distinction between a sense of very strong preparation in "Creativity" and a considerably less strong preparation in "Mathematical Skills" is clear. In fact, the overall score of 4.81 given to the broadly labeled skill "Creativity" is the highest of all results in this section of the questionnaire. The second highest score goes to a skill that could hardly be distinguished from the first: "Creative Capacities" with 4.61 points (see Table 6.9 below). Creativity and creativeness are also implied in the fourth highest score, of 4.47 points, given to "Create New Ideas" (Table 6.3).

In contrast with this high valuation of a generally named creativity, we should note in advance the relatively low scoring of an item titled "Practical Knowledge" exemplified by "how to fix a bicycle." It received a score of 3.37 points, one of the lowest overall in this section, with just under 50% of respondents saying they were well prepared in this area (Table 6.9).

"Mathematical Skills" not only receives the lowest score (3.30) on the above list of general skills, but is also second to last among all the skills listed in this section. The apprehensiveness that alumni feel in this area becomes even clearer when we note that only 18% of respondents give it the highest score (5 points for being "very well" prepared), which contrasts dramatically not only with Creativity's 84.5% but also with the highest score of all other skills on this list such as "Critical Thinking" (65%), "Reading Comprehension" (58%), or even the one-to-last item, "Information Literacy" (41.6%). Furthermore, the cumulative negative scores ("not too well" + "not well at all") of Quantitative Literacy/Mathematical Skills add up to 25.5%, which is the second to highest negative score in the entire section. The highest negative score, or the area in which alumni feel they have been the least prepared for, is given to the ability to "Use Multiple Media Technologies," as we shall observe shortly (Table 6.6).

More Creative and Holistic than Analytic and Systematic
The skill of creativity, in which alumni feel so well prepared, does not simply denote preparation in the arts. Rather, creativity appears to be linked to the innovative, more associative, less rule-governed mode of thinking dubbed "holistic." As previously summarized, holistic thinking is characterized by looking at the "whole picture"—focusing on the value of the whole rather than the relation between parts—and exploring issues in terms of whole fields and full cycles. Holistic thinkers focus on contexts, relationships, and general meanings; they explore alternative points of view to a problem. Holistic thinking is contrasted with the systematic procedures of breaking down and reconstructing elements that characterize analytic thinking, which is strongly invested in causality, functionality, and logical reasoning.

The recognition by Waldorf alumni that they were strongly prepared in creative, holistic modes of thinking is evidenced by the higher overall scores of the first two items on the list below (Table 6.2)— "Thinking in Whole Pictures" and "Analyzing Alternative Points of View"—both of which are defining features of holistic thinking. The high support for "Thinking in Whole Pictures" is evidenced by the overall top score it receives on this list—4.49 points, the third highest score in the whole section—and by its 88.8% of positive votes ("very well prepared" + "well prepared"), almost 10 percentage points ahead of the next item on this list. Most, if not all, of these subsequent skills, which received lower scores, are more characteristic of an analytic thinking that breaks down problems into their parts and reconstruct them as an explanation. The lowest score on this list, granted to the ability to "Analyze Evidence" (3.92 points), indicates that Waldorf graduates felt less prepared not simply in analytic skills but specifically in empirical analysis, which requires drawing specific implications and conclusions from observed evidence.

We should emphasize, however, that the relatively lower scoring of these analytic skills cannot be seen as an indication of *insufficient* preparation, for they are still scored on the highly positive end.

Table 6.2: Cognitive skills

	Very well (5)	Well (4)	Somewhat well (3)	Not too well (2)	Not well at all (1)	Score average
Think in Whole Pictures	**61.6%**	27.2%	7.7%	1.6%	0.8%	**4.49**
Analyze Alternative Points of View	**50%**	29.6%	15.4%	3.2%	1.7%	**4.23**
Use System Thinking (the ability to analyze how parts of a whole produce overall outcomes)	**47%**	32.5%	12.8%	5.2%	1.7%	**4.19**
Solve Unfamiliar Problems	**41.8%**	34.7%	16.6%	4.9%	1.6%	**4.11**
Synthesize Information in an Argument	**40.1%**	35.2%	18%	4.1%	2.4%	**4.07**
Draw Conclusions Based on the Best Analysis	**39.5%**	35.1%	18.25%	4.9%	2.1%	**4.05**
Analyze Evidence	33.65%	**35.9%**	20.85%	7.3%	2.2%	**3.92**

Responses to another set of skills, which focus on thinking strategies in relation to new ideas (Table 6.3), offer another indication of alumni's sense of stronger preparation in holistic and creative thinking. With all items on this list scored above 4 points, it is the hierarchy formed by their scores that provides further insight.

The generally labeled ability to "Create New Ideas," suggesting spontaneity and bubbling creativity, tops the list with 4.47 points (89.2% stating they feel either "very well prepared" or "well prepared" in this area). The second item, the ability to "Brainstorm" (4.28, 84.2%), suggests a more prolonged or process-oriented mental activity involving an extended period of turbulence or turmoil, as the very word "storm" suggests. The most exacting and demanding item on the list, "Develop a Plan Based on New Ideas," is ranked at the bottom with 4.13 points (76.6%), following the precision skills of *evaluating* new ideas and *identifying* problems. In short, it appears that alumni feel that their preparation in systematic analysis and planning might have taken a back seat to their preparation for outbursts of originality and invention.

Table 6.3: Creativity and innovation

	Very well (5)	Well (4)	Somewhat well (3)	Not too well (2)	Not well at all (1)	Score average
Create New Ideas	**60.7%**	28.5%	8.1%	1.4%	0.95%	**4.47**
Brainstorm	**47.9%**	36.3%	11.7%	2.2%	1.3%	**4.28**
Evaluate New Ideas	**46.7%**	37.1%	11.3%	3.2%	1.3%	**4.25**
Identify a Problem	**46.4%**	35.9%	13.3%	2.4%	1.6%	**4.24**
Develop a Plan Based on New Ideas	**42.3%**	34.3%	17.7%	3.35%	1.75%	**4.13**

A comparison of these results to responses by NAIS alumni (Table 6.4: Creativity and Innovation Compared) offers further insight into the way Waldorf alumni perceive the creative and innovative aspects of their education.

Firstly, we note that *all* items on this list of creative thinking skills are scored higher by Waldorf alumni than by NAIS alumni. Secondly, a considerable gap appears between the two groups concerning the ability to "Create New Ideas." While this skill is at the very top of the Waldorf list, with 4.47 points and 60.7% of votes stating "very well" preparation, it appears at the very bottom of the NAIS list, with 3.99 points and 36.9% "very well prepared" votes.

Table 6.4: Creativity and innovation compared (score averages)

	Waldorf Alumni	NAIS Alumni
Create New Ideas	**4.47**	3.99
Brainstorm	**4.28**	4.03
Evaluate New Ideas	**4.25**	4.12
Identify a Problem	**4.24**	4.23
Develop a Plan Based on New Ideas	**4.13**	4.09

Indeed, if we reorder these five skills according to their ranking by NAIS alumni, we detect an inverse relationship in which what is uppermost for Waldorf alumni is bottommost for NAIS alumni (with some variation in the middle). The order of progression on the NAIS list appears to be from the most pinpointed task, *identifying a problem*, to the least defined task, *creating new ideas*:

Identify a Problem (4.23)

Evaluate New Ideas (4.12)

Develop a Plan Based on New Ideas (4.09)

Brainstorm (4.03)

Create New Ideas (3.99)

We read this contrast between the two scoring orders as the difference between NAIS alumni's sense of stronger preparation in analytic, systematic, and clearly defined thinking strategies captured by the verbs *identify*, *evaluate*, and *develop a plan*, and Waldorf alumni's feeling of being better prepared in the holistic, general, creative, and somewhat ambiguous strategies denoted by the terms *create* and *brainstorm*.

The differences observed here are substantiated further when we compare the two alumni groups' responses to the list of cognitive skills summarized in Table 6.2:

Table 6.5: Cognitive skills compared (score averages)

	Waldorf Alumni	NAIS Alumni
Think in Whole Pictures	**4.49**	N/A
Analyze Alternative Points of View	**4.23**	4.16
Use System Thinking (the ability to analyze how parts of a whole produce overall outcomes)	**4.19**	4.03
Solve Unfamiliar Problems	**4.11**	**4.11**
Synthesize Information in an Argument	4.07	**4.25**
Draw Conclusions Based on the Best Analysis	4.05	**4.30**
Analyze Evidence	3.92	**4.19**

Here we clearly see that NAIS alumni give somewhat higher scores to their preparation in the structured, analytic kind of thinking that proceeds from analysis to reconstruction to conclusion. Waldorf alumni, on the other hand, feel better trained in exploring multiple perspectives or alternative points of view and in using system thinking.[6] And while thinking "in whole pictures" was not offered as an option on the NAIS questionnaire, we note that the score it receives from Waldorf alumni (4.49 points) is considerably higher than the item receiving the top score on the NAIS list. This item is the highly-analytic ability to "draw conclusions based on the best

---

6   The notion of "System Thinking"—focusing on the contribution of particular components to the overall effect of the system in which they operate—is a tricky feature in this comparison: it could be seen as the very meeting point of holistic thinking, which privileges the view of a system as a whole, and analytic thinking, which focuses on the components that make up a system.

analysis," which receives an overall score of 4.30 points. In other words, *thinking in whole pictures*—a hallmark of holistic thinking—does not only appear to define a general attitude of Waldorf education; it also appears to mark a fundamental difference between Waldorf education and the dominant approach in other independent schools in the United States.

Community Oriented

A second major theme arising in this section of the survey concerns the social perspective of Waldorf alumni. The various indicators reviewed below suggest that Waldorf students graduate with a perspective that leans toward considering others and the needs of the community as a whole rather than centering on their own personal needs and priorities. We see this as a contrast between individualistic and communal perspectives, between a worldview that centers on one's own needs and personal priorities to one which is more group and community oriented. This distinction becomes especially apparent when comparing responses from Waldorf alumni, who appear to favor the latter posture, to those by NAIS alumni, who tend to favor the former perspective.

Focusing first on aspects of communicative and collaborative skills, we notice a somewhat complex picture.

Table 6.6: Communicative skills

	Very well (5)	Well (4)	Somewhat well (3)	Not too well (2)	Not well at all (1)	Score average
Listen Effectively	51.6%	34.2%	11.9%	1.3%	0.95%	4.34
Articulate Ideas through Oral Communication	52.7%	32.9%	10.8%	2.2%	1.4%	4.33
Articulate Ideas through Written Communication	50.6%	30.95%	12.9%	4.1%	1.4%	4.25
Communicate Ideas through Non-Verbal Communications (body language)	34.6%	33.2%	20.2%	7%	2.4%	3.93
Communicate Effectively in Diverse Environments (including multilingual and multicultural)	31%	30%	23.5%	9.6%	4.9%	3.73
Use Multiple Media Technologies	7.95%	11.6%	25.3%	27.7%	22.1%	2.53

Waldorf alumni give high scores to the communicative skills they were taught at school, but their grading strongly emphasizes oral communication over the use of media technology. In fact, the overall score given to "use of multiple media technology" is the lowest of the entire section, 2.53, and it is also the only item where the negative evaluations greatly outweigh the positive ones: 49.8% ("not too well" + "not well at all") vs. 19.6% ("well" + "very well"). We read this not only as a criticism of preparation in media or communication technologies but also as the outcome of a more limited exposure to advanced technology in general, a view substantiated by comments offered in several free-form sections of the survey.

The general trend of this scoring suggests that alumni feel best prepared in the immediate or non-mediated context of oral communication, in which they share a space, a language, and perhaps even a culture with their interlocutors. The higher scores drop slightly when we move from preparation in oral communication (4.33) to written communication (4.25), and the positive votes dropping from 85.6% to 81.6%. The drop is more pronounced when we move further to non-verbal communication, with 3.93 points and a decline of the positive votes to 67.8%. And the downward trend continues when the alumni are asked about preparation in effective communication "in diverse environments (including multilingual and multicultural)," to which they give a 3.73 score and 61% of positive votes. Nearly a quarter of respondents state they were only "somewhat well" prepared in this area.

These lower numbers, while still considerably above the scores concerning preparedness in the use of media technology, tell us something not only about communication but also about the extent to which Waldorf students interacted with diverse and multicultural communities; had these kinds of interaction happened more regularly, alumni would more likely have felt more well-prepared to communicate effectively in such environments. On this point, alumni repeatedly say their Waldorf experience afforded little exposure to diversity and diverse communities.

That said, a somewhat different picture is formed when Waldorf alumni responses are compared to those of NAIS alumni.

Table 6.7: Communicative skills compared to NAIS (score averages)

	Waldorf Alumni	NAIS Alumni
Listen Effectively	**4.34**	4.09
Articulate Ideas through Oral Communication	**4.33**	4.02
Articulate Ideas through Written Communication	4.25	**4.44**
Communicate Ideas through Non-Verbal Communications (body language)	**3.93**	3.53
Communicate Effectively in Diverse Environments (including multilingual and multicultural)	**3.73**	3.59
Use Multiple Media Technologies	2.53	**3.54**

In this comparison, we see that Waldorf alumni give considerably higher scores than do NAIS alumni to all aspects of direct, immediate communication with others—whether they are required to listen or speak, use words or non-verbal means of communication, whether they are within their own community or in "diverse environments." The only two areas in which NAIS alumni rate their preparation higher are those in which a medium is placed between them and their interlocutors—written language or media technology. (We also note that NAIS alumni, too, give one of their lowest scores to preparation in media technology, 3.54, though it is still a full point higher than Waldorf alumni's low score of 2.53 points.) In other words, Waldorf alumni feel better prepared in coming into *direct* contact with others than NAIS alumni say they feel.

And while Waldorf alumni report limited exposure to diverse, multicultural communities, this exposure still seems to be somewhat higher than that of their peers from other independent institutions, as suggested by a moderate score difference of Waldorf's 3.73 to NAIS's 3.59.

In short, when we view the question of communication skills as framing social capacities—a person's facility and sense of comfort in interacting with various others, we can conclude that Waldorf alumni feel more confident socially than their peers from other independent schools in that they feel more comfortable with and better prepared for the immediate encounter with others, even with the culturally other.

This impression receives further support when we compare the two groups' evaluations of their preparation for collaborative work.

Table 6.8: Collaborative skills compared to NAIS

	Waldorf Alumni Score	NAIS Alumni Score	Waldorf Very Well Prepared (5)	NAIS Very Well Prepared (5)
Value Individual Contributions in Teamwork	4.39	4.05	56%	41%
Assume Responsibility in Teamwork	4.38	4.21	56.3%	48.4%
Exercise Flexibility to Achieve a Common Goal	4.29	4.00	49.8%	37.9%
Work Respectfully with Diverse Teams	4.21	3.87	51.0%	37.2%

With higher scores in all four aspects of collaboration listed above, and a much stronger sense they were "very well" prepared to work in teams, Waldorf alumni acknowledge a collaborative bent to their education. With its emphasis on working "respectfully with diverse teams," and exercising "flexibility to achieve a common goal," Waldorf education appears through these responses to be directed towards community and collective goals more than the education experienced in other North American independent schools.

On Self and Other

Through other questions concerning work and study skills, we are able to construct an even clearer picture of the Waldorf alumni's social outlook. These questions touch on the ability to see one's own strengths and weaknesses, to consider alternative perspectives, and to take into account other people's views, values, and ways of thinking. In other words, they alternate between a focus on self-awareness and the awareness of others in the work/study environment. In effect, the responses sketch the social relation of self and others in the work/study context. We find that Waldorf alumni generally recognize that their education prepared them to be attentive to the place of others, and of the community as a whole, in their view of life and work.

Table 6.9: Perspectives, self-awareness, and awareness of others

	Very well (5)	Well (4)	Somewhat well (3)	Not too well (2)	Not well at all (1)	Score average
Creative Capacities	**69.4%**	23.6%	5.2%	1.1%	0.5%	**4.61**
Development of a Meaningful Perspective on Life	**55.1%**	27.7%	11.15%	4.3%	1.6%	**4.31**
Ability to Step into the Thoughts and Feelings of Others	**50.9%**	32.1%	11.7%	3.3%	1.6%	**4.28**
Interest in Discussing Points of View Different from Your Own	**50.5%**	30.5%	14.1%	3.2%	1.4%	**4.26**
Awareness of Your Strengths	**39.6%**	36.25%	16.4%	5.7%	2.1%	**4.06**
Ability to Resolve Conflicts with Others	**38.5%**	32.1%	11.7%	3.3%	1.6%	**4.02**
Self-Confidence	**38.3%**	32.1%	18.3%	6%	5.2%	**3.92**
Awareness of Your Weaknesses	26.5%	**36.2%**	25.6%	8.5%	3.2%	**3.74**
Spiritual/Religious Orientation*	22.2%	21.2%	**22.3%**	9.4%	5.7%	**3.55**
Practical Knowledge (e.g., how to repair a bicycle)	22.35%	**27.3%**	24.6%	15.85%	9.5%	**3.37**

Nearly 20% responded to this item with "Not applicable"

First, as already noted, Waldorf graduates report a wide spread between the "creative capacities"—with an average score of 4.61 points and 93% positive responses ("well prepared" + "very well prepared")—and "practical knowledge," with 3.37 points, just under 50% positive responses, and 25.5% negative responses (prepared "not too well" or "not well at all"). Second, we note the high score (4.31) awarded to the "development of a meaningful perspective on life." Of course, we are not privy to the specifics of such "meaningful perspectives," and yet, further items on this list and the following one (Table 6.10) do suggest a certain commonality in life perspectives. This commonality concerns elevating the place of others over oneself in the context of work, study, and social interactions.

We note that the two other-oriented skills—"ability to step into the thoughts and feelings of others" (4.28) and "interest in discussing points of view different from your own" (4.26)—score considerably higher than the self-oriented items—"awareness of your strengths" (4.06), "self-confidence" (3.92), and "awareness of your weaknesses" (3.74)—and that the latter two are preceded by a higher scored "ability to resolve conflicts with others" (4.02). The differences might be subtle but the trend appears to be clear: Waldorf alumni recognize they were more strongly prepared to respond to and respect others than to maintain a greater focus on themselves.

This trend is reflected again in Table 6.10, where being "fair and tolerant regarding other people's opinions" (4.32), as well as the ability to "express your views and attitudes to others" (4.16), come before self-promoting capacities like the ability to lead (4.05), or the qualities of self-knowledge and self-governance that allow one to know one's capacities and limitations (4.00), balance workloads (3.66), and handle criticism (3.65) or competition (3.57). We also note that the ability to "resolve conflicts," which weaves together both aspects of strong self-governance and respect for others, is situated in the middle of this other-oriented and self-oriented distinction. It receives a score of 3.86 points—lower than the items concerning leadership and self-knowledge but higher than those concerning the self-control of balancing workload and handling criticism and competition.

Table 6.10: Self-Governance and relation to others

	Very well (5)	Well (4)	Somewhat well (3)	Not too well (2)	Not well at all (1)	Score
Be Fair and Tolerant Regarding Other People's Opinions	**52.6%**	32.1%	10.8%	2.7%	1.4%	**4.32**
Express Your Views and Attitudes to Others	**43%**	37%	13.4%	4.5%	1.6%	**4.16**
Lead	**40.4%**	34.5%	16.8%	5.7%	2.4%	**4.05**
Know Your Own Capacities and Limitations	34.5%	**39.4%**	18.5%	5.7%	1.6%	**4.00**
Resolve Conflicts	29.2%	**38.6%**	22.9%	5.7%	2.9%	**3.86**
Balance Workload	26.7%	**31.8%**	25.6%	11.9%	3.6%	**3.66**
Handle Criticism	21.9%	**38.7%**	25%	9.5%	4.1%	**3.65**
Handle Competition	22.7%	**33.4%**	26.3%	10.9%	5.6%	**3.57**

The suggestion that the subtle differences in the rankings are significant, and that the significance they reveal concerns the place of self and other in the Waldorf students' experience, is further supported when compared to the NAIS alumni's responses to similar questions. (Note that the NAIS questionnaire contained some, but not all, of the items included in the Waldorf survey. Only shared items are presented in the table below.)

Table 6.11: Self/other orientation compared (I)

	Waldorf Alumni	NAIS Alumni
Development of a Meaningful Perspective on Life	**4.31**	3.95
Awareness of Your Strengths	4.06	**4.13**
Self-Confidence	3.92	**4.07**
Awareness of Your Weaknesses	3.74	**3.90**

Table 6.12: Self/other orientation compared (II)

	Waldorf Alumni	NAIS Alumni	Waldorf Very well prepared (5)	NAIS Very well prepared (5)
Lead	**4.05**	**4.05**	40.4%	**43.9%**
Resolve Conflicts	**3.86**	3.79	29.2%	**30.8%**
Balance Workload	3.66	**4.03**	26.74%	**44.5%**
Handle Criticism	3.65	**3.92**	21.9%	**34.7%**
Handle Competition	3.57	**4.17**	22.7%	**48.3%**

Table 6.11 clearly shows that in comparison with Waldorf alumni, NAIS alumni feel much better prepared in assessing themselves, specifically in assessing themselves positively. Like Waldorf alumni, NAIS students feel better prepared to recognize their strengths rather than their weaknesses, but all their scorings regarding self-awareness, confidence, and self-governance are higher. The difference in scoring increases considerably when the questions move from issues of self-assessment and self-awareness to questions that focus on self-regulation and self-control, such as balancing workloads and handling criticism and competition. In the first kind of questions, NAIS alumni score their preparation only slightly higher than Waldorf alumni, with differences that range between 0.07 and 0.16 points. The subtle difference between the two groups grows when we turn to self-regulation and self-control, where NAIS scores are 0.3-0.5 points higher than Waldorf scores, and almost twice as many NAIS respondents say they were "very well" prepared for these tasks, compared to Waldorf alumni.

Despite these differences, in which NAIS alumni appear more self-assured about their abilities and Waldorf alumni appear to be focused more on community than on themselves, the two groups are much closer to each other in evaluating their capacities at the meeting point of self and other. This meeting point is found in the question regarding one's ability to *lead*. Leadership frames a self-other relationship that can be viewed from the opposite perspectives of either service or superiority, but both perspectives presuppose a feeling of self-confidence. Here Waldorf and NAIS alumni offer the exact same score, 4.05, with a slight advantage in NAIS alumni's highest score ("very well" prepared) of 43.9% to Waldorf's 40.4%. Similarly, on the self-other relationship question of the ability to *resolve conflicts*, the two groups are very close—Waldorf 3.86, NAIS 3.79—with again a slight advantage in NAIS alumni's highest scores, 30.8% vs. 29.2%.

Still, the greatest contrast is to be found in the difference in responses to the question of *handling competition*, which is the lowest score listed by Waldorf alumni,

3.57, and the highest score listed by NAIS alumni, 4.17. Furthermore, while almost half of NAIS alumni give this capacity the highest score ("very well" prepared or 5 points), less than a quarter of Waldorf alumni do the same.

This stark difference invites further reflection on the issue of competition, in itself a core element of a leading American ethos. This ethos defines and measures success by an entrepreneurial navigation of a competitive free market. To be able to handle competition well, to be ready to compete, means to be ready to position oneself over against others with the intention to win, which often means to advantage oneself to the detriment of the other. To be well prepared in handling competition would indicate a readiness to view oneself and one's interests as taking precedence over those of another or of the community as a whole.

While the relationship between individual success and collective benefits can be debated to different ends, as can the comparison of behaviors in the economic and social arenas, we want to emphasize here the significance of competition: namely, that its first and defining step is the promotion of self over others. Such an attitude can be expected to take a dominant role in one's overall worldview when it appears to be the most promoted attitude in the course of an influential education. What we want to suggest here is that the observed difference in the approaches to competition signifies an essential difference between the social orientations of Waldorf education and the education proffered by other independent schools.

It is on this background that we conclude that Waldorf education, according to reported outcomes rather than simply declared intentions, promotes a life-perspective which is more other-oriented or community-oriented than it is self-centered, and that this approach distinguishes Waldorf education from the approach of other independent schools in the United States.

Is this the difference suggested by the different scorings of a school's influence on one's development of a "meaningful perspective on life"? Waldorf alumni give this the top score of 4.31 points, while it is third-to-last (3.95 points) on the NAIS list of skills that we associate with the self/other perspective. We cannot answer this question empirically, but we can affirm that Waldorf alumni highly agree that their education has brought an overall meaningfulness to their lives. It has done so not through some taught content but rather by nurturing a way of seeing, a perspective on life that enables a person to see life as full of meaning. The evident difference between the observations of Waldorf and NAIS alumni in this regard suggests that different educational approaches—whether they are promoted at home or in school—lead to different outlooks on life.

COLLEGE PREPARATION: SATISFACTION AND CRITICISM

A decisive majority of Waldorf alumni are satisfied with the way Waldorf education prepared them for college. This majority consists of 82% respondents (41.5% are "very satisfied" and 40.5% are "satisfied"), while only 5.3% profess to be "dissatisfied" and 2.3% to be "very dissatisfied" with their college preparation; 10.3% are neutral on this question.

Narrative comments on the preparation for college provide a more detailed picture, including some pointed criticisms. The majority of respondents are highly appreciative of their overall experience and college preparation, but a few report they found the academic norms in college highly challenging and some of their own learning skills lacking. With few exceptions, respondents emphasize their strong preparation in writing, conceptual thinking, and the liberal arts in general, while 28% of respondents complain that they felt underprepared for college in the fields of math and/or science and technology, even as these complaints at times come from alumni who proceeded to higher studies or even a professional career in these same fields. A handful of respondents felt that, in retrospect, their lessons in American history were selective, partial, and sanitized.

While most respondents emphasize a warm community and harmonious social setting, some confess that the transition to college made them realize that their social experience in high school was less than optimal and that they felt shut down and shut out by strong personalities and a male-centered culture. A handful of these comments are bitter and angry, complaining about an insufficient education and inattentive educators. These and other highly critical comments are by far in the minority, still they do testify to the fact that students in the Waldorf schools of North America do not experience a uniform standard of academic program, nor a fully welcoming social climate or sufficient attention to social challenges.

The Positive Overview

Positive evaluations of their college preparation, emphasizing different aspects of Waldorf education, are exemplified in the following comments by Waldorf graduates:

I was better prepared than anyone else I met in university. I knew how to learn, I knew how to think flexibly, and I was engaged. I had been given a good grounding in reading and writing.

I felt very prepared to enter into the larger educational conversations of literature, culture, art, politics, as well as felt a deep confidence in my role as a student, citizen, colleague, leader, and friend.

An ability for cognitive thought and problem solving put me ahead of my peers during undergraduate. Social and interpersonal skills helped me succeed in my career field. All learned at Waldorf.

Waldorf education may not have prepared me for the specific academic material of my post-high-school education, but it prepared me to handle anything.

I am satisfied with my level of preparation. Generally, I would say that Waldorf education spends more time preparing students to be people than to be good college students.

In pursuit of my degrees in Architecture & Building Science, I found myself exceptionally well prepared, both for the technical as well as the design aspects of the curriculum. In particular, the university tracks concerning sociology and the built environment contained readings and philosophies that I'd covered in high school and with which none of my college classmates from other private schools or public education had any familiarity.

Waldorf School prepared me very well for college in terms of academics. I graduated likely within the top 1% of my undergrad class and am now pursuing a Ph.D. at one of the top universities for science and engineering in the U.S.

Shocks and Challenges

Certain positive evaluations emphasized an initial difficulty in adapting to college culture in general:

There was big shock switching from my small, caring Waldorf community to a large college without a close relationship with teachers or one on one guidance.

Because my early education was in such a small, and nurturing environment, I find my adult self lacking in a core life skill: how to compete. At my Waldorf school, it was easy to usually be "one of the best" at something. In a high-end liberal arts school, this was not the case.

Any system of education which does not breed conformity but instead individuality and deep connection is bound to be in conflict with systems which demand conformity. Hence, I did not find that my education prepared me to function well in conventional higher education, but although this brought with it many struggles, the value it gave me far exceeds the detriment. The audacity to question is today more relevant than ever and Waldorf Education supported me in that audacity. What more could I ask for to be able to give a valuable contribution back to society and the Earth.

I went to a very academic college which was very challenging. In my first week I had to learn to type and produce a 500-word essay. I learned quickly and adapted but my self-esteem suffered initially. I was not used to the competitive behavior of my fellow students and that too took some getting used to. Would I go back and do it differently? No. My Waldorf education has been of value then and to this day.

Some Deficiencies

Other respondents identified general deficiencies in their Waldorf experience, some of them diametrically opposite to the positive experiences cited above:

Would have loved to have been challenged more, especially in my senior year. When I started English classes at college, the critiques were hard, letting me know that if I didn't step up the quality of work, I wouldn't make it.

Needed more U.S history, less focus on European history.

Less prepared for standardized tests.

I was very prepared for college socially and in the arts – I was not prepared for the math, bio, and chem classes.

I feel like my school did not adequately prepare me for the type of testing administered in a more traditional education. Specifically, how to study for and take college level midterms and finals.

Well prepared in some areas, but badly unprepared for the workload and academic rigor and tools/skills required in engineering school. My first year in undergrad was miserable.

There should have been more hands-on guidance for college preparation. As a first-generation college student, navigating the process was a major obstacle, esp. in contrast to my peers with parents who were able to assist in the process.

I had learning disabilities that went unnoticed and undiagnosed until I was on severe academic probation. I distinctly remember having horrible difficulty in school and somehow coasting by on my eloquence.

I don't think that I was prepared enough with practical study skills, goal setting, task management, importance of networking and organization. I don't think that I was held accountable enough or encouraged to reflect on my lessons of failure, then perhaps setting goals and evaluating myself and resetting goals or dreaming bigger.

The Problem with STEM

As stated above, math and the natural sciences were repeatedly mentioned as areas lacking in preparation—a criticism expressed in various degrees of acceptance as sampled here:

Overall, I felt I was extremely well-prepared for university because Waldorf education on the whole does an excellent job developing critical thinking, writing skills, and community engagement capabilities, all of which are highly valued and useful at university and in life. However, as someone who entered a STEM field, I think I could have received a stronger grounding in mathematics and basic sciences from my Waldorf education. While I understood concepts well, I was not well-prepared for the mathematic rigor of university-level scientific study. I think Waldorf schools could incorporate the mathematical aspects of science more, while still maintaining the inquiry-based, holistic, and arts-integrated approaches of the science curriculum that make it conceptually rigorous.

I found that my math/science skills were behind other students in the STEM program I entered. Although I was able to learn the new subjects, some of the holes in my high-school math education have continued to be weaknesses in my math skills as I moved forward.

I was woefully behind my college peers in nearly every aspect of science & technology.

My terrible mathematics and English literacy skills were extremely apparent. My computer skills were non-existent. Overall, it was embarrassing and the amount of catch up work I had to do on my own was frustrating.

Social Critique

A different kind of criticism was targeted at a problematic social environment and a lack of awareness to social issues:

Academically I felt very prepared. Socially, not as much. At the time I was there, [my Waldorf school] had many social problems with bullying, sexism, sexual harassment and abuse, and this has affected me more than I realized at the time. I was very intimidated by men in my college classes, mostly because I was used to men in my [Waldorf] class shouting over me, mocking all women, and getting away with it.

Looking back, I see that the environment at [my Waldorf school] was not healthy for students who were not white or were of mixed race. The faculty members were particularly unaware of how and why they should provide an inclusive education and to try and include different cultural perspectives. I would call my school, at that time, a bastion of white liberalism in the most problematic ways. The "Native American Block," for example, was an example of all that was so problematic in that perspective. In that class there was no mention of Native Americans still living today, the words "relocation" and "genocide" were never used; the entire class was designed for the entertainment of the white liberal. This environment, then, was also problematic for all students who walked away from that course believing they had, in fact, learned a solid overview of Native Americans but had been provided with an incredibly misrepresentative narrative. Equally as problematic, if not more so, was the phenomenal degree of patriarchy and even misogyny in the culture at school. There are teachers who may still be teaching that I regard as having broken my spirit so many times and with such innate disdain for me because I was female.

The Bitter View

Several respondents clearly came out of their high-school years harboring some negative memories, causing them to describe their education in harsh terms:

I almost failed out of freshman year of college. I was grossly unprepared for math and science classes. I graduated Waldorf without crucial skills to succeed in college. My hand-working skills were excellent but the remainder of my educational foundation was severely lacking.

Lacked educational merit. School failed to teach science and math. Most importantly, it promoted separatism and classism.

I was not at all professionally accompanied by my teachers to prepare me for my further education. They were all psychological wrecks and were not able to cope. The social aspect of my school was horrible and I was mobbed up until I left in 9th grade and came back in 11th.

In regards to history, Waldorf's view of making History into some hyper-PC Lala Land and trying to sugarcoat the past does more harm than good, and I felt like I was not taught history properly until college.

Balancing It Out

Finally, a finely-detailed, mostly appreciative, evaluation of college preparation, with attention to both advantages and drawbacks, is demonstrated by the following two comments:

Waldorf taught me to think creatively, critically, and compassionately. Did I learn calculus? No. Am I a better version of myself, who understands the value of dialogue, the power of community, the importance of kindness and empathy, the dangers of cynicism, and who has been able to learn new skills and forge lasting bonds with people everywhere I go? Yes. I am grounded in who I am as a being on this Earth. And if I need to learn calculus later, I will learn calculus later.

I deeply appreciate the rich quality and broad scope of the education I received. When I met my husband at the age of 25, he asked me what I had gained from my grade school education. I said, "A sense of the full range of my capacities as a human being. What about you?" Having graduated from one of the top-ranked public schools in Silicon Valley, he answered, "Preparation for college." I am without a doubt grateful for the fact that my education prepared me to approach the world—college and everything else—with a sense of openness and possibility. Having completed so many practicum experiences, lived overseas and gone to school in a foreign language at the age of 15, etc., I've never been daunted by stepping into new and unfamiliar settings or embarking on new personal endeavors. Likewise, I've always had the feeling that my learning should be relevant to my life and work in the world; that it must feel inspiring and alive in order to be worth my while. Coming out of high school, I also knew with certainty that college was but one means of learning and finding my way into my life's work. All of this prepared and didn't prepare me for my actual college experiences. My creative writing was strong enough to pass me right out of any writing requirements at Oberlin, where I began undergrad, but once I had to write a formal paper, I found myself back in Comp 101 because I didn't know what a thesis statement was or how to do citations. Likewise, though I'd always been at the top of my class in math and science, I had no idea how to do college lab work and felt intimidated and at a disadvantage. I also had to defer enrolling in Bio and Chem classes I wanted to take because I had to go back and make up algebra work we'd never covered in high school. (I know that shortly after I graduated high school, these shortcomings were addressed.)

OVERALL RETROSPECTIVE CRITICISM & INSIGHTS

In general, an absolute majority of Waldorf alumni have positive feelings towards their former schools. Of the 82% that say so, a little more than half qualify their current feelings about their school as "*very* positive." At the other end of the spectrum, only 5.5% of respondents say they have negative feelings towards their school, and 12.75% are neutral. 70% state they are proud of their affiliation with their former school and no less than 83% strongly agree that their school forms part of who they are today (10.5% are neutral on this issue while 6% reject the idea).

These positive feelings translate into a strong endorsement in that 87% of alumni would recommend their Waldorf school to a friend or family member. This figure covers also the 70% of alumni who would *highly* recommend it; about 8% would *not* recommend their former schools to others.

Still, alumni are not without suggestions for improvement, and some offered pointed criticism regarding their former school. Several free-form questions solicited such reflective criticism, while other sections invited respondents to rank areas of strengths as well as areas in need of improvement from a given menu. While the latter method allowed us to compile the lists presented below, the elaborate critical comments produce a more detailed picture. We read of continuing or belated appreciation of various aspects of the education, as well as recurring critiques of the instruction in STEM subjects or preparation for the practicalities of life. At times the criticism can turn acrimonious, fueled by some unpleasant high-school experiences and couched in bitterness that refuses to abate.

The Best and the Wanting

Individual rankings of areas of strengths in their former school produced this collective top-five list (the percentage of respondents who named each area is included in parenthesis):

1. Arts Program   (53%)
2. Faculty   (50%)
3. Individualized Attention   (38%)
4. The Culture of the school   (33%)
5. The Core Academic Program   (28%)

While the list speaks for itself, we do note that it captures, in items 2-5, what can be seen as the most essential elements of a school: the teachers and the kind of attention they afford the students, the overall culture of the school, and the core academic content. The arts program tops the list of strengths, with more than half of alumni citing it, while only a quarter name the humanities program. Math and science programs did not evaluate nearly as well, with only 2.8% naming the latter as an area of strength at their school and 2.5% naming the former.

Aspects that may appear less essential, such as extracurricular clubs, academic facilities, and school location, all received very few votes, and a total of zero respondents named IT/computer studies as an area of strength. An indication that some alumni do not remember their school appreciatively is demonstrated in the response to the invitation to name three areas of strength, "I am struggling to find three." On the other hand, we do find several variations at the diametrically opposed side: "Goodness, only three?!?"

Interestingly, the items on the top-five list of areas of strength assembled from NAIS alumni responses are practically identical to the Waldorf list and at times even follow the same order (see table below). The notable difference lies with the arts program, ranked at the very top of the list by Waldorf alumni but listed very close to the bottom of the NAIS list (and singled out among the top-five areas in need of improvement). First place in the top-five list compiled by NAIS graduates is taken by Honors/Advanced Classes, an option that is rarely available in Waldorf schools.

Table 6.13: Waldorf and NAIS listings of school strengths:

Waldorf Top-Five Areas of School Strength	NAIS Top-Five Areas of School Strength
1. Arts program	1. Faculty
2. Faculty	2. Core academic program
3. Individualized attention	3. Individualized attention
4. Culture of the school	4. Culture of the school
5. Core academic program	5. Honors/advanced classes

Waldorf alumni were also asked to name up to three areas they felt needed improvement at their former schools. At the top of this list we find the following five items:

IT/computer studies program	(44%)
Diversity	(43.5%)
Science program	(30%)
Math program	(28.5%)
Academic facilities	(28%)

The critical view of limited instruction in technology, math, and science, expressed in several other sections of the survey, is reflected clearly in three out of the five items on this list.

What is also made clear here is that many alumni believe that diversity was lacking at their school. (Diversity topped the NAIS alumni list of areas in need of improvement.) Indeed, a perceived lack of diversity is a central point of criticism for post-college Waldorf alumni. "As I look back," one alum writes, "I realize the Euro-centric nature of the content we studied, and I wish I had been exposed to a more diverse curriculum, a more diverse student body, and a more diverse teaching staff." Another adds: "It is a homogenous culture that lacks diversity. Sometimes there is a major disconnect between the wealthy families that get to drive costs and policies. I thought I was getting a diverse view of the world, and it has been true time and time again that the lens through which the Waldorf community [views the world] doesn't encourage diverse viewpoints."

CRITICAL COMMENTARY

A more elaborate picture of the schools' strengths and weaknesses is offered by individual responses to open-ended invitations for comment. Asked whether they have changed their view of elements they were critical of at the time, some alumni write that they have in fact become more critical of their education in later years, finding fault in what they accepted at an earlier age.

> *I viewed everything in my education as pretty good but realized after the fact that I really wasn't challenged much and that we did a very poor job of supporting students to understand a diverse, multi-cultural, multi-religious world. Additionally, the disdain for technology was not helpful.*

> *In all honesty, with the benefit of time and life experience, I have a much more negative view of my Waldorf school experience than I did 14 years ago when I graduated.*

> *I would never send my child to a Waldorf school. The failures I experienced during school have only become grosser and more outrageous in retrospect.*

Positive overviews of school experiences, gained through an understanding earned later in life, are demonstrated by statements like these:

> *As a student, I often thought the curriculum was too soft, too based in feelings and broad ideas, rather than fact. As an adult, I'm appreciative for that, because I feel like I learned how to learn, rather than learning a rote list of facts (facts which, by the way, I have access to through the internet anyways).*

> *Having to participate in all subjects with no choice in the matter at the time seemed unnecessary, however now it gives me confidence that nothing that comes my way is beyond my abilities and that I can find a way to excel at anything.*

> *Post-Waldorf, I understand now why so many different practices were instilled during my time at Waldorf. I feel capable of taking on any situation because of the diversity of subjects studied in school. There's is nothing I don't feel capable of doing.*

> *Throughout elementary school and most strongly as I entered adolescence, I was critical of Waldorf's abstract approach to learning. For example, I didn't understand why we weren't learning "real" facts about the world, but rather we were being told stories and drawing mythological gods. It was only after I graduated that I understood*

the essential effect this had on my development as a child; that I was encouraged to keep my mind open and imaginative rather than filling it with irrelevant and quantitative facts too young. I often felt like a "Waldork" when I was in my early teens, but this also contributed to a deep and self-affirming confidence to stand on my own later in life.

I often bristled against the more limiting maxims of the education – media policy, being treated too childishly for my taste, etc., but I look back on those years with such clarity and fondness because I had so much time to explore and be unfettered by cultural imperatives of what a pubescent girl was meant to be in mainstream media.

I both blame and credit Waldorf education for my hardworking ethics and willingness to work for little financial gain. I "have the will to work...."

Repeated topics of criticism or praise include the following:

Mismatch between Waldorf education and "the real world":
There was a tangible lack of dissension—stemming from a similar lack of diversity— that I remember recognizing as potentially harmful. I knew that the world outside of my safe "Waldorf World" would not be so obliging and wondering whether I could levy my education to settle disagreements. Turns out, I couldn't. And can't. It's not enough to have read Homer when the rest of the world is thinking about food, sex, and money. Go figure!

Stifling individualism in favor of collectivism:
I really hated that we were often held accountable for other people. For example, our whole class would be held late because a few people were misbehaving. I really wanted to be seen and evaluated as an individual. As an adult I can see some of the benefits to this approach, but I'm still not sure I agree with it!

Discouraging competition:
On the question of handling competition... Waldorf Schools are so very uncompetitive (which is fine) that I think when I went into an environment (university) that WAS competitive I didn't know how to handle that. It turned me off so much that it almost discouraged me, but that's not a slight at all to the Waldorf education – it's praise of it.

Appreciation of creative and artistic instruction:

The drawing and painting seemed like a great way to "waste" time in school, but now my ability to imagine what the answer to a complex problem might look like allows me to share with others that solution. They are then able to understand and adopt my point of view.

The emphasis on art and writing has been invaluable in my current career.

I was not a big fan of the physical classes (woodwork, knitting, etc.). But I have found a real joy and practical use for these abilities as an adult and credit my confidence in these types of endeavors to my experience in school.

Public speaking:

Being forced to public speak at the time was an issue and challenge, but probably one of the most beneficial things I experienced, since the majority of my colleagues have no experience with that at all.

Teachers' personal involvement:

As a teenager I thought my teachers were over-involved in my personal (e.g. non-academic) development; however, I now recognize how the two are connected and how much more support I received in my overall growth as a result.

Dogmatism:

DOGMATIC. I experienced this as relatively harmless at [my school]. None-the-less and unfortunately, I have found this dogmatism is widely present in many anthroposophical organizations. This is a serious problem completely counter to the ideas of Steiner which needs to be addressed.

I used to think that the teachers were "Steiner worshipers."

Math and Science:

As stated in previous sections of the survey, criticism of science instruction is often expressed by alumni who proceeded to obtain higher degrees and even professions in scientific fields. Such comments include:

I genuinely loved my learning environment and was thrilled to attend every day. The one aspect I was a bit unhappy with while there was the level of rigor in the science and math classes. I still became a professional scientist and science educator, so it wasn't crippling by any means. However, I look back and remain disappointed in the level. I think we could have had higher quality science education.

Lack of science. I completed a science-based degree and did not find myself to be any further behind other students. Waldorf education taught me to think and this enabled me to quickly become adept in the more science-based subjects.

I wanted more "real" science, but am now grateful for the phenomenological emphasis we were exposed to.

Technology:

Similarly, criticism of a school's approach to technology and electronic media is often stated with a mixture of initial disappointment, at times bitterly expressed, and later appreciation:

Media policy. It felt like an unfair limit on my out-of-school time that didn't seem fair. I look back now, especially being in a position in the same sector as I was forced to abstain from, realizing that not having exposure to media helped me learn more efficiently and have more creativity. I don't think young children should have very much exposure to media because there are far better things they can spend their time on. [...] I work in videogames and my limited exposure to media as a child helps me bring new ideas and perspectives to my work. I know that when I have children, I will adopt similar policies until they are at an age where they have developed more.

I hated and still do have issue with the ludditism [sic], especially with regard to computers and digital technology. Eventually, thanks to my uncle and my high school, I developed a love for and facility with digital technologies but only to a certain level. I think this really held me back professionally and economically. However, now I do see value in the way my school developed my whole self. I'm happy with that, though I think it could have been done without so limiting me in terms of advanced technical and future-looking skills.

Other:

The older students weren't given enough space to grow into adulthood and develop autonomy.

I didn't appreciate the underlying Christianity. Not sure I appreciate it anymore today, but I do understand it better now.

Eurythmy:

Finally, the subject of Eurythmy is singled out many times in this section. Many statements acknowledge a belated recognition of Eurythmy's value, at times expressed in depth and other times with pithy humor:

> *Eurythmy always seemed like a joke as a student. But I now realize how important spatial awareness is. I used to skateboard around NYC. Now I play ice hockey with many people who have had several concussions. I have never had a concussion and am very skilled at avoiding collisions. I attribute this partly to Eurythmy and also to outdoor play in lower school.*

> *I sometimes did not understand the importance or relevance of Eurythmy, but I now value this because I see it as offering so much in helping the human being foster awareness of that which we cannot see.*

> *Eurythmy. As soon as I left, I missed it. It uses all the parts of yourself and your brain that nothing else honors.*

> *Nope, sorry, still don't like Eurythmy.*

> *Ugh, fine, Eurythmy has a purpose.*

MAIN THEMES OF GENERAL CRITICISM

In response to an invitation for a final overview of their former school, three main themes and one notable feature emerge out of alumni's comments. The themes deal with elements of the high-school curriculum, with aspects of the school culture, and with the question of diversity, which touches on both. The notable feature mentioned by several alumni could be named the "crisis of indecision," wherein alumni feel that the richness of their education has made it hard for them to limit their many possibilities and decide on a single avenue to follow in adult life.

Aspects of the High-School Curriculum

The high-school curriculum receives various and, at times, conflicting critiques. While one alum launches a vigorous complaint against the shift from narrative evaluations to letter grades, others say they felt a need for a stronger break with the "soft" approach of the lower school to a more "rigorous" high-school curriculum and academic expectations. STEM subjects, as observed previously, become a repeated target of criticism, with many alumni complaining of insufficient instruction and others suggesting that their school did not take math and science as seriously as it did the humanities and arts.

A second complaint in this area regards what is perceived as missing components in the education. These include electives and extracurricular activities, either as advanced courses or expansions and alternatives to the main curriculum, as well as athletic offerings that would allow for more opportunities for students to excel.

A missing component mentioned by several alumni is instruction in some life skills, such as balancing a personal budget, basic computer literacy, managing a household, or understanding a rental contract. This criticism is often couched in terms of a felt disconnect between Waldorf education and the realities of practical life.

School Culture and Personal Relations

While we remember from other parts of this survey how much the personal instruction, attention, and support is appreciated by the vast majority of alumni, we also note that a host of critical comments address issues concerning the intimate nature of the Waldorf school community. Specifically, some alumni complain that students were often aware of personal or ideological conflicts among faculty members that seeped into the classroom and negatively affected the school climate. Other graduates commented on the effects of a familial community, with faculty children appearing to receive preferential treatment because teachers (parents and their colleague-friends) were intimately familiar with them and their immediate circle of friends. This familiarity decreased the ability of some teachers to apply the same standards to all students.

Another undesirable outcome of the intimate setting, one alum writes, was that it caused some teachers to hold a settled view of their students. One comment read: "I remember feeling often, especially in high school, that my teachers had already decided who I was," thereby not seeing the student's wider potentials and capacity for change.

Conversely, the close view students had of their teachers invited close scrutiny, and while many teachers are remembered as inspiring figures, several alumni also state that some faculty members were misplaced and ineffective. These suggestions are often supported by two kinds of perceptions: that the school was under-resourced and at times had to make do with under-qualified personnel, or that the close-knit nature of the community could lead to collegiate protectiveness and an inability to see the limitations and shortcomings of colleague-friends. A related criticism suggests that such myopia was linked to a dogmatic adherence to some blueprint of Waldorf pedagogy, and that remaining close to this blueprint overrode the reality of classroom dynamics and the effectiveness of the teaching. We see this in the following comment:

> [I]t feels that whenever issues crop up, no matter how large, long-time Waldorf teachers have a "my way or the highway" approach and there is no room for real change, conversation, or growth. For instance, our math teacher was... not teaching us. We'd get out of class 30 minutes early, never really be graded, and there was no standard of evaluating him because he was a long-time teacher and anthroposophist.

... then he went on to teach at other Waldorf schools and was lauded as an exceptional teacher.

The critique here is clear: the fully-immersed scholar of Waldorf pedagogy or well-learned anthroposophist does not always a good teacher make. While colleagues in the school leadership may not see this, students certainly do feel it.

In this context, we note that several alumni regret the absence of a school counselor who could have helped with personal and interpersonal issues in the community.

Diversity

The multifaceted issue of diversity holds a special place in the alumni's critical comments. It is clear that they are attentive to the need for diversity and inclusiveness in various domains and that in retrospect many of them view their school communities and curricula as lacking in this area.

More than a third of respondents say that while at school they had rarely or never interacted with people of a different race or ethnicity than their own; the same number of respondents say they *did* interact with such individuals regularly or almost always. Interactions with members of different economic and religious groups or with people who came from other countries or cultures took place more often—for each such group, about half of respondents say interactions took place usually or almost always. Still, a third of respondents say that interactions were only occasional, indicating that their social others were not part of their daily school community. Things are decisively different in these alumni's current lives, where 75% or more report having frequent interactions with their social and cultural others, while less than 5% say that such interactions are rare.

In their comments, alumni at times link the lack of diversity at their former school with their reservations about sending their own children to a school that they still perceive as privileged and predominantly white:

I loved my school. Looking back and forward, as I consider options for my own child, I would value more ethnic and economic diversity. Price makes it almost exclusively for white, upper class families.

Another alum writes, "Waldorf education should be more accessible, not just to the white and wealthy." And another comment reads: "The school needs to do everything in its power to diversify. ... This applies to teachers as well."

Comments like these echo previously noted criticisms of a "Euro-centric" curriculum, suggesting a need for a wider variety of perspectives and cultural-historical content, as well as a change in the socio-economic and racial makeup of the community. We place in the same context the several calls to improve accommodations for learning disabilities, seen as a recognition of diverse learning styles and strengths, as well as the remarks about a lacking awareness to issues of gender and sexual identity. About the latter, one respondent writes: "There could have been more attention to acceptance/ bullying LGBTQ students and engaging in conversations of feminism (awareness of male dominance)," while another states:

> *I think there was really a lack of racial diversity at the time that I graduated from high school. I also think that there were prejudices very apparent amongst students (e.g. anti-LGBTQ) that did not make for a welcoming environment for all students, attitudes that are overall detrimental to community.*

Even a brief sampling of comments demonstrates how alumni's own use of the term "diversity" brings together a variety of social justice issues, underlined by an expectation of a fully equal and equitable society. These critical comments show at times a dissatisfaction with the level of diversity in their past school communities; at the same time, they testify to an acute sensitivity to diversity and social justice by alumni who have been educated in these very same communities. The comments also reflect an awareness of the entangled relationship that education has with equality and opportunity, and express alumni's expectations that their former school community will adapt itself to meet the emerging norms of social equity.

These new norms are very much a sign of the times in contemporary American culture. In this social critique, Waldorf alumni show that they are in tune with the current *Zeitgeist*. We also see in their embrace of this social critique a manifestation of a deep-seated valuing of equality and justice. In other words, they are the manifestation of values instilled in them in the formative years of adolescence by the pedagogical community that finds itself on the receiving end of their retrospective criticism. In short, the critique of insufficient diversity carries an important message regarding what needs to be corrected in Waldorf schools, while at the same it reflects a significant pedagogical success.

The idea that an integrative moral perspective is inherent to Waldorf education is something we find in the alumni commentary itself, expressed in the feisty tropes of an emerging generation of self-assured justice warriors appearing to have newly found their voice:

> *My opinion of all Waldorf schools is that they should be thought of as leadership training academies, whose purpose is to create a generation of leaders in every sector uniquely educated to see systems, think from a whole-system perspective, and bring personal ethics and strong morality back into their industry of choice.*

At the same time, another alum offers the view: "I resent how elitist and full of hot air your entire philosophy is."

Between the sense of confidence and empowerment of the former comment, and the caustic dismissal expressed by the latter, we insert a third voice, which is heard several times throughout the survey. It says that the supportive and wide-ranging preparation of the Waldorf school years can have harmful effects on life post-graduation, when the time comes to face the challenge of choosing among all the many possibilities one has been prepared for:

> *The education did a fantastic job of teaching me that I could do anything if I applied myself, but that information can be crippling. After high school I was often running into the problem that "anything" is not "everything" and choosing between many good options means not doing most of them. Many of my Waldorf peers stalled out in life because they did not want to choose a path, and therefore chose nothing. I was lucky to have good guidance on my career path, but I think that is rare.*

The message to Waldorf educators contained in this comment is the need to prepare students for this crisis of indecision, which seems to afflict more than one or two Waldorf graduates. Such preparation could perhaps be found in Steiner's directive, which could serve well as a school's parting words to its graduating students:

> *Observe that in your life all joy and sorrow, all happiness and pain will depend on the finding or not finding of your own individual initiative.*
>
> (Rudolf Steiner, *Karmic Relations*, Volume III, p.151)

THE IMPACT OF WALDORF EDUCATION ON PARENTING

A final issue to observe in this chapter relates to the perceived impact Waldorf education may have on another major stage in an alum's life: parenthood.

One third of this post-college alumni group report they have children, while about 15% state that they are not planning to have children at all. The vast majority (85%) of those who are already parents or are planning to become parents respond that their experience as students in a Waldorf school has influenced their actual or planned parenting practices. When asked to further elaborate, alumni mostly describe parenting elements that are relevant to early childhood and the early school years, rather than to adolescence. This could be explained by the age group of the respondents, who, for the most part, graduated from high school in the past decade or two and therefore are expecting to have younger children, if any at all. At the same time, these responses could also be interpreted as an indication that Waldorf education is much more pronounced, distinctive, and recognizable in its practices in the early grades than it is in the high school.

The elements of Waldorf education mentioned in these responses are listed here in descending order, from the most frequently mentioned to the less so:

- Restricting media and screen technology
  (mentioned in 40% of responses)

- Type of play, with emphasis on the outdoors (20%)

- Role of creativity, imagination, and the arts
  in the life of the child (20%)

- Spending time in nature (18%)

- Attentiveness to the stages of child development (12%)

- Attentiveness to seasonal and other festivals,
  rhythms, and rituals (10%)

- Using natural material "Waldorf toys" (8%)

The ways alumni see and express, in their own words, the influence of their past education on their parenting priorities are demonstrated in the sample of quotes below. The aspects and practices mentioned in these representative responses also provide a glimpse into what alumni identify as a Waldorf upbringing:

Limited screen time. Imaginative playtime. Having to think through problems and realize that an adult won't always be there to tell you the answer.

Emphasis on nature, multiple intelligences, the arts, diversity.

I attempt to make sure he sees the whole picture when learning and foster his creativity.

I feel that Waldorf education greatly influences how I raise my children. We limit media/technology. We spend a lot of time outdoors and encourage a home environment conducive to creative play. We bake, sing, do art, and follow routines and purposeful actions in our day. We try to encourage empathy and kindness and try to help our kids understand their contribution to the community (e.g. they have "chores").

Engaging with people, kindness and respect, understanding the natural world, not being selfish and self-centered.

We celebrate the festivals, say a blessing at every meal, have our kind of seasonal table, balance playing structured games with just being creative with tree stumps and rocks, read and sing a lot together, and engender values of kindness and contribution that were strongly cultivated in my Waldorf experiences.

Having a picture of a healthy human being and how to nurture that.

We use meal time and bedtime rituals and also see an anthroposophical doctor. Our diet is organic/biodynamic and local foods with health and person in mind, cooked at home. We incorporate many activities similar to a Waldorf school, such as watercolor painting, baking, building forts, using natural materials, etc.

I like the idea of teaching "the right thing at the right time," not rushing children to learn too fast. Not focusing on developing the intellect too soon, preserving a sense of wonder, especially in the early grades.

No screen time! Trying to have a calm home environment, letting the children physically explore their surroundings and spend some time outside every day (they are under five years old). Eating a plant-based diet, reading stories, learning a second language, being open minded to other people, caring for the environment, pursuing hobbies, learning practical skills. Almost all of what I want to share with my children is based on my experience at Waldorf.

Wonder, gentleness, beauty, careful observation of who this individual child is, value of outdoor play, value of learning with hands and body, not just intellectually, spiritual perspectives on people and kids.

Do alumni also choose to send their children to Waldorf schools? The answer is complicated.

Only a third of the survey respondents answered this question, with 54% saying that they would send (or are sending) their children to a Waldorf school, while 46% stating they won't. The free-form responses provide a more detailed picture, in which many of the naysayers point out that the costs are prohibitive for them or that there are no Waldorf schools in their locality. Among those who say they are planning to send their children to a Waldorf school, some qualify their response by saying their final decision will depend on the quality of the teachers at a given school and the suitability of Waldorf education to the specific needs and preferences of their children.

Otherwise, alumni who are positive about their children attending a Waldorf school explain their reasons by saying that in their own school days they had a positive experience, which they would like to give their children as well, and that they believe in the pedagogical approach, specifically the emphasis on unhurried childhood, gentle attitude, absence of technology, outdoor play and relation to nature, practice of the arts, and the attention to the whole child. In addition, they believe Waldorf will instill in their children the love of learning, give them emotional support, and raise them in a wholesome atmosphere.

On the other side are those who do not subscribe to at least some aspects of the pedagogy, such as the absence of technology, or who say that Waldorf education is not changing with the times. Others prefer to support public education, either on the principle of equality and diversity, or because they are pleased with the specific public schools in their area; some choose to homeschool their children. A sizable group of respondents say that they cannot even imagine being able to afford the costs of a Waldorf school or that there are none available to them, while several others don't trust the Waldorf school in their area.

Here is a representative sample of responses to the question, Why would you/ would you not send your child to a Waldorf school?

It's the best and only option for us!

No good option where I live.

I believe in public education.

My wife and I are both students of Waldorf, we'd like our children to be as well.

A no-technology approach is outdated.

It is the best school in our area. I value their emphasis on quality materials, quality time and developmentally-appropriate curriculum.

I can't afford to.

Lack of diversity is a major issue for me and my husband in choosing a school. Our daughter is mixed race and we feel she would be one of the only children there who is, and are not comfortable with that.

It's the responsible thing to do. All other forms of education, especially in the states, would hurt my children. Not good.

I am not aligned with the philosophy.

I want my children to enjoy going to school, to be curious and interested about the world and compassionate to other people who may be different in many ways. I want them to have an education that encourages them to think for themselves and solve problems in innovative ways. I believe that this kind of creativity is increasingly vital to any kind of success.

Because I can't imagine sending them anywhere else.

I want him to build a love of learning, the ability to see people for who they are, to appreciate nature, and to have the arts as a significant part of his learning.

I value the hands on, low tech, whole person approach to education.

I want them to experience what I did.

VII In Their Own Words (1)

ALUMNI SHARE EXPERIENCES AND IMPACT
OF THEIR WALDORF EDUCATION

Where is the book in which the teacher can read about what teaching is? The children themselves are the book. We should not learn to teach out of any book other than the one lying open before us and consisting of the children themselves.

Rudolf Steiner

One method of gathering information and impressions for the current Survey of Waldorf Graduates consisted in a set of 22 personal interviews with alumni from various Waldorf schools across the United States. The present chapter presents an overview of these interviews along with a summary of the main themes and perspectives featured in the conversations. In addition, we include at the end of this chapter the transcripts of two full interviews, one with two siblings who graduated from the Waldorf School of Garden City in the late 1990s, and the other with a 2011 graduate of the Hartsbrook School in Hadley, Massachusetts.

The full groups of interviewees represent seven different Waldorf schools, with nine individuals hailing from the West Coast, eight from the East Coast, and five from Midwest schools. Several interviewees were referred to us by their graduating schools, others were approached directly by the interviewer, Connie Stokes, who was assisted in two interviews by Liz Beaven. Both women are veteran Waldorf teachers, school administrators, and parents of Waldorf alumni. They relied on their professional and personal networks to locate some of the interviewees.

Interviews were conducted in various face-to-face settings, including one-on-one sessions and small groups of two or three interviewees at a time. The interviewees ranged in age from 19 to 45. Nine of them graduated from high school in the past eight years and are regarded "college-age" graduates, while the other 13 already completed at least a first round of undergraduate education and are representative of the group of "post-college graduates" surveyed in this study. The same number, 13, represents those interviewees who have attended Waldorf schools from early childhood through 12th grade. In addition, the wider group includes two sets of two siblings and seven alumni who are children of Waldorf teachers. We found no significant differences between responses provided by these "faculty children" and the rest of the interviewees, except that faculty children were more familiar with Anthroposophy. Still, most of them admitted that their knowledge of Anthroposophy was cursory. The final transcript included in this section, an interview conducted with two siblings who are also children of Waldorf teachers, demonstrates how following a similar path in Waldorf education, and even being raised in the household of Waldorf educators, can still lead to very different life choices and career paths.

SOME PERSONAL IMPRESSIONS

Several common characteristics stand out when looking at the full group of interviewees engaged over a period of a year. They all appeared to be guided by a certain moral compass: their words and actions expressed a deep interest in humanity and the human condition, in serving the world, and in helping others and especially mainstream society's "other."

Reflecting back on their Waldorf education, the interviewees were generally appreciative, adding some constructive suggestions for adaptation or change. A common suggestion for improvement focused on the study of science and math. However, this perceived lack did not seem to impede the few interviewees who chose to major in college in scientific or medical fields. Interviewees who were still in college or graduate school tended to focus more on their current learning experiences and aspirations, while those who were long out of school tended to relate their Waldorf experiences to their family and work life. Graduates who attended a Waldorf grade school referred back to these earlier years, emphasizing the role of their class teacher in forming their experience and outlook.

It was clear from many of the comments made during these conversations, that these alumni were aware during their time at school of faculty and staff discords, and that they believe now that aspects of school administration, such as effective hiring and release practices, could be improved. Only two of the whole group of alumni interviewed seemed well-read in Anthroposophy and the writings of Rudolf

Steiner, while the rest showed little theoretical knowledge of or interest in exploring Anthroposophy more broadly. Instead, these Waldorf graduates appeared to be "walking the walk" of Anthroposophy rather than talking its talk.

The interviews followed an outline of 19 questions, which are included at the end of this chapter. However, not all of the questions were included in every interview, while additional questions were posed in response to the interviewees' comments or life stories. Below, we have organized quotes and summaries of the responses according to major topics shared in the conversations.

SPONTANEOUS ADJECTIVES

Asked to spontaneously come up with five adjectives to describe their Waldorf education, the interviewees, while often resorting to the word "creative," produced a wide variety of responses with very few words or phrases repeated. Their responses included the following words:

adventurous	positive	community oriented
engaging	beautiful	invigorating
nurturing	holistic	sweet
well-rounded	protective	different
alternative	bizarre at times	magical
enriching	incestuous	tight-knit
painful	safe	diligent
worldly (class trips)	colorful	motivational
appreciative	interesting	transformative
flexible	social	diverse (curriculum)
playful	comforting	natural
balanced	intuitive	wholesome
fun	supportive	

as well as:

"perfect because it was not so perfect"

"quality of relationships with teachers"

PROFESSIONS

A wide variety of professions and directions is displayed among alumni who are already on a career path. Current or past positions held by the interviewees include:

Vice President of Ticket Sales and Services for an NBA team

Executive Director of a non-profit watchdog organization protecting labor unions

Owner and Director of an urban design company for building and landscaping

Corporate book publishing employee

Professor of mathematics at a community college

Associate Producer in a family-owned ensemble theater

Production Coordinator at Netflix

Team Member at Morningstar Financial Services

Employee in the field of e-marketing for fashion and interior design

Team-member in a company producing and providing patients with medical equipment

Content and Strategy team-member at an agency creating museum exhibits

National Oceanic and Atmospheric Administration officer, working to protect endangered species

Financial Day Trader working from home

POLITICAL, SOCIAL, AND PERSONAL CAUSES

We asked about the various causes—political, social, personal, or other—that interviewees support or are engaged with in one way or another. A follow-up question asked about their views as to what are the most important causes to be pursued for the benefit of humanity at large. We recorded the following (partly paraphrased) responses:

I am indirectly associated with my family's cause to help the poor and specifically children in Ecuador.

I am involved in the World Refugee Fund.

I volunteer as a board member at my former school and am interested in finding ways to use my work to influence civic engagement.

Parenting is a major priority for us. We want to raise our kids to be thoughtful, good human beings who go out into the world. [I am] committed to a renewal of the labor movement, not [only] working for good wages but also to have time for personal endeavors and family... I don't think we can truly achieve this notion of free individuals without having economic freedom and economic freedom means having control of your workplace.

I am committed to social justice and educate myself on these issues [in order to ask] myself how we will affect change through my work.

I have lobbied for incarceration reform with the racial aspects, the environment, and immigration. I have been an activist since high school protesting, organizing events. I am into politics and very liberal. I think young people like us can make a difference with the current issue of gun rights.

I lobbied for immigration rights.

We try to be as environmentally conscious as possible; I send money to children and women in countries where just a little bit can really make a difference in their education or lives; I support the ACLU in their work on social justice and equity.

I am environmentally conscious.

I have demonstrated in the political protests of late. My company is focused on dedicating money and resources to non-profit charity causes. I donate to environmental organizations.

I am not particularly active in things separate from my job. I focus on family, friends, and health.

For a while I taught in a program for adult literacy as a volunteer. I am involved with my local Waldorf School as a volunteer. We make in-kind donations.

I don't get involved with politics at my college, because opinions seemed to be locked down without the possibility of a real dialogue.

Operating a community theater, creating partnerships with neighboring, financially disadvantaged communities, offering scholarships and internships to high-school students to work with a professional performance group. Working on transforming a large farm space into an arts campus, which will include a section prioritizing First Nations people to use as they see fit. Projects are done in partnership with locals who serve as a guiding equity committee.

I am a filmmaker interested in exploring and promoting women's causes.

I try to live in the middle of things and see more than one perspective. My ideal is to understand the other.

One interviewee is working on immigration reform with the Center for a New America. She has developed interest in these issues while learning about migration in college, leading to research in Senegal and the writing of an undergraduate thesis on the role of Senegalese rap artists in social and political resistance and reform in their country. She places the immediate question of immigration issues within the wider historical (and academic) context of colonialism and its effects.

Another interviewee is a team member in a financial services firm, involved in the "I-Mentor" program where he leads a program in which company employees engage in one-on-one mentoring of first-generation, first-year college students from low-income, underrepresented demographics. The interviewee reports: "I am very interested in economic inequality. A former CEO challenged me to put a working group together to determine if and how [the company] can help those who are underrepresented or economically disadvantaged. I am also fortunate to have a 6-week paid sabbatical to work in Tanzania as an intern exploring financial inclusion. There are many people at [the company] who are my age and are also doing something that is greater than just getting a paycheck every week."

REFLECTIONS ON WALDORF EDUCATION

A good portion of the interview questions invited graduates to think back on their time in Waldorf education, reflect on perceived strengths and challenges of their education, and discuss the effects of Waldorf on their current standing in life.

The perspective of one interviewee, viewing her past experiences through the lens of the mother she has become, touches on several aspects of the Waldorf experience. Here she is in her own words:

You've got to have teachers who care, since as a kid you are spending more than half of your day in school. I think that is why I am also obsessing about it as a mother because I find education to be more than an academic experience. I really want my children's experience to be what I had. The learning component is the emotional component as much as it is self-growth and American History and they are all equal because you had that emotional stability and intelligence. You can continue to learn those things and you have the confidence to know that you are not going to be good at everything. I am very confident in that and I can go out and accomplish other great things. This is one of the most valuable things a person can feel about themselves because you are not going to be great at everything ... to have confidence.

I have always felt that there is a kind of elitist view of my education. I benefited from something that was remarkably special that differentiates me from so many other people that I know were not Waldorf graduates and I have never been able to fully put my finger on exactly what that would be except for that. The one thing that I can really hone in on is that if you have a classroom environment where ... every single class focuses on a kind of original thought, kind of ... the cornerstone of what makes you a thoughtful human being. That is the one thing that you can graduate from school with—original thought.

I wish we had been taught why or what we were taught the way we were. I feel like it would have been ingrained even more deeply. I feel like I would have gotten even more out of it if I understood the process. Things just seemed random and in retrospect they weren't random, but they were never explained ... I would have appreciated a map of what your education is going to look like for the next six months.

Other reflections on the perceived value of their Waldorf education included the following:

Waldorf was a very social way to go to school; you are engaged with your peers from kindergarten all the way through high school. But you are also getting on stage, doing plays and performances, from kindergarten on and you have to give a speech in your senior year, and there are all sorts of ways in which Waldorf makes you a social person. We were conditioned by Waldorf to relate to people and understand people, but I don't think I was pushed enough ... they should not have allowed me to go into the lower level math class, it should not have been an option. That is just one example. ... Maybe this has all changed, but I just felt there was a little bit of getting away with things that we probably shouldn't have, and I don't think it served me well.

Being able to work through a problem by having true discussion is something I gained from Waldorf Education. ... I understood science metaphorically. We were given everything we needed to know. Then we had to figure things out for ourselves. Then there was the visual aspect, verbal, writing. There was no angle from which we couldn't learn. We were taught every way, for audio learners, visual learners, from writing it down. ... There was no way not to get it if you put in the effort.

Everything about the way the education is structured influences the capacity to create healthy, balanced relationships. I love the academic humanities as a whole and taking them apart and examining the details. Being exposed to this over and over in all my classes brought into focus all the details.

I was able to be who I wanted to be. I was colorful in plays. I was able to be an athlete. I sewed something. I knitted things. I sang in the chorus.

I feel very set apart from many others and incredibly, incredibly grateful for the education that I have had. To this day I feel like a "Waldorf evangelist" because I go out and spread the word on what an incredible system this is and how it can do amazing things...the way it approaches the human and the child and the mind and development. Waldorf education made me who I am today. I would not be that person without it. That is the core. The multi-disciplinary approach to training your mind to look at something from all sides is extremely valuable. It lends itself to flexibility in thinking, creativity and confidence and being able to teach yourself something.

You can either teach someone what they need to know or teach someone how to learn what they need to know, and I feel like both my [mainstream and Waldorf] high schools were teaching me how to learn what I need to know.

RELATIONSHIP WITH TEACHERS

I valued how loosely you relate to your teachers. It is the primary reason I do so well in school now. We got so familiar with our teachers here we always felt we could go to our teachers' offices and ask questions. A sense of community that you get here. I don't think people in other schools have the same experience. I assumed that this was the same at college, so I just felt at home going to [my professors to] ask questions. My professors were very open, both with class-related problems and problems unrelated. This is something that my high school prepared well.

I appreciate the high-school teachers who were close to us in age. Our math teacher offered himself big time at lunch. I wouldn't go out during recess. I would rather hang out with the teacher.

The close relationship between students and teachers can result in lack of professionalism in communication and boundaries which can then affect decisions that otherwise should be more objective regarding discipline, curriculum or personnel.

MAIN LESSON BLOCKS & BOOKS

Waldorf encouraged in me ownership over my creative projects. I really loved creating my Main Lesson books and all the details working on it for weeks. I got a lot of satisfaction out of this, and it has helped me do my commercial projects now. I have to put together a binder after all my preparation and it is the outcome of my [education]. Attention to detail is essential in my nature. I also remember suffering during woodworking, working on one thing for a year, but at the end of the year being proud of it. In 8th grade I made a stool. It taught me long-term work ethic. If you can put off the reward a little longer—realizing that you focus on something for, let's say ten years, and won't see the result until later. It is similar to making a movie. Working really hard for years and years and a long time until the finished product. I remember thinking that making a movie was like a Main Lesson.

Definitely making our own textbooks. I really appreciated that, you know, writing basically our own entries. There's something really, really reinforcing about, you know, the lessons that we learned when you have to rewrite it and think it out for yourself rather than in the words of a textbook. Coming out with our understanding of it was [what] I found really helpful in solidifying the lesson.

I studied international affairs in both undergrad and grad school, but the common thread through all of that was a desire to use storytelling to effect some kind of outcome or change. ... At the company that I currently work for I am doing research and content development. We are telling stories to impact people that come into spaces. So, while it is not international affairs related, that story could be anything. It is about creating a story and an experience that is going to do something to the people there.

ART IN WALDORF

Art is everything. There was rarely a class where an art medium did not appear and was brought into our learning process. ... I don't think of Waldorf education as being based in the arts. Everything about the education is so deeply integrated. Those are the moments in class in high school that I remember.

I appreciated that Waldorf allowed me to get a taste of the arts ... metal-smithing, basket weaving, sewing, knitting, crocheting... [Back] in the moment I didn't care but I recognize its value now. No one I know who attends a different kind of school had this in their curriculum.

VARIETY AND FREEDOM

I like how my school allowed me to pursue my interests outside of class: AP Calculus, I started a newspaper, all the extra-curriculars, you could play basketball and baseball; it was encouraged.

What I found valuable was the flexibility of it and the fact that the teachers' work with me was really valuable. Travel was also very important to me. We went to Costa Rica for the senior trip. We had a class trip every year. That was really important to me. Having the older students as mentors was also very important to me. I think the Math program could have been better, although I was ADHD.

I felt really comfortable with my senior project. It was hard not to keep going. I wouldn't change anything in the actual educational philosophy, nothing. I would add AP courses. A lot of my [college] classmates transferred in with quite a number of credits. I would have liked my 12 years of German to count for college credits.

ACADEMICS AND PREPARATIONS FOR COLLEGE

I felt more prepared than I expected to be for college because my whole life I have been told that I would not be prepared enough, especially with Math and Science. I can't speak yet about the sciences but with every other subject so far, I felt more than prepared, even better than my peers. I was confident in people skills, group work. I know how to work with people, I know how to get my thoughts across. College is hard, but I was able to stay above average with everything, which was a really nice feeling. I feel the same way, especially with writing and humanities and reading. I am in the top tier with my school in those subjects.

My [college] biology class was really difficult, and I definitely had to teach myself but I think others did as well. Our science in high school was so sporadic and broken up in different styles of teaching. I felt a little let down by that, and it is okay for me because I am not going to go into sciences, but I know a couple of friends from my class that want to do pre-med and the other wants to be a nurse or bio major, and they are really, really struggling because most people leave public school way, way ahead. If we had one or two science [Main Lesson] teachers throughout the school year, we had to relearn things – people would use different terms or different styles. It is important because in college you do need to know those terms to be able to understand what is going on when you go into your first class. So, I think it would be super useful to have a track class like we did with English because then it is consistent. Having a science track class would be very beneficial.

Our high school was very academically focused for me. We had a lot of homework and I know that other Waldorf schools do not. Always having this academic pressure made me turn down some other opportunities in high school that would have been cool. I gave up some sports activities because it was just too much.

I noticed in college that my creative side was where I was strongest, and I still remember taking more English classes ... I was using my imagination which more than anything just enabled me to write things in certain ways that were very attractive to the teachers and to get points across. I think this also carried over into my work. I read a lot of stock market articles and can form things really quickly.

Being in a small classroom allowed us to feel comfortable speaking up. I got used to speaking in front of the class. I feel pretty good about public speaking.

I am taking a biology class and I thought I was going to be terrible at this. I haven't taken science since I left high school. Now I am so excited about it. It is just figuring things out. What is so astonishing to me is that I love history and German, literature, and reading books. I didn't like the sciences as much as I liked literature. But [now] I love science and I am thinking back on my zoology class in high school.

My interest in my major—Political Science with a History minor—was not inspired through academia, but through student organizations and campaigns and relevant occurrences. One aspect of this which was fostered in high school: my high-school science teacher would start all his classes with reading a story in the newspaper. We would take 15 minutes to discuss the issue of the day, whether it was local or national to give us a political issue every morning.

I am a mathematician graduated with honors from a California University. [Waldorf education] only affected me positively.

I am liberal and I grew from my high-school years through the humanities curriculum. … High school taught me about ideals and college taught me that ideals don't do what they are supposed to do all the time.

PARENTHOOD

The way we raise our child is also related to our education. Our kids will go to Waldorf for sure.

It has helped me be a parent. I want my son to be passionate about who he wants to be as an individual, whether it is sports or arts. I treasure a lot of those characteristics.

CRITIQUE

I would change the hiring process and allow students to weigh in after the prospective teacher does a sample lesson.

There is so much in my freshman general education classes that I had already done and that I already knew.

I do think that the running of the school probably needs something different. I think when I was in the school it was run by a bunch of idealistic hippies, and when I went to Germany as an exchange student it seemed so organized. Waldorf Schools in Germany are like the pinnacle of amazing.

The world is different than in 1919. There has to be openness to change. There are new discussions happening in the world and there is a new group of people in the world that need acceptance and need places to be seen and heard and acknowledged. I think it is important to bring in the LGBTQ community, Black Lives Matter community, just like teaching history from every point of view, from what is honest and what is true and what is hard to acknowledge about American history. ... I wish we would change our emphasis on White European history and bring more Native American history into the curriculum.

The most important area of change needed in Waldorf is the lack of diversity, both ethnicity and racial. What is in the curriculum is often very Christian-centric, which I understand is how Steiner was. We need history that is more than just an American perspective. We were introduced to African-American literature that had never been in the school before, and it was really a good class. The only books I ever read were written by white men and women. I think we need more than European and American history. I don't feel very knowledgeable about other topics. I am starting to educate myself because I want to know more about it.

My most critical feedback would be the hard sciences where the teaching part wasn't developed enough, but every other aspect of my education I felt did a tremendous job of advancing me as a person.

More life-skills could be interesting ... one class for one trimester about taxes, how to be an adult, how to fix a car, how to balance a budget, how do you live your life, how to change a tire. Maybe it would be appropriate for Senior year when people are checked out of more rigorous academic courses. It could be a good time and have a lot of practical rewards: You are about to enter the world after high school, saving money, this is what an IRA is...

If anything, I guess I would have maybe liked to have a little bit more kind of insight to how our education is different from traditional education and what differences I might encounter when I went to the university. You know, I felt like I was kind of in a bit of a culture shock when I went to a college just because things were so different, and the learning and teaching styles were really different. I felt like I needed a lot of catching up and lacked a little bit of confidence in that area. ... Having a little bit more introduction to what the convention is might've been helpful, might've given me a little bit more confidence going into a big public university like I did.

HOW WOULD YOU DESCRIBE WALDORF EDUCATION?

I would describe it as a holistic approach to education. I think it is an opportunity to be exposed to far more breadth whether through different approaches to history in different times throughout human evolution to arts and crafts. I think even the sciences are taught using a broader holistic approach. ... A holistic approach to education that really enables individuals to be creative in their own way as opposed to a mainstream approach.

I always say it's a developmental education, so it follows where the child is in their life and growing up and it tries to educate towards that. It is developmental learning. You educate the child in love and freedom because it is true and good. When you say that to someone they relate to it, then I think they just Google it.

I realize that I can have a normal human conversation with an adult without being uncomfortable. This is how I can describe Waldorf education.

I call it an education that educates the whole person rather than just the mind. I am using my hands, color, movement, singing and it just makes you a well-rounded person. ... It is super small and kind of hippy-ish and in the woods.

Waldorf educates the head, heart, and hands. These are not just buzzwords that I have heard in the household. I think it is an education that wants to help you learn how to think as opposed to just know things, how to think about things that help you come up with your own opinions. So critical thinking and critical reasoning are major aspects of what the education is. They want you to be a well-rounded person, contributor to society.

It makes you a really well-rounded person. I had all the regular English, math, science classes, and then I also did woodworking and a blacksmith thing. I learned my time-tables with bean bag games, so I talk about turning theory into practice and how we went to Hermit Island and we had the opportunity to learn in the ocean what we were learning about the ocean. It is very interactive learning.

I would say holistic education. It works both with kinesthetic learning, oral learning, visual learning. It lets people progress at their own pace ... so there is no pressure to conform and everyone will come to their fruition when their time is right. There is no pressure to be anything because you will become who you are eventually.

It is surprising how many people ask me about Waldorf. A couple of professors asked me about it. It is really difficult. Kind of hard to explain: We have the same teacher, curriculum tries to bring things at the right age, small class sizes, being able to speak with my teachers. ... I can't really talk about the philosophy. I also talk about the arts. We had one or two blocks ("Becoming Human," "Parzival") just touching on the philosophy...

I feel like I went through it without really knowing the philosophy behind it, except for the little slogans like "education from the inside out" or something like that. I never really learned about the philosophy and I honestly don't know that I would have been interested.

RELATIONSHIP TO ANTHROPOSOPHY

My wife relates to Anthroposophy more than I do. My eyes glaze over. My wife and mother discuss the ideas and enjoy their conversations. I stay out of it.

Aha, well, right now there is no way I can't have a relationship with Anthroposophy because it has been such a key piece of my life. I am an atheist, but I have a fondness for things like Anthroposophy and an appreciation for all religions because I grew up with Anthroposophy, which respects all religions and itself isn't really a religion, although my Mom and I debate this. … I have read some of Steiner's works and have had a lot of conversations with my parents, as you can imagine, but I have lots of respect. Because of Anthroposophy there are a lot of wonderful things that exist in the world. Waldorf education is certainly at the top of the list, but also biodynamic farming and Camphill.

I think it is more of an abstract relationship than concrete. I think by the time I was a Senior, it all came together, and it just made sense when it was described. I don't know if I would have a concrete understanding, but it is interesting.

We had a child development thing, but we didn't get into depth very much. Basically, we went back to the grades and observed some classes. It was more of a personal reflection. My Dad is always talking about it. He is obsessed with it. I think it would be kind of cool to have a block on the origins of Waldorf education and Anthroposophy, maybe an elective. I really don't know anything.

When I was 21, I joined the Anthroposophical Society and for a number of years I went to a few conferences and to a study group in the area where I was living at that time in Virginia. I was pretty involved for a few years, but once I had kids it was just too much. Like it was another responsibility on top of my career to stay involved in. … But ever since I was maybe a Junior in high school, I began reading. Theosophy was the first book. I have read all the basic books and others to get a knowledge of my upbringing and education. I did keep reading some things like the Calendar of the Soul and did some meditations. It is off and on for me because of my family but I had the drive to learn about the origins but have not done much with it myself.

I know our parents go to meetings and do their kind of thing … and they've talked about it, but I haven't myself done a lot of research or reading on it. And that wasn't the purpose of it really.

Anthroposophy? Yes and no. I have very peripheral knowledge. I read a lot of Steiner books on nutrition and health, but I have not really delved into theosophy very much or the roots of Anthroposophy, so I know there is more reading. It is close to my heart.

I will probably explore Anthroposophy at some point later on in my life. I would say at this juncture I have more of a relationship to the outputs or the physical manifestation of the philosophy, i.e. Waldorf or biodynamic farming. I got to be a farmer for many years, my teenage years as well. More of the practice of it, but I am not very familiar with the philosophy.

THE INTERVIEW QUESTIONS:

1. What is your profession? Are you happy with your profession? Is it the one you would aspire to have should you be able to start all over again?

2. Do you feel that your profession defines who you are? If not, what are the things (roles, characteristics, social and personal traits, etc.) that define you?

3. What are the causes (personal, social, political, etc.) that you feel most passionate about?

4. What are the causes (social, political, etc.) that you think are most important for humanity at large?

5. Can you list a set of skills you feel you have, ranging from the personal (e.g. the ability to listen, comfort, entertain) to the professional?

6. Can you list a set of skills you wish you had?

7. Do you feel that you have accomplished your goals so far? What would you still like to accomplish? Do you believe you will?

8. What do you do today that you can relate to your Waldorf education, e.g. lifestyle, child rearing habits, advocacy, rituals?

9. How does your former education contribute to who you are today? Considering our time and culture, do you see necessary changes or modification in Waldorf education and its general approach?

10. How has Waldorf education made a difference in your life or influenced changes in our world?

11. Imagine you are going back to visit your high school, see your teachers and walk through the hallways. What would you want to see that is the same as when you were a student? What would you want to see that is different?

12. How is your health and well-being? Do you relate this to your education?

13. How much do you keep in touch with your Waldorf classmates and/or your former teachers?

14. Do you see yourself as a leader in your community?

15. If you worked for an airline, what role would you like to fulfill: pilot, co-pilot, navigator, flight attendant, ground staff, maintenance, public relations, company owner...?

16. If you were handed a million dollars, what would you do with it and why?

17. When you were a teenager, did you have any heroes or role models? Today?

18. What are the first five adjectives that come to mind when you think of Waldorf education (not necessarily your own experience of Waldorf)?

19. When people ask you what Waldorf education is, what do you say?

TRANSCRIPT I:

Cariel Klein, Hartsbrook School, 2011

Cariel Klein attended the Hartsbrook School in Hadley, MA, from which she graduated in 2011. After graduation she trained at the New England Center for Circus Arts and the Circus Warehouse and received a degree in the Political Performance of the Self from NYU. In 2016, she started a marketing/IT business and worked as a Marketing Director for her family's ensemble theater, Double Edge Theatre. A year later she assumed a permanent role as Associate Producer of the theater, engaging in all performance, production, and business activities.

I am an Associate Producer for the Double Edge Theatre, an ensemble-based theater that belongs to my family. After I left high school I went to school at NYU and I was a professional circus performer, working as a flying trapeze artist for six years. I left that profession because it was economically unsustainable. I loved it but I wasn't feeling like it was the right place for me at that time. At NYU, I studied a mix of performance studies, anthropology, and political theory. I started working at a tech company to make ends meet and I was very bored, but I was picking up a lot of skills like how to fix computers and how to use Photoshop. One person asked me to do marketing for their business, and so I started building up my own marketing business, which I still run, but for fewer clients now.

And so I was working in marketing and the theater needed a marketing person, so they were like: Would you work remotely? Can you do our marketing? And I said, yes. In a weird sort of circumstances, things happened. One of the people who was working at the theater company and was supposed to be producing an event left, and the theater said to me, Oh, we just need somebody to run it in person for two weeks and we'll pay you for the job. So they did and then decided to hire me full time.

Is that a skill you had growing up? Was that related to anything you did at the high school?

Hartsbrook allowed me to split my schedule during my last two years there. I spent a lot of time at the New England Center for Circus Art, so they would let me go instead of, for instance, some PE lessons, fencing or something like that. I would go and do circus instead and they really allowed me to mix my schedule. My senior project was based on that. So, yeah, a lot of it came from the flexibility at Hartsbrook.

Is your current profession something you aspired to? I mean, if you were to start all over again, is this something that you really wanted to?

I would have started with this. I think I would like that to be further along, but I just didn't know it was my thing until later.

Does this profession define you? Do you think that your profession defines who you are?

No, I think that I really like the theater. It is very hard to explain, but it's a very different kind of theater from a normal type of theater. I would say it's like a Broadway show would be like a regular public school and my theater would be sort of like a Waldorf school in that analogy. It is very community based. The whole goal of it is that the artists are making a living wage by doing what they love, but they also all have a stake in the business. I really believe in the cause because also we have a lot of background working with equity, working with different types of communities in the area. So I think that the job activates parts of me that are important, but I don't think it defines who I am.

It doesn't define who you are in terms of characteristics or traits?

Well, OK, in that sense, yes, I would say that the job does define me right now. In that sense, yeah.

Tell me more about some political or social causes that you might have.

A lot of what we do is believing in equity and we make a huge effort in this area. We have a huge scholarship program and we really try and engage. For instance, where we live in Massachusetts is an economically wealthy community, although not exclusively, but it's also next to Springfield and Holyoke, which are two of the poorest communities in the area. We partner with a high school there and have a multi-year partnership where we bring two high-school students to work with us over the summer so that they can have that opportunity to, like, you know, be a part of a professional performing show. We made a commitment. We received a big grant last year that is helping us renovate old farm buildings into part of our, sort of what we call our arts campus. The whole space is converted into a hundred-acre dairy farm.

One of the spaces that we're converting is going to prioritize First Nations people. We were speaking to First Nations people and we realized that there were no spaces that prioritize them without compromising them. How can we provide a space and not tell people what to do, but just say here's a space, you can use it? We're also partnering with locals, what we would call the equity committee of people in our community that have a stake in this and also guide us in this journey. So that's one thing that we're really involved with.

Your social or personal causes seem to be connected to your profession.

They're very connected. Yes.

Can you list a set of skills that you have from personal or professional life?

I have the ability to listen, collaborate.

What would you say that you excel in?

I excel in organizational work and planning. I also excel in group efforts, like executing projects. It's something that I feel confident in my ability to excel. I also find alternative solutions to issues where you might not have the easiest option, or it may not be the best option, or it doesn't work the way we need it to work. I think I am able to fix that or go outside the box a little.

Do you feel you've accomplished the goals that you set for yourself or do you still feel like you are working towards other goals in your life?

I think that I accomplish goals that I didn't know I had or like; I thought that I would find them someplace else and I found them in this job, but I do still think that I have a lot of goals that I want to accomplish.

I think one of my goals was to find a job that traveled. I thought that that was going to be through circus. I want to travel the world, and through producing I'm able to see the world. I try and get tours and to make connections with other theater groups in the world. Another one of my goals, I would say, was to be a little more financially stable and I certainly did not get that through circus. So finding that through my current job has helped me.

What kind of places do you travel to? Where have you visited?
Most recently I was in Cambodia. It was partially a vacation, but also we were looking at spaces to perform there. I went to San Francisco for a conference. I'm about to go to Louisville for a conference and then in two weeks I'm going to Poland for 10 days to work on a tour that we're trying to go there for the last month, but I was on tour in New Jersey.

Do you have any sense of your feeling of your health and well-being and any relationship that you might relate to you Waldorf education experience?
Like, that my health or well-being is connected to my education?

Have you thought about that?
I have not thought about, maybe, yes, in a weird way. I've always known that people call me the social butterfly of my friend group. I knew that my ability to communicate and express myself clearly and work through problems was a product of my family, but also my Waldorf education. I don't know if health is the right way to put it. I mean, I was only in Waldorf school for high school; I wasn't a baby Waldorf student.

Do you see anything in it that contributed to who you are today?
Oh, a lot. Totally. I mean, so I went to a Waldorf high school and the college that I was lucky enough to go to is an individualized study college, so it was like a continuation of Waldorf education in college. I have a great ability to see relationships between ideas and to really delve deeply into topics and I have a great relationship with teachers in a way that a lot of my friends who went to other types of high school just don't have. I am still friends with some of my teachers from high school and I still really admire a lot of them and what they did. And I think it comes from my high-school education and I'm still close with a lot of my classmates, which is not something a lot of people can say.

What do you remember about the schools you attended before Waldorf and the change you might have experienced when starting high school?
I was in an all-girls middle school. I didn't enjoy being in an all-girls school. It was very strict and I wasn't diagnosed until after I transferred, but I have ADHD, so being in an environment that's very strict and that doesn't allow for any sort of flexibility was very difficult for me. I think it was only because of Hartsbrook that I was able to get out of that sort of box. There were other reasons that I switched; it wasn't a very interesting environment. I think it was sort of sterile, and most of the kids boarded, and I didn't want to board.

Do you keep up with your classmates?

I had 20 classmates in my grade and I keep up with 8. The rest of us keep up with each other through social media. We have a private Facebook page. I was in Massachusetts last Saturday and got together with my closest friends.

What did you find valuable and what did you think needed change at your school?

What I found valuable was the flexibility of it and the fact that the teachers worked with me. That was really invaluable! Travel was also very important to me. We went to Costa Rica for the senior trip. We had a class trip every year. That was really important to me. Having the older students as mentors was also very important to me. I think the Math program could have been better, although I was ADHD.

Was it a handicap when you went to college?

I did well with writing papers, but standardized testing was difficult. I appreciated not having it in high school but then when I got to College, I just didn't have the experience of taking tests. Being in a class of 500 where people know more than you do, you have to stay awake. I wouldn't really want to replace the education I had in high school, but it would have been helpful to know how to take a test.

Did you have testing in your other school?

I did have little tests, like quizzes in 7th and 8th grade, but we did have a state standardized test. That was the big test that I had in seventh and eighth grade.

Was it hard catching up with your classmates who went through the lower school and years of Waldorf experience in public speaking and theater work?

I was already pretty outgoing. I think the word "precocious" was used by my teachers, fondly. I was lucky and I was very comfortable with that. But I remember even the other people in my class who did join in high school, there were four of us, we were really encouraged to come out of our shells. And I think that there was, there might have been a moment of acclimation problems, but it didn't take long for us to catch up.

What I struggled with was that everybody else and to this day was so much better artistically than I was. They could all draw and I always remember being the last person to hand in anything that had to be drawn, because it would always be the worst, and I would always apologize. The teachers were fine and only I cared about it.

How did you do with crafting or woodwork or the other handwork?

I did really well with that. I enjoyed that kind of thing. We had woodworking, I'm still friends with the teacher of that class. We also did ballroom dancing. I love that stuff. Anything active I was really into.

Can you give me five adjectives to describe your Waldorf education?
Diverse, alternative, flexible.

Do you think that Waldorf education can make a difference in the world?
So the high school that I went to was very new when I went there. I think it was like the fifth graduating class. So I remember they were still working out the kinks of like, what does it mean to have a high school? But I think that it was really great and I really enjoyed it. I think that it gave me skills. I'm thinking about this, to be in a foreign country and do an exchange like teaching that type of idea of exchanging with the world in a real way, in a way that you're taught that your vulnerable is extremely important to me. And I actually was lucky enough when I was going to Cambodia, I saw my exchange student on the way there. She lives in Japan and it felt like nine years have flown by, but I remembered that feeling of being vulnerable. And I think that it's, it's too easy for us to pretend that we're not vulnerable and that, you know, to just tough it out. But if you, if you actually extend that, I think you can have a deeper appreciation of a lot of things. It also helps us to be more sensitive. It is important to be sensitive.

TRANSCRIPT II:
Genevieve Soloway Angle, Waldorf School of Garden City, 1996
Gareth Soloway, Waldorf School of Garden City, 1999
Genevieve Soloway Angle and Gareth Soloway both attended the Lexington Waldorf School in Massachusetts before moving to Hempstead, Long Island. They attended the Waldorf School of Garden City, from which Genevieve graduated in 1996 and Gareth in 1999. Their parents were both Waldorf class teachers while Genevieve and Gareth were growing up, and they continue their work in Waldorf education as visiting mentors and evaluators. Both siblings, their families, and their parents live today in Portland, Oregon.

Genevieve: *I am a biologist. I work for the federal government in the National Oceanic and Atmospheric Administration. My work involves protecting endangered species and their habitats.*

Gareth: *I have a company where I do investment education and stock trading. We focus on quicker investing based on technical charting. The terms are "day trading" and "swing trading." Day trading focuses on holding stocks for minutes, looking for disparities in price action while swing trading is holding a stock anywhere from a couple of days to a month or so. The education program helps young people to retirees manage their money in a much more hands-on approach versus the buy-and-hold mentality.*

How long have you both been in these professions?
Genevieve: *After I graduated from college, in 2000, I went to teach English in Japan for two years, then went to graduate school from 2002-2004, then started working for the government. I was going to graduate school in Washington, DC at George Washington*

University, so I started off working at headquarters and then I moved out into the field office in Portland, after about four years.

Gareth: *Following college in New York, I worked for MetLife for one year as a financial planner. But I hated the cold calling, so after a year and precisely on that date I quit to focus on stock trading. I started to trade for myself, but with limited capital it wasn't really something that I was going to be able to do fully right away. So, at that point I started to work a couple of different jobs to build capital. Ultimately, in the next couple of years, I began to trade profitably. I met a couple of people that had the same mindset. We studied the markets together and we ultimately came up with a unique way to analyze stock charts, giving us an edge in finding winning trades. We wanted to educate the public and started the company in 2007 with the goal of helping people learn how to manage their money more effectively than long-term investing. It's now 2019, so we have been operating the company for 12 years.*

Do you feel that your job defines you?

Gareth: *I don't think any more or less than other aspects of my life. It's convenient to sometimes let it define me as people see me as the "stock trader." Also, through owning a company, it becomes your main focus, at least until you are successful. You have no choice but to live and breathe it.*

Genevieve: *Not particularly. I mean, I don't think of myself as a scientist unless somebody says, oh, what work do you do?*

Gareth: *Anyone that knows what I do is always asking me what I think the market's going to do or what's a good stock to buy. And then, you know, I have a relatively large following on Twitter and that's who I am, at least online. However, I also love gardening. I have a big garden at home, and I use that as a therapeutic side of things because of the high stress of my job. I go to the gym as well. And obviously now that I have a little daughter, she's really taken up a lot of time, so, yeah, I'd like to not think it totally does.*

Genevieve: *And you're a little different because you have your own business, right?*

Gareth: *Yes, so I've had to live and breathe it to get it to be profitable early on and to actually make money and not go out of business in the first year or two, you know. I really had to. Everything I was doing was focused solely on that. But I do think now that it's running smoothly and well. I've been able to kind of focus on other things and take a step back a little. The nice thing about it is if there's a high-speed internet connection, I can work from anywhere in the world. Of course, it is good and bad on vacations. I still work, but at the same time I can go anywhere at any time.*

Are you happy with what you do?

Genevieve: *I am. I enjoy the science side of things and as time goes on I've gotten more and more into management. I mean, I've been doing this for 14 years and I'm still learning all the time and there are opportunities if you're self-motivated to always keep learning. So I really do enjoy it. And then I also enjoy the fact that unlike Gareth, I can just leave work at* *work. Now, whether I do or not is another thing because I tend to also check emails while on vacation because I don't want to come back to 300 emails, things like that. So yeah, I would say I am happy.*

Gareth: *I do enjoy it. I mean, it obviously has its ups and downs, but if I'm helping people make money, then there's nothing better in the world. People saying you've made a difference in their life, or they bought a new car because I helped them make money or they saved more money for retirement. However, it does have its downside where occasionally I'll be wrong on a market/stock call. When you mess with people's money, they can be pretty mad. But luckily I'm good enough at it, the wins far exceed the losses. I'd been around for long enough and for the most part everyone does very well. It's very rewarding and the freedom to work from home is awesome. I love the markets from the perspective of everyday when you get up, you don't know what you're going to get, some days it's wild, crazy, and exciting. Sometimes it's slow, but, but overall you just never know. It also is never the same day on repeat. It's never that same repetitive kind of nonsense every single day. And that's cool.*

Genevieve: *Our jobs are both pretty flexible. And it's great having that kind of freedom when you have a family to go and see a performance at the kids' school, or, whatever you need to do during the day, like this interview.*

Gareth: *It makes your life more in balance. I start working very early since the markets open at 6:30 in the morning (Pacific Time). I'm up at five, but my main computer terminal, it's in my detached office. Sometimes, 15 minutes before the markets opens, I just roll into that seat in my pj's and off to work I go. So that's cool.*

It sounds like you're both very happy in yours jobs. Do you think about doing anything else 10 years from now? Do you think that far ahead?

Genevieve: *Well, I don't think about doing another career so much. I thought at one point about going back to school for accounting or something, but I think at this point, with the government job, your pension builds over time, so they joke about the golden handcuffs, right? It's to my benefit to stick with it and I enjoy it. I think I will stick with it for now. Whether I put in my full 30 years or not is up in the air. What I mostly think about now is how long do I actually still have to continue doing it before I can completely have freedom. Saving up for that and then just choosing at some point to maybe live overseas or do something different.*

Gareth: *It's kind of a give and take. Sometimes the stress will really get to me, I tell my wife I don't know how long I can do it. Granted, that is about 5% of the time. The other 95% of the time I love it, the reward for helping people is great. However, there is a time limit. At some point I will hang it up and just trade my own capital or maybe just teach an investing class here and there. I will always trade for myself though, it is in my blood.*

Tell me a little about your personal causes, socially and politically motivated causes.

Gareth: *We try to be as environmentally conscious as possible. We put solar panels on our roof. We do our best to recycle everything we can. In addition, because I am tuned into every stock market move, I am tuned into news instantly. Some people can tune out and not watch the news, that is not an option for me. Ever since the 2016 election it's definitely caused more stress on me because I am environmentally conscious, and I am aware of the hate that's been popping up. I try and do my part and have been speaking up more and more. So when the EPA is rolling back these pollution standards it is affecting companies I deal with every day. It's this negative nonsense. So I do notice that it is in play and it is not fun.*

Genevieve: *Yeah, I feel like I put a lot into helping the environment with my work. I don't think I get quite as stressed out about it. Even though ultimately the President is my boss, I see all the people who are actually doing the work and that they have their hearts in the right place. They're really doing good work where I am in the government. Even though in the news you always hear all these bad things. So I'm happy to be involved with that, and it gives me an insider's perspective that's different from what a lot of people have.*

But outside of work, when I think of causes besides environmental ones, it's ones that help women that interest me. There are groups that you can send money to for girls or women in countries where just a little bit can really make a difference in their education or their lives. So I've done that ever since I was in high school. And then, every time I get outraged about something, I send some money to the ACLU or a similar organization. After the election I was constantly calling senators and representatives from Oregon about issues, but then I started to realize that our senators were already doing what I want them to and I don't know that my calls were making a difference. So I pulled back on that a little bit, but I have no problem getting involved in all sorts of things.

Gareth: *Yeah, it's interesting because I have to walk a little bit of a finer line. While I have become more vocal on Twitter and inside my trading services, I have many members that are supporters of the current administration. It is a fine line between being vocal but not hurting the business. I try and use economic facts to discuss and vocalize things. It is the only way that comes across as middle ground with big money players. So it's a weird kind of dynamic where I have to be careful. Like as strong as my feelings are about certain things, I don't want to crash my own business, you know. It's tricky.*

Can you list a set of your strong skills, both personal and professional skills?

Gareth: *Communication for me, and that's part of what I do for my job too: being able to communicate ideas, concepts to people and connect with them.*

Genevieve: *I don't actually think communication is one of my strongest skills, although I do think I'm a good writer, which is a type of communication. I would say determination and the ability to see something through, like if somebody needs to get something done, I'm a* *good person to be on the job. I like to do things. I don't like to talk about things. I like to just jump in and do things.*

Gareth: *I think in terms of caring and backing someone up and doing what's right. When I was at school, I always hated to see any bullying and I always tried to stop it. I always thought that doing what's right was important. Also, thinking outside the box, that's one of the things I think Waldorf gave me: that ability to be creative. I think in terms of the business, almost everything that we've brought forth in the business that has been successful has been my brainchild. I would say that we're one of the few online education and stock firms that have been around the longest, at this point, and we do not even advertise. If we grow, we grow by word of mouth. If you search InTheMoneyStocks.com online, we pop up everywhere. Being creative is everything when it comes to starting or growing a business.*

Did you have any issues or difficulties in the transition from high school to college?

Genevieve: *No, I did not. I went from high school to a small liberal arts college in Bar Harbor, Maine. It wasn't that big of a leap. I mean, maybe going from conservative Long Island to this very hippie kind of college was a little bit of a cultural transition. But that was what I wanted, and as far as the academics, it was not a big* [transition]. *I worked really hard in high school. Our high school was very demanding, at least it was when I was there. I don't know what you are thinking, Gareth.*

Gareth: *I was happy with B pluses while Gen wanted an A plus on everything. I went to a very big college, Binghamton University. A New York state school. I think initially, maybe the first year, it's just, it's a little bit surprising because you have so many people in classes and stuff like that. But I would say I adapted pretty quickly. I think the biggest thing for me was that it was that first real life experience. I think Waldorf keeps you in this bubble, which is good, but then at some point you've got to get out and really meet so many new people. And in many ways, it was, I don't think you did this, Genevieve, but definitely by Junior year I was happy to party and, you know, it was a little different for me. I mean, I still got decent grades. It was definitely kind of those new experiences I tried to get under my belt. I mean, we were at Waldorf before we even went to school.*

So, did you have a media free home because your parents were Waldorf teachers? If so, was that a problem with your friends outside of school? Did you experience that as an issue in your lives?

Genevieve: *We didn't have a television early on. When we were in high school, we had a TV downstairs in the basement and we were allowed to watch certain programs.*

Gareth: *I think when I was in high school, I was allowed maybe an hour on weekends. We watched Star Trek and basketball. I still remember that when I was probably in third grade, though, I would have friends in the neighborhood and I would go to their houses to watch cartoons on a Saturday (without my parents' knowledge).*

Genevieve: *When we were very young, we had a whole outdoor life going on. We built elaborate forts in the woods and things like that. And my parents had this little black and white TV that they kept in the closet and would occasionally bring out so we could watch sports with them on it. And then when there was a really big event, like when the Berlin Wall fell, they would bring out the TV and we got to see a few minutes of whatever was going on in the world at that point. But that was when I was a pre-teen, I don't remember anything from when I was really little. There are certain things that are really big and in the memories of people our age, for example, the Challenger disaster. I had no idea about that until much later.*

Gareth: *I remember the OJ Simpson trial. I listened to it on the radio a lot. I think I was 13. But yeah, by then I think I was in high school, and we had a little media and, yeah, I definitely liked it. There was no Facebook, obviously.*

So how is that for you today? Do you find yourself wanting more media?

Genevieve: *I've always had a little bit less interest, I think. I have always been into reading books, so TV has never been a priority. Occasionally I have gotten into a show, but now I never watch TV. I have a TV but we use it for DVDs, watching movies we borrow from the library or things like that. We are still in the stage with our kids where we miss practically everything new that comes out and if there's a movie that we want to see, we'll wait till it comes out on DVD and then watch it at home after the kids are in bed. But my big thing as far as media now is my phone, I'm on the phone and computer a lot, because my work is so connected to that. And that's where I get my news. That's where I manage my finances. That's where I get my work emails and my personal emails and keep my schedule and tasks and everything. So it's a struggle, you know, and the kids are always giving me a hard time about how much I'm on my phone. Well, everything is on my phone, and it's hard. I think we're different in that respect.*

Gareth: *I'm much more of the type that will binge watch something on Netflix, you know, or catch certain shows that I like when they come on. I am definitely more into the shows than you are, and because that's just my work, I'm on my computer all day long.*

Genevieve: *I have a feeling that maybe when our kids are older and they leave home we will ask about what we missed* [on TV]. *I'd love to catch up at some point, i.e., Game of Thrones. But it's just not a priority right now.*

Gareth: *Since my daughter was born, we try not to have the TV on in front of her, so occasionally I'll have a stock show I watch and she'll just get very excited, but it's very rare because obviously I think it was very beneficial that we didn't have a ton of exposure when we were younger. It made us use our imaginations to go outside and do stuff.*

Genevieve: *And the only downside of that at all, I think, was just when we got to college and everybody was very nostalgic about all the things that we never saw, like the Molly Ringwald movies and the stuff that went on in the eighties that we never saw, and I just had no clue. So I would look at that stuff and think that's really not that great. But it was very nostalgic* [for my peers], *and they would all get together and I did not really feel part* *of it... That's a very minor thing compared to everything I think we got from not having media though.*

Another thing: I always wanted those teen magazines that were for girls, like Seventeen and Teen. And so [my parents] made me wait until a certain age before I was allowed to get those magazines in the mail. Then finally I was reading them and thought it was so great, like I'm finally getting this experience that all my friends have had. But then I noticed that after I finished reading them, I didn't feel good about myself. Everyone in the magazines always looked so perfect compared to me. And so I stopped getting the magazines. I feel like if I'd started reading them earlier, as a kid you don't have that ability to step back and say that's not good for me, I can stop, I don't have to do that. That's still a struggle. I mean, it's the same with Facebook now, I've been off Facebook now for a year or more. Still there are a lot of other things online that I probably could do without, but I still do them. It's difficult.

Do you do anything today that you can relate directly to your Waldorf Education?

Gareth: *I noticed in college that my creative side was where I was strongest, and I still remember in college I would take English classes because, for me, I could whip out five-page papers in an hour and all my other friends were pulling all-nighters. And I was getting A's on those. I used English classes to actually keep my GPA up really high, you know, and I think that was so big because it was all in, in school, we always were writing. Everything was about writing. And then just using your imagination more than anything just enabled me to write things in certain ways that were very attractive to the teachers and to get the points across and so forth. And then I think that carried over into, into work. I write a lot of stock market articles and I can really just, you know, formulate things very quickly. I do think that for sure there's probably lots of other stuff too. I mean, as far as our approach to Juliana (my daughter), for sure we relate our education to the way we're raising our daughter and she will go to Waldorf.*

Genevieve: *As far as raising kids I don't know if it's from Waldorf specifically or just how our parents raised us, which was kind of Waldorf based, but it's been natural for us to be relatively media free and send the kids outside all the time. Just playing in the neighborhood with other kids. We really looked for a neighborhood where the kids were outside all the time so that our kids could have a group of built-in friends in the neighborhood, and they've had so many adventures out there. And then, as far as something that I've thought about over the years, is that you do so many different things in a Waldorf school and you have to be good at so many things. Even things that you wouldn't naturally be good at. And eventually I think, with me, it kind of built confidence that I could do whatever. I can do this. If life throws something at me, I can handle it. From writing research papers to going out and volunteering in places where you wouldn't necessarily find yourself otherwise. I think just all those various experiences really helped to build confidence in me that I could take whatever comes and do whatever.*

Gareth: *I agree with that, that's a good point. I think the connection to nature and probably the fact that you are in an environmental field potentially had its roots in Waldorf education.*

Genevieve: *I chose to go to an environmental college as well, so yeah, it probably did have a lot to do with that. Not only caring about the environment but wanting to be outside.*

If you were to go back to your high school today, as a student, while knowing what you know now, what would you keep the same and what would you change?

Genevieve: *I would maybe focus more on the non-academic stuff. Our high school was very academically focused. At least it was for me. Maybe that was me more than the high school, but there was a ton of homework. And I think always having that kind of academic pressure maybe made me turn down some other opportunities in high school that would've been cool. I think at one point I stopped playing sports because I just couldn't do everything. Eventually I had to make a choice because I didn't have enough time in the day to do everything. So maybe if I went back, I would like it to be more balanced than it was.*

Gareth: *I would say for me, you know, I had some good friends in terms of teachers and even relationships that I have kept up with today. But I think my class was a little rough on certain teachers and looking back I feel bad because, obviously they were just trying to do their job and do the best they could. But, my class was, I mean, it wasn't necessarily me, but I still remember it would be like a mob mentality and I swear we were known as the worst class in that respect.*

But yeah, just looking back on things, I think I might've been a little bit too hesitant or shy to try lots of things, and now, looking back, is like, man, I should have done that or tried that.

Did you each have your class teachers all the way? Eight years?

Genevieve: *In the lower school—we moved from Lexington to Garden City—so once we arrived in Garden City, we had the same teacher until 8th grade. I still keep in touch with my class teacher and a couple of teachers from high school.*

Do you keep up with your classmates?

Gareth: *Not on an active basis. Facebook connected there. So I see lots of pictures of kids and different things like that. I'd like to get back for the next reunion. But in terms of talking on the phone and really being connected, not as much for me.*

Genevieve: *Yes. I mean, we had a very small class and we got together for our 10-year reunion and recently for our 20-year reunion. We got together in one location and had an evening or a couple of days together. It was great fun. I mean, we've all gone in such completely different directions. It's so cool to see what everybody has been doing. You know, we've got somebody in marketing in New York City who lives on Wall Street. We've got somebody who's directing in Hollywood. We've got somebody who is an oncology nurse. It's just random how* *people branch out. It's interesting too, because you think coming from Waldorf, people are all moving towards a specific type of work, but that's really not the case.*

Gareth: *You know, you just see people excel in so many different ways. A lot of times people look at me and they're like, how did you end up in day trading and swing trading?*

It is important to recognize that our artistic approach to education supports the potential for creativity and flexibility in wherever life leads one.

Gareth: *I think it does. I think that's probably one of the biggest things is that you just have that flexibility. I feel like I could go do something completely different and be good at it. There was this variety that you were exposed to and you have that flexibility.*

Did you have any experience where you felt that your gender identity was not being met by Waldorf education?

Gareth: *I didn't feel that way. I think it met me greatly, especially in the sports side of things. I love basketball, and if I was in a public school, I probably wouldn't have made the team, but I got on the team and I think I was captain even Senior year. I don't think Waldorf ever didn't allow you on the team or anything like that. So, I think in that respect it was great for that side of things. I mean some of my favorite subjects were woodworking and stone sculpture. I could see maybe how if someone enters Waldorf without going through the early years, I could see how a parent or child could look at Eurythmy and ask, what's going on?! But it makes sense to me later in life, more than ever, especially in our high-paced life. I do think that most of the time anyone who started in first, second, or third grade, I feel like most of them really carried through.*

Is there a subject that you had in high school that you hated back then but appreciate now? Was there any subject that you didn't like?

Gareth: *I would say, looking back, if I could put more into certain things I would have paid more attention to the languages. I took German and I, I did the minimum, you know, it just wasn't super interesting to me back then. Looking back, it would be cool to be a little bit more fluent in German. What about you? You did German. You were a little bit more into it.*

Genevieve: *I feel like I did German well. I can now help my kids do it, but I couldn't go to Germany and carry on a conversation at this point. I did not like Eurythmy in high school. That was probably the main class that I didn't see the point of. I was always really stubborn. If I don't see the point of doing something – I am stubborn.*

Did you give your Eurythmy teacher a hard time?

Genevieve: *I did, but I didn't give her as hard a time as others did. I was more just rolling my eyes. I wasn't actively disrupting the class. I understand now one of the benefits of Eurythmy that I didn't see back then: there are so many sedentary activities that we engage in all day long, and even in high school, if you gave me a book to read or an assignment, I'd* be sitting there for hours, not even moving. And I think Eurythmy got us moving and that was good.

Gareth: *I'm looking back on it. But looking back like if, if, if there was an hour and I had to do [Eurythmy], I actually wouldn't mind it. And the reason I say that is because actually I think it's not only moving, it is kind of getting yourself moving, it almost reminds me of tai-chi, kind of a meditation type thing for stress, But I think looking back on it, it probably was a great way to gain an understanding of calm, controlled motion and calming me down. However, at that age, you don't understand. And when you hand a bunch of kids a copper rod, I mean that's just asking for trouble.*

Genevieve: *I think it's true. Thinking back, I don't remember everything from Eurythmy, but you're jogging my memory. I'm sure it did help. But in high school I was focused on what I needed for college, i.e. math, science. I just wanted to do that.*

If you were to work for an airline, what role would you like to fulfill: Pilot, Co-pilot, Navigator, Flight Attendant, Ground Maintenance, Public Relations, or Company Owner?

Genevieve: *He'd be the owner of an airline.*

Gareth: *I don't think I'd want to be the owner. I think at this stage in my life I want to be a flight attendant. Pilots have a lot of responsibility. I've entered a phase in my life where I'm de-stressing. The stress was the first 10 years of getting the business up and going. Now I want de-stress. So I think that I'm just conversing with people. I enjoy making them smile, stuff like that. So I think customer service. Yeah, that's probably good.*

Genevieve: *I think I would like to be the navigator. That would be super interesting – to do charting. You probably don't even do that nowadays, but it would be cool. I've always thought it would be amazing to sail a ship and use the stars for navigation. Maybe when I retire.*

So now, if you had a million dollars, what would you do with it?

Gareth: *Um hmm. Or maybe 10? These days it's all relative, isn't it? But, I mean, I've always wanted to give a lot away. If I knew that I had my family and I was safe financially, then that would be where the next stop would be, you know? Giving away, helping things, and doing things. I'd love to help the environment; anything else really. Helping the homeless or people with mental issues, or you just see so many things these days that break your heart and, you know, I always say that when the lottery is like $500 million, we're going to play this time. We'll just take this much money and put it in and make five percent a year. Just live off the interest. And then with the rest of it we'll do good things.*

Genevieve: *I'd love to do something good for the Waldorf school. If I had a million on top of what I needed to live, then I would give it away. And I would travel. I would take time and just see the world and find adventures, because I've always wanted to travel a lot and it's been a long time since I've been able to do that with the kids being little.*

Thinking of your physical and emotional health, do you relate any of that to your education?

Gareth: *Well, to some degree my physical health, because we've been able to keep up with getting outside and moving and that—that was central to our upbringing. It has obviously been good for both physical and mental health.*

And again, I'm not sure if it goes back to my education or not, but I like to think that when problems arise we have one of those brains that can figure out solutions versus some people that get overwhelmed. I've never had that issue. I'm like, this is what we have to get done. Let's just tackle it right away instead of fretting over it or whatnot. So maybe something like that.

Genevieve: *Also self-knowledge. I've learned that if I sit at the computer all day, I'm a wreck in the evenings. Like I can't just be still and have only my brain doing anything all day. I've got to be up and moving around, be more balanced. So, you know, I think being able to know yourself and what you need to be healthy is maybe part of it.*

Gareth: *Yeah. I don't know how directly that can be related back to Waldorf, but possibly it can. It's hard to know. That's the thing. It's very, very hard to know if it comes from your education or your family life.*

Genevieve: *I mean we're both pretty healthy so maybe that's one of the reasons why.*

Can you give me five adjectives that come to mind when you think about your relationship with your Waldorf education?

Quality; well-rounded; sweet; protective and nurturing; more demanding as you get older; quality of relationships with teachers; free play; human connection.

Genevieve: *Several years ago, my younger daughter's class teacher had given her a poem for her birthday. I think she was in first grade and I recalled that my class teacher had done the same for me. You know, when I was young, when I was her age. I messaged her on Facebook and I said, look at this, do you remember when you used to do this for us? And she actually wrote me back a new poem for my 37th birthday. That's amazing! It stays with you and keeps you human.*

Tell me about your relationship to Anthroposophy.

Genevieve: *When I was 21, I joined the Anthroposophical Society and for a number of years I went to conferences and to a study group in the area where I was living at that time in Virginia. I was pretty involved for a few years, but once I had kids it was just too much. Like it was another responsibility on top of my career and family, to stay involved in. And so I cut back on that, but I've been interested in it ever since I was maybe a junior in high school, when I read Theosophy and later the rest of the basic books plus a few others that covered areas I was interested in. I just wanted to get a knowledge of where this whole upbringing and education came from, the origins of it. I did things like working with the Calendar of the Soul and did some meditation with the Foundation Stone and things like that. So, so I've done a lot* *over the years. And then I started to get involved with Waldorf with my kids. So it's been kind of off and on, but I definitely had the drive to learn the origins of it. For that purpose, mostly.*

Gareth: *So I know our parents go to meetings and do their kind of thing. I know the basics and they've talked about it, but I haven't myself done a lot of research or reading on it.*

Genevieve: *I think if Mom and Dad hadn't had bookshelves full of all those books—I love to read, you know—I probably wouldn't have done anything but it was there and I was like, okay, this could be interesting. I read philosophy books of all sorts at one point in my life, when I had time for that. I think we both had very positive experiences in the school and appreciated it much more later on. I mean, it's like you have no picture of the wider world when you're a kid and I think it takes a few years. It was very quickly after I left the school, though, even at college, where I started to appreciate it, because you'd see so many kids who didn't have the... the skills that you just took for granted, basically. I think the only thing I struggle with in sending my kids to Waldorf is the social justice aspect and how I'm spending a vast amount of money to send my kids to the school and how much that money could do if I sent it to educate other children elsewhere. It's not enough of a bother to me to make me not give my children the education that I had though. But it's definitely something I think about and it doesn't sit right with me that I could every year pay for 100 kids in a developing country to go to school with that money.*

VIII In Their Own Words (2)

FOUR GRADUATES LOOK BACK

> *The human being is not a being standing still, a human being is in the process of becoming. The more human beings enable themselves to become, the more they fulfill their true mission.*
>
> Rudolf Steiner

The present chapter offers a sample of first-person narratives by Waldorf alumni who have attended schools in different parts of the country at different time periods, from the 1990s to very recent years. Next to the personal stories and unique personalities presented in the speeches and essays that follow, we get a glimpse of some common themes that kept showing up in the various testimonials collected for this study. These themes, reflecting the signs of the time in contemporary North America, include a focus on social justice and diversity, a realization of one's personal passion through a professional vocation, engagement with cultural institutions such as organized sports, and attentive reflection on lessons learned in one's personal and professional life.

A clear message coming from the more recent graduates is that the times are a-changing, and an important facilitator of change is the voice of a new generation. It is extremely important, they say, especially for an educational mode that is progressive in its values, to listen carefully to this rising voice. This is one of the reasons we decided to include here these four monologues, in their original voice.

Ben Tindall, Maine Coast Waldorf High School, Class of 2013

In May 2018, five years after graduating from Maine Coast Waldorf School, Ben Tindall returned to his alma mater to speak to a Grandparents Day audience. His speech addresses the "life toolbox" he feels he has acquired at the school, beginning with the very ability to speak in public—a shyness overcome through the yearly school play and other gentle prodding. Waldorf education, Ben concludes, did not teach him "any one thing in particular ... but how to APPLY what I DO know in unfamiliar situations ... it gave me a set of building blocks which let me do anything."

Here is an abridged version of Ben Tindall's speech:

I was asked to speak to the value I see from my Waldorf education, and, to begin with, one very obvious impact it had on me is actually visible simply by virtue of my even standing up here in front of you right now. When I was younger, I was incredibly shy. I would go to great lengths to avoid speaking in front of larger groups at school, let alone up on a stage in front of a crowd. But, as some of you may know, it is a tradition here for each grade to perform an annual play. I remember one year in fourth grade when my class was performing a play about the Norse gods, where not only did I choose a role with no lines, but a character from the land of the dead where I could even have my face completely covered, like I wasn't even there. However, as time went on, I was given bigger and bigger roles (not always voluntarily) until I began to actually enjoy being on stage. I know I will always be grateful for being pushed and encouraged to overcome what was, at the time, one of my biggest fears.

Public speaking is just one tool in what I think of as sort of life toolbox. When I think of my life, I want to have as many life tools as possible because not only do more tools mean more options, but living a life with variety is just more fun. I see the defining part of my Waldorf education as the breadth of experience I was fortunate enough to gain during my time here. To name just a few outside the ordinary, I cross-country skied, blacksmithed over a forge, slept in a lean-to made of branches and leaves I built with my own hands, carved wooden chairs and sewed clothing, learned to ride a unicycle, made a topological survey using handmade inclinometers, and studied the properties of fractals. This is all a day in the life for a Waldorf student who goes through if not identical experiences, then equivalently broad and varied ones.

After high school, I went to Middlebury College, a small liberal arts college in Vermont. When I arrived, I had absolutely no idea what I wanted to study. I switched my anticipated major from math to political science to economics, before I finally landed on philosophy and computer science. I loved that combination because it was a compromise between the philosophical, big picture part of my brain and the part that likes clean, technical solutions. Both of these subjects were ones I had very little experience with beforehand, but I never felt constrained about what my options should be or what I could do with my choice of studies, and I think that was due, at least in part, to an impression that Waldorf had given me that I didn't need to know all or even most things up front to start something new. [...]

The important thing that Waldorf taught me wasn't any one thing in particular, like how to interview an enterprise architect, but how to APPLY what I DO know in unfamiliar situations. I believe that all of the "tools" Waldorf equipped me with make me more flexible, adaptable, and confident in a world that's changing faster than it's ever changed before.

I read an article a month or so ago which made me think a lot about my Waldorf background. It's called "The Indigo Era" and was written as an introduction to a journal called Global Perspectives that was started by a Russian billionaire named Mikhail Fridman. In this article, Fridman argues that, historically, the global economy has been largely controlled by access to natural resources. Wealth was derived from control of national borders and access to farmland, gold, trade routes, oil, and gas. But the world's biggest company isn't Exxon mobile anymore, it's Apple and Google and Facebook – companies that don't control access to a natural resource, but that use materials that already exist in new and creative ways. The people of the future who are able find solutions to global problems from political instability to global warming to economic inequality will be able to do so due to their imagination and ability to see possibilities and opportunities that haven't been revealed yet. I used to get so annoyed because no one would give me answers at this school. We would do a science experiment and instead of giving us a textbook with the answer we would have to come up with our OWN explanation for what was happening. It seems to me this is exactly the kind of thinking Mikhail Fridman is talking about. I share this story because it reminded me so much of the values I always heard growing up in this community. [...]

I think a lot about the future, primarily because I think it's exciting. But one big reason for this excitement is because it seems like anything is possible. I doubt I'll still be doing the same thing in another five or even three years, or living in the same city, and I'm not sure what the next step I'll take is. That doesn't bother me, though, because I believe that I'll know the right opportunity when I see it. More importantly, I'll have the skills and tools to make it happen. Waldorf didn't teach me how to do anything in particular, it gave me a set of building blocks which let me do anything. Well, almost anything... let's be real, pretty sure my career as an NFL linebacker is probably not my best option at this point.

John Beaven, Sacramento Waldorf School, Class of 1998

John Beaven spent his entire childhood in Waldorf schools. Having moved to the United States at age five, he first attended the Rudolf Steiner School in New York, from Kindergarten through fifth grade. Then, upon moving to California, he attended the Sacramento Waldorf School from sixth grade through graduation. While the essay below does not mention the word "Waldorf" even once, it portrays significant aspects of the life story, values, and perspective of a Waldorf graduate. These aspects materialized in John's personal and professional engagement with the world of sports, which provides John not only with an occupation but also with a prism through which he sees the social world. A Vice President for Ticket Sales & Services with the Golden State Warriors NBA team in California, John describes a worldview infused with the core values of teamwork, collaboration, and joy, which come to life for him in the sports arena. "In an age when social interactions are quickly being replaced by social networks," he writes in words that evoke immediacy, equality, and support, "arenas and stadiums offer a gathering place for fans from all walks of life, setting aside life's difficulties or personal differences for a few hours of blissful support. Sports foster unity. They connect us."

John's narrative expresses social sensibilities in ways that appear to demonstrate the effects of a Waldorf education without revolving its story around the explicit elements of a Waldorf world. It tells, instead, the story of the child he was and the adult he has become. It also serves as a tribute to his father, Alan, who perished on September 11, 2001, along with 39 other passengers and crew members on board United Flight 93. This is the flight that crashed in a field in Pennsylvania after the passengers took action to prevent the hijackers from causing monumental harm of the kind perpetrated that day in New York and Washington. Alan Beaven had a profound influence on his son's love for sports and, therefore, on his embrace of the life-skills that sports reinforces.

As I reflect on the passage of another 9/11 anniversary and ponder our current, complicated societal landscape, I find myself in a place of contemplation and introspection. The ideals that I hold dear—respect, trust, and sincerity—have slowly been eroded by an environment in which disrespect, mistrust, and untruths have become acceptable. As a father, this is of particular concern. How can we ensure our children are exposed to the good in humanity? How do we navigate today's stormy waters and make it safely back to the shore of stability and civility? This reflection has caused me to consider my personal relationship with sports, and why I feel the games we play matter now more than ever.

As far back as I can remember, sports have been synonymous with my identity. Through life's ups and downs, sports have served as an unwavering beacon of hope and stability. Teamwork, optimism, and the reality that hard work can indeed pay off are valuable lessons honed on the playing field that I now apply to every aspect of my life. I also see how sports can impact society at large. In an age when social interactions are quickly being replaced by social networks, arenas and stadiums offer a gathering place for fans from all walks of life, setting aside life's difficulties or personal differences for a few hours of blissful support. Sports foster unity. They connect us. Together as one.

As a wide-eyed five-year-old, I moved to this land of hope and opportunity with my parents. We barely made it off the JFK tarmac in New York before I begged them to take me to Central Park. You see, while living in England I had been introduced to baseball through a softball league my dad played in, and amidst a huge transitional moment I found both familiarity and comfort in a simple game of catch. Sports do that. They create common ground. They provide a sense of familiarity and happiness. Above all, they provide hope.

Throughout my childhood, sports (for me it was baseball) was a constant. This was never more applicable than in the relationship I had with my dad. After my parents separated when I was six, there were periods of my childhood in which I would see my father once, maybe twice a year due to travel. And yet, whenever he came, we always had a game of catch or an occasional and highly anticipated trip to Shea or Yankee Stadium (and later Candlestick or the Coliseum, once we moved to California) to help us re-unite. Throughout my childhood, my father staunchly supported my desire to pitch in the big leagues. With the exception of recreational softball he never played baseball himself, yet he understood what this dream meant to me and, more importantly, recognized the power baseball had to bring us together. For that I am eternally grateful. And through countless hours of practice, I came to recognize that he embodied many of the values sports taught me. Family, character, selflessness, and working hard to achieve a goal.

Before my senior year at UC San Diego, my dad told me he would be travelling to India with my stepmother and young sister to work, pro bono, on clean water legislation. We said our goodbyes, and he went back to New York to wrap up some business. There was one last case in California that needed his attention, so he boarded United Flight 93 from Newark to San Francisco. That was September 11, 2001. He and 39 other passengers and seven crew members lost their lives that day when they stood up for what is right, and put others ahead of themselves by confronting evil head on.

A week later, when friends finally ventured into his sparsely appointed upstate New York office, they found a hand-written note taped to the wall with a simple phrase—"Fear? Who Cares." Whether or not you believe in fate, he boarded the plane subconsciously prepared to embrace and overcome fear. And guess what—the ability to acknowledge doubt, stand up to fear, and push through adversity are all skills reinforced through sports. In a comforting way, this realization also gave me the tools needed to heal. And I am not alone in this fact—sports have served as a beacon of hope for countless individuals after moments of tragedy. Sports can have a powerful healing effect and remind us that life does go on, that looking ahead is not only warranted but needed, and that together we can overcome any obstacle life places in our path. Sports are a catalyst for hope, and they provide lessons of inspiration and triumph. They build character, encourage perseverance, and have the profound ability to showcase the best in all of us.

So, as I think about my father and the impact he has had on my relationship with sports, I am thankful that my life has been intertwined with the values I've been exposed to through years of competition. I was introduced to the Golden State Warriors in the aftermath of 9/11, and have been blessed to be a part of this organization for 14 years. I'm part of an environment that champions all that is right about sports: teamwork, collaboration, and joy. These are not just buzzwords, but are core values this organization exudes. It's why I feel so at home here, and why I have so much faith in the power of sports to impact society at large. Because they have for me.

My personal experiences leave me with no doubt that sports can be the vehicle of change we so desperately need right now. So I am hopeful that the games we adore can serve as the catalyst needed to refocus the core values our children should embody. We need to embrace each other instead of hide behind avatars. I believe we can use the lessons that sports provide to make this world a better place. For us. For our children. For our future.

Avi Bowie, Chicago Waldorf School, Class of 1998

During the 2018 AWSNA teachers conference in Washington, D.C., 20 years after graduating from the Chicago Waldorf School, Avi Bowie delivered a message of LGBTQ awareness. Avi shared a personal story of struggle and self-discovery which was made possible by the support and love of family and the encouragement afforded by Avi's educational community:

For my entire young life, I fought hard to be who I was expected to be. It was lonely, and stressful, and exhausting. But I also had many protective factors that supported and enabled my resilience. I have never wanted for anything material. As a child my curiosity was nurtured. I was showered with affection and my family was rich in love. I had a formal education that encouraged and celebrated my creativity that did not judge my melancholy nature, that instilled in me, unequivocally, the value of service to others. I had parents who supported me unconditionally when I came out to them—twice—first as gay, and then as non-binary. I have had incredible privilege and all of the concurrent protections that made it possible for me to survive and thrive.

Avi's personal history paved the way to a life of social activism, fueled by the values instilled in childhood and dedicated to supporting LGBTQ youth. These efforts not only offer protection and guidance to those who need it, they also aim to strengthen the principles and practices of justice of our society as a whole. Here is an abridged version of Avi's speech:

My name is Avi Bowie and I'm a social worker, a therapist, a trainer, and a co-founder of the Chicago-based consulting group, "Resilience Rising." Our work is centered around supporting individuals and organizations in the creation of cultures of healing. Much of my career has been spent working with and on behalf of LGBTQ youth. I'm also an alum of the Chicago Waldorf School, and the child of Waldorf teachers. [...] This month marks 20 years since my high-school graduation and I think my continued connection to this community speaks to the lasting impact that my Waldorf education has had on my life. [...]

Like all of you, my passion lies in creating such a world for and alongside young people, especially those [...] who are still being rejected by their families, still taunted by their peers, still murdered by the police, and by men who are emboldened by unchallenged toxic masculinity. I am specifically committed to engaging in that work with adolescents, a group of people one of my mentors once described as being the most difficult to love and also the most in need of love.

So many young people suffer from a lack of real, abiding love, and from a deep and justifiable fear born out of the resultant isolation. There is a loneliness in the margins that begets an almost constant questioning of your own worth, your inherent value, your right not only to survive but to thrive. It is not ok that young people are made to feel this way, that adults don't intervene, that we don't take responsibility to make the necessary changes to ensure that every young person has what they need to succeed. I am by no means an expert in how to do this but there are three words that speak to efforts that have helped to clarify my understanding of how we might move forward. They are: equity, representation, and bravery. [...]

We also spend a lot of time concerned with safety—making sure that everyone feels safe. The question I grapple with when that is our focus is whose safety are we considering? I want to name that the value of safety is important and that these conversations tend to be difficult. I want to also encourage you all to enter into these conversations with openness and some degree of bravery. By not working to understand and explore and call out the oppressive experiences navigated by marginalized individuals and communities, and the ways in which "good meaning" folks enable oppression through prioritizing safety and comfort, we are, essentially, saying that those experiences don't matter as much as the safety and comfort of those with the privilege to choose whether or not to engage in these conversations. We will not get free by being quiet and polite and not addressing the root causes of oppression in our communities. If we can challenge ourselves and each other by engaging in difficult and uncomfortable conversations with the goal of growth and healing, then we demonstrate to young people who are on the margins that we are truly committed to their well-being and that we are willing to be with them in their pain and willing to be brave enough to challenge our own sense of safety in order to support theirs.

Another part of exorcising loneliness and instilling worth lies in representation. Think back to your own childhood. Did you see and read and hear about heroes and heroines like you? Who and what was portrayed as beautiful? Who was portrayed as brave? Whose image and story were uplifted and centered and celebrated? For me, as is true for many girl children, for many queer kids, for many black and brown kids, I didn't see myself, or stories like mine, reflected very often, if at all, and when I did the images were often not favorable. Girls and women often needed to be rescued, people of color had little if any power, and there was hardly a whisper of LGBTQ lives. As is true for most students, the centralized narratives that I was shown in school were those of straight, white, cisgender, men, women, and children. [...]

If you are poor, or black, or brown, or queer, or female, or undocumented, or living with a disability, or anything outside of the privileged majority, the systems of institutionalized oppression that you are forced to navigate can create a seemingly impenetrable cascade of trauma dominos, where suffering begets suffering, where you can't catch a break, where justice is not proffered, where healing cannot occur. The cycle continues uninterrupted unless we, the adults, recognize that we have the power to effect change, to stretch beyond our comfort zones, to create more space and opportunity for young people to determine how they want to exist, who they want to love. Unless we recognize that we can choose to take responsibility for the youth who need for us to be that beacon, the youth whose very life depends on it. [...]

Let's work together to ensure that every young person in our lives can [...] say that no matter who I am, my parents will love me, no matter who I am, my teachers will support me. Let's work together to ensure that on the days when it feels too much to bear, there will always be someone, even just one person, to turn to.

A mantra to which I return time and time again is this: "Be the person you wish you had when you were younger." [...] Take a moment and think back to your younger self. Was there a part of you that had to exist in the shadows? Was there a need, a yearning that went unmet? Was there something you were desperate to hear from the adults around you? Was there a person who came to your rescue? Was there someone who acknowledged your pain, your loneliness, your beauty, your infinite worth, your power? Was there a passion that was cultivated that helped you to survive? Now, think about what you can do to ensure that you are that person for those queer kids who walk into your classroom, your school, your life. They are there. They are waiting for you. They need you.

Cecilia Twanmo, Washington Waldorf School, Class of 2016

After returning from freshman year at College, Cecilia Twanmo, a graduate of the Washington Waldorf School in Bethesda, MD, spoke to an audience of Waldorf educators at the 2018 AWSNA annual schools' conference. Cecilia told the story of the joys and pains of a mixed-race, Asian-American student in a predominantly white Waldorf school. With rich understandings earned during an insightful first year at Bard College, Cecilia was able not only to tell a personal story but also to provide the perspectives of the current generation of college students and present their engagement with the question of diversity, which is central to the current social and political climate.

At least two particular messages ring loud and clear in this address: First, that the Waldorf school Cecilia attended shaped the person we saw in front of us at the conference. Second, that Waldorf education and Waldorf schools must listen carefully to the rising voice of a new generation, with its unique perspectives and sensitivities in a world and a society that have been and still are undergoing fundamental changes. With all the good intentions and all that is good about Waldorf education, there is yet much to be learned through attentive listening to this rising voice. Here is a sample of this voice, in Cecilia Twanmo's own words, presented in this abridged transcript of the 2018 AWSNA address.

I am a Waldorf lifer and alum and a rising sophomore at Bard College in the Hudson Valley. I am so honored to be speaking today. It's a hard feat to accomplish, to represent the voices of the current and graduated students, a voice that is vast and diverse in opinions and perspectives. It is a hard task to unify and summarize a diverse selection of experiences, so I am both excited and nervous to attempt to give you an idea of the perspective of the students through one voice.... I'm also extremely excited about this opportunity because I think the importance of a young voice is growing rapidly in today's social and political climates. More and more young people are voicing their opinions and needs, and although we're still figuring out how to articulate these needs, they are crucial to the growth and adaptation of educational institutions, social and political issues, and in turn, the world.... What I will try to do today is provide a window into the student perspective, from both a current standpoint, and one from after graduation.

When I attended the Washington Waldorf school, I loved it (for the most part). I loved my relationships with my teachers and peers, I loved the familial feeling woven into the academics, and most of all I loved the people that the school was forming us into.... It was a wonderfully caring and supportive relationship and environment.

When I was younger and wanted to tell people something about myself that I thought they didn't know, I told them I was half Chinese. (Little did I know, everyone could tell.) ... It wasn't until later on, in middle school, when I learned that this piece of me that I only felt connected to by using it as my secret badge, was in actuality an obvious difference that separated me from my peers. Asian jokes and stereotypes followed me to every piano recital and failed math test. My secret badge of honor was not only exposed, it was exposed on someone else's terms, an identity placed on me based simply on my appearance and not at all on how I felt inside.

In high school, I grew more into my skin and began really thinking about who I was and what I wanted from life.... My self-expression became more and more important to me.... I began thinking more about what it meant to be mixed race, specifically in a predominantly white environment. ... My friends were supportive whenever I'd talk about being the only mixed-race Asian student in my high school, but I could see that none of them fully understood where I was coming from, as most of my friends were white. ... One thing that hurt me the most was that most of the racist comments were coming from my closest friends, possibly because they knew that because of our relationship, I would take everything as a joke and carry on. Just as your stomach starts to hurt after eating a whole pound bag of cherries, my stomach began to hurt at each joke that was directed to me, hearing them year after year since middle school.

With all the reflection that came with college essays and preparing for my entry into the world outside Waldorf, I became more confident in voicing what was okay with me and what was not in terms of my identity and the ability to grow into it. I was no longer confused about my identity and became more confident in who I was and how I was expressing it.... After speaking to both students and teachers, I realized that although they listened, the severity of the issue was not quite seen.... I didn't know how to effectively make my voice heard, so it was not. ...

The transition into college was tough, like any change... but at Bard, I gained what I didn't know I was missing. I gained solidarity amongst my peers, who had gone through similar searches for identity, and who were confident enough in their skin to help me along my way.... We are a school of activists, artists, and rebels of the social norm. By leaving Waldorf and arriving at Bard, I went from being an ambassador of my heritage to a student of it. Just by having friends in the LGBTQ+ community, friends of color, and friends with backgrounds more mixed than mine, I gained a greater understanding of what being mixed race meant to me and the people around me. I went from identifying as white, as it was the only culture I knew, to seeing myself as a person of color and ready to explore this new culture that had always been a part of me. There was no big moment or event that sparked this new understanding, but simply being in an environment that supported and encouraged all identities and being able to converse and share stories with people who I knew understood. ...

After being immersed in this environment, I looked back at my time at Waldorf with anger and resentment that I hadn't been provided with the same support as I was getting at college. But just as I didn't know what I needed in high school, neither did they. Much of this has to do with time. The times in which faculty grew up held significantly different ideals than today. Even five years ago, the ideals were different. The legalization of gay marriage and movements such as Black Lives Matter and #MeToo show how much the focus of a society can change in a short period of time. So, it is understandable that schools wouldn't be immediately prepared to accommodate the changing times. ...

When I was beginning to think about what I wanted to say today, I put a note on my social media asking Waldorf students and alumni if they had any comments on their experience at Waldorf, as I could be their representative.... From their stories and mine, I found two things that stood out. First, the general desire was for role models, people to look up to, to relate to, to know we are not alone. This applies not only to diversity in faculty and students, but to authors, artists, and the academic curriculum. With a small school, I know this is easier said than done, but the simplest task of replacing a male author with a female, gay, or author of color makes a bigger difference than you may think. It provides diversity in learning and may give even one student the commonality that she or he needs.

My second conclusion—and this is the part in my speech where I need to be frank with you, because there is no rainbow silk to cover this ugly and unfortunate truth—is that our stories not only need to be heard, but taken seriously.... So, I ask you, on behalf of all students, please do not turn your backs on these controversial yet crucial issues. Without being addressed, problematic students learn in effect that what they are saying and doing is okay, while those hurt by these actions are left unheard and unappreciated.... Girls should not have to amend their comfort and expression for a boy's misbehavior; closeted students should not feel as though they need to stay closeted; and students of color should not be subjected to the ignorance of their friends.

When I talk to people who know about Waldorf but never attended, they tell me two things: first, there's this thing called eurythmy where you dance your name or some-thing, and second, that the community is very warm and loving. Both are mostly true, but lack a piece. Eurythmy is not just dancing your name, it juxtaposes movement with sound, stories, and music. The Waldorf community is warm and loving, but has neglected to address controversial issues in order to uphold this sense of "warm and loving." This is blunt, maybe even harsh, I am aware of that, and some of you may disagree with me. But this is why I'm here. To give you a look into the perspective of the student, to share our concerns and complaints with the hope for change. Because when you ignore these issues, not only are the students affected made to feel unheard, but the bad behavior of the perpetrators is encouraged, never learning that what they are doing is wrong. ...

For the hardcore Waldorf enthusiasts who believe in sticking to the original Waldorf philosophy and sense of community that dates back to the 1920s, I have a message for you: The world is changing rapidly. Everything is more accessible through social media and the internet, meaning that more people are exposed to new ideas and worlds. Kids are now growing up faster, the playing field is being leveled, and our voices are louder than ever. So, just as the curriculum provides support for the developing child, so must the school support the developing needs of children in a world that is rapidly changing, and move with them. ...

I hope that after hearing my story, you can take at least one thing back with you and change someone else's story. I have been blessed with going to two schools that I love. I cannot thank my teachers at Waldorf enough for helping shape me into the young woman I am today, for teaching me how to knit, how to dance my name, and most importantly how to understand myself. It was only after I left and saw the school from a different perspective that I became troubled by what I saw was missing. So, I ask you all to take a step back. Take a look at yourself and your school from a different perspective. Listen to your students and try to understand where they are coming from. They can teach you more than you think, even if it's not perfectly articulated quite yet. Let their stories be your role model for change.

IX Through a Teacher's Eyes: Waldorf Students In and Out of School

To supplement our survey of Waldorf graduates, we invited high-school teachers with long years of experience to reflect on the students they had taught in various Waldorf high schools and to comment on what had become of them as alumni. Since the questions were open-ended, we received a wide variety of responses, ranging from the simply factual to the poignantly effusive. We made no attempt to tabulate the teachers' answers in any statistical form, given that their comments were, by design and invitation, largely qualitative and anecdotal.

Of the several dozen responses we received, perhaps the most comprehensive reflection came from Cedar Oliver, a trained Waldorf teacher who has taught physics and math for over 20 years at two Waldorf high schools. An accomplished writer of books and manuals on computers, Cedar offered the following thoughts on the students he had taught at High Mowing School in Wilton, NH, and at the Waldorf High School of Massachusetts Bay in Belmont, MA:

After teaching in Waldorf schools for twenty years and staying in contact with many of the hundreds of alumni I've taught, one thing stands out to me: Strikingly often, the students whose path was not smooth through high school become the most respected and inspiring leaders as their lives unfold. I am thinking of several young people who came to Waldorf education partly because they felt different—a debilitatingly shy girl, a boy whose thoughts never seemed to come quickly enough, others whose nervous energy kept them "in trouble," the dorm "drama queen," the classroom fidget, the girl who refused to go to class and stood her ground, yelling indignantly, the boys who debated more assignments than they submitted.

When I reflect on these particular students, the "handfuls," the ones who sometimes made me wonder whether teaching was a fruitless profession, who could make a classroom into a battleground, I smile. And I smile not only from the knowledge I now carry of their powerful, memorable deeds as adults. Nearly every one had already begun to become extraordinary leaders even before leaving school. That shy freshman girl ended up co-teaching calculus with me. That slow-thinking boy discovered he was incredibly talented in both academics and the arts, when given time for his meticulousness. The nervous ones, the fidgets, the stubborn ones fighting every assignment, became in case after case the visionaries, the award winners, the only student left completing a project long after others had abandoned it. The differences that made school tough turned out, again and again, to be the differences that led to unprecedented achievements in one studio or subject where they thrived. The dyslexic discovered his genius in digital electronics, the drama in the dorm was exceeded by dramatic talent on stage. The girl refusing to go to class was yelling that she needed to finish a yearbook that turned out to be one of the best in the school's history.

I like to think that Waldorf education, perhaps even Waldorf teachers, get a little credit for some of the moving work that these "difficult" students have brought to the world. They have started industry-leading businesses, saved countless lives as activists around the world, created award-winning and awe-inspiring art, from music to cinema to pottery to mathematics and writing. They earn and deserve admiration and respect for their medical care and medical illustrations, for their parenting and elder care, for inventing new risky careers and yes, for old-fashioned careers like teaching too. But along with troubles transformed, I see another thread that unites their stories: In each case, at least one Waldorf teacher dared, sometimes against all reason, to believe in them. I don't mean this in a trite, generic way, but rather in very specific individual ways tailored to each: appointing the least dedicated as the director, letting a brilliant student spend "too much" time mastering the art of pottery or wandering in the woods, giving unconventional assignments designed to help a young man truly earn his first A+. At times, being "permissive" and making space for her to follow existing passions. At other times, fighting intensely to convince her she could achieve what she'd never dared to try.

In the end, little credit goes to mentors in comparison to what youths themselves bring into our world. As Waldorf teachers, our first—perhaps only—task is to recognize that mysterious, unpredictable, uncontrollable gift brought by each young person. It seems to me now that the struggles of youth may be a measure of the greatness of those gifts. The world is not, after all, calling for sameness or people who "fit" easily in it. The world most needs those who will challenge its teachers and teachings, who each come with the difference they will make.

CONSTRUCTIVE OUTLETS

Greg Shultz, a high-school teacher of life sciences and math at the Santa Fe Waldorf School for some 20 years, submitted an example of how Waldorf education was able to channel a student's passion into positive action. Greg described a graduate from 2007, an "environmental activist . . . always a bit of a quiet rebel, whose Waldorf education helped him find a constructive outlet for his activism." He went on to describe a student who graduated two years later as being "extremely ambitious, but her Waldorf education helped ameliorate this sometimes extreme attitude."

A RECURRING THEME: LIFE AS A BALANCING ACT

A few common themes kept recurring among the responses of Waldorf high-school teachers. Several teachers noted that students they had followed in their post-college careers combined a rare mixture of *the ideal* and *the practical*. David Barham, first a class teacher and then high-school teacher of humanities in three New England Waldorf schools, described one graduate who put his lofty political ideals to the practical test, going door to door in the bitter winter months canvassing for candidates whose platforms he was willing to support, and sticking with this work despite disappointing results at the polls. Lisa Babinet, a math teacher on the West Coast, described a graduate who pursued simultaneously a rarified field of experimental physics with a hands-on career in the practical and mechanical aspects of building and marketing computers. Another Waldorf alumnus, who graduated from college with a degree in engineering, traveled to Africa, where he set up a company to turn dung into energy for poor farmers. He credited his experience of the arts in the Waldorf school for his ability to balance abstract study with practical interests.

In a related vein, teachers told us of Waldorf graduates who deliberately sought out a balanced lifestyle in their college life even before forging a career. One student, for instance, was accepted into MIT but agreed to matriculate there only if the university would give him credit for taking a course in pottery at another university, so that he could continue to balance practice in the arts with the study of abstract theoretical science.

Leed Jackson, a long-time practical arts teacher at the Toronto Waldorf School, framed this search for balance by Waldorf alumni in a more general way:

What strikes me about graduates or even high-school students (beyond their obvious social intelligence) is Practical Wisdom (Rudolf Steiner might characterize it as the synthesis of the Knowing-Doer)—the ability of the soul (consciousness as a capacity) to mediate between the practical worldly sphere and ideal content.

One of my students, a fourth-year Engineer who still knits, was repeatedly given responsibility in a nuclear steam engineering company even before she graduated because she could not only see the   overview or theory but also the practical blueprints and paper layouts. She could see the need for spaces within the technical designs for forklifts or people to navigate around all of the heavy machinery, as just one example. She could think and perceive whole to parts. Mobility of heartfelt thinking gave her the ability to move between the soul structures of inner space and the external demands of outer physical structures. She demonstrated what Steiner calls the "moral technique" needed to accomplish the moral imagination or intuition concerning individual needs in a practical or social setting.

Another theme recurring in several teachers' assessments is the claim that Waldorf graduates are likely to think and act "out of the box" and to attribute this quality to their Waldorf education, often thanks to the practice of the arts. One teacher reported speaking with a number of Waldorf graduates who became entrepreneurs and who credited their education with the confidence and skill needed to start a new business. By contrast, self-employed graduates who opted to make a living in the arts (a surprisingly small number, given the emphasis placed on arts in Waldorf schools) reported they struggled to find their way after leaving the Waldorf school. That is to say, the rich experiences in the arts that the Waldorf curriculum offers do not necessarily smooth the path to a career in the highly competitive fields of the fine arts and performing arts. The emphasis placed upon artistic practice in Waldorf schools is not intended to prepare students to become professional artists. Rather, this practice is embedded in the Waldorf curriculum in order to develop in students the inner capacities of fortitude, resilience, and moral sensibility.

Combining practical careers with personal passions also came up in several reports by teachers. One student, drawn to writing, music, and psychology, "was determined to find his way to work outdoors in nature," his high-school teacher wrote. "He started working with conservation organizations in the field, but eventually found his way to working for a wilderness therapy company which combined his love of the outdoors with his wish to help people."

David Sloan, a veteran teacher of three Waldorf high schools (two of which he actually founded), opted to write to some of his former students, asking what they had done with their lives. One wrote back to him:

During the last day of High School, our class gathered in a room and we were asked by our teachers where we want to be in 10 years. I responded "Not too comfortable." I made the mistake of telling that to my husband, who has made making me uncomfortable his life's mission ever since. In all seriousness, I think that going to Green Meadow [a Waldorf school in Chestnut Ridge, NY] taught me to never settle and to always look at the bigger picture, to try new things and to feel confident about navigating the insanity of life regardless of how uncomfortable I felt.

After completing 12+ years at Green Meadow, I went to Bard College in upstate New York. In my classes there, I found myself asking all of the questions that no one else thought to ask. I loved trying to bring a different perspective to the table and seeing how convincing the complete opposite view on a subject could be. I thought for myself and I like to think that I still do. I thank my Waldorf education for that.

After graduating from college, I helped build an online start-up business into a multi-million-dollar operation, I worked at a top marketing agency in Hamburg, Germany, and in recent years have combined my passion for photography with brand consulting and marketing. I started working freelance so that I can create my own hours and work from anywhere in the world.

I've lived in Germany, New York, Northern California, and now I'm back in New York, close to Green Meadow, so that my 3-year-old son can have the same education that I had.

My priorities are family and finding purpose and meaning in my day-to-day life. I'm always trying to find the balance between taking risks and providing safety and comfort for myself and my family—life is too short to stop growing and learning.

I can't wait for my son to find his place in the world and I'm grateful for Waldorf Education for helping me do so.

We see here how the theme of "balance" is extended beyond the weighting of the ideal and the practical to a desire for a healthy juxtaposition of risk and security in professional as well as private life.

Another one of David Sloan's former students, a professional plumber, opens up a further commonly expressed theme among Waldorf graduates, namely the way they value and cultivate relationships with others:

I've been able to build up my clients organically through referrals, and since there is so much money and work in town I never have to spend time looking for work and almost never have to travel outside of San Francisco either, which is great.

I think the main thing that differentiates me from a lot of plumbers is that I take the time to explain problems to my clients and just generally have a more personable attitude to customer service. Most plumbers are pretty rough around the edges, and that's probably my biggest differentiator, as well as offering reasonable prices.

And I must give some of the credit to my Waldorf education that helped me learn to treat people as unique individuals rather than as client numbers. The personal connection is almost as important for customers who are letting you into their houses and trusting you with their property.

And I must also credit the Fellowship Community [an old-age home connected to the Waldorf school] with how to be comfortable speaking and being with the elderly, since I have quite a few retired clients that I serve, and of course they often need special attention and patience to deal with their concerns. (I always offer senior discounts.)

SEEKING DIVERSITY

A third student of David's sounds a note that also re-echoed through our online survey—namely the feeling that Waldorf education does not provide the breadth of socio-economic diversity in its student body that Waldorf graduates would wish for their own children. In the words of one alumnus responding to the question, "Looking back on your Waldorf education, would you say it has helped or hindered you as you've navigated subsequent life stages?":

I would say that my education has helped me in that I feel like I can do various things in my life and that I have options. At the same time, I felt very strong about sending my older son to public school (he had attended a private school in Costa Rica and in our first year in Oregon) because I felt like I wanted him to gain and share experiences with people of different backgrounds (economic, racial, etc.) and I felt like I didn't really get that opportunity. I still feel that I am a bit elitist and I think that my Waldorf education partially instilled this in me and I don't feel like that's a positive.

The advent of Waldorf education in the public sector, along with initiatives among independent Waldorf schools, are intended to address this concern. One such initiative is described by Roland Rothenbucher, who for more than three decades has served as high-school chair and German teacher at the Waldorf School of Garden City. He relates the following example:

The Waldorf School of Garden City has made a commitment to representing diversity in our student population. The following high-school student highlights the challenges and benefits of this commitment. A 14-year-old boy (whom I will refer to as Jim) joined our school in his freshman year, after attending a small local academy serving underrepresented populations on Long Island. His attendance at our school was made possible through an endowed scholarship which augmented his tuition assistance.

The transition into our demanding program of main lessons and daily subjects was not a cakewalk for him. Though his educational background was less than ideal for the level of learning in our school, Jim made a commitment to stay after school from 3:30-6:00 p.m. each day of his high-school years in order to take advantage of extra help with completing assignments.

During his 9th and 10th grades, it was rare for Jim to ever raise his hand or voluntarily participate in class. When called upon, Jim always gave polite though barely audible responses. Unlike 90% of our high-school student body, Jim did not travel to school by yellow school bus. It soon came to light that he and his mom frequently had to move from one place of residence to another; at one point they lived in a room with no kitchen—just a room for sleeping. High-school faculty members donated school supplies, a calculator, and a laptop. Staff members rallied to offer him rides to and from school, and school administration arranged for him to be fed two square meals at school each day. For many days of his high-school years Jim biked and/or walked a considerable distance to get to school but always arrived on time. At parent-teacher conferences, his mom, who did not speak English, communicated with each of Jim's teachers with the help of our Spanish teacher, who served as interpreter.

In his junior year, Jim discovered a passion for basketball, and he joined the Varsity team. At every free moment, Jim could be seen on the playground or in the gym "shooting hoops." As the years passed, he became ever more physically fit and trim; at the same time, there was an upward trajectory in his academics—so much so, that he ultimately earned a full college scholarship. Ever appreciative, ever helpful, ever full of gratitude, Jim never complained about anything. At the end of the day, we all learned from him about courage and dignity in the face of real adversity.

In college Jim majored in computer science. He recently wrote: "I am a passionate learner seeking to leave the world a better place than the way I found it."

MATURING THROUGH THE ARTS

A more common theme sounded by Waldorf teachers involved cases of students who during the course of their high-school career—or in one case only after graduating from high school—blossomed from a timid teenager into a confident young adult. While this profile is by no means unique to a Waldorf adolescent, it is interesting to see how often the arts played a role in opening up a diffident student. Bev Boyer, teacher and counselor at High Mowing School, which is both a day and boarding school, offered three such examples:

[1] Jack [not his real name] was a skinny kid with huge blue eyes that looked half-frightened much of the time. He was a poor student and needed support with his academics. Shortly before entering high school he had started learning the guitar

(teaching himself, I think), and he could be heard quietly—and tentatively—playing it in his dorm room. During his years at High Mowing, his interests carried him strongly in two directions: towards the outdoors-based naturalist program and towards a deepening of his music. It was clear that he was profoundly affected by both.

By the time he graduated Jack had become a master naturalist: he read nature like a book and adored it like a lover. Further, his growth as a musician was astonishing. He teamed up with three schoolmates to create a band, spending endless hours together and performing both on campus and at local venues. Jack moved from being a background guitarist to lead guitar and vocalist/songwriter. The timid and retiring   freshman had become a grounded, confident, creative senior.

At this point in time Jack is a professional musician. He is currently recording his third album and has toured extensively in the U.S. and in Europe. Recently I heard his name mentioned on NPR. He credits his years at High Mowing as being the turning point in his life.

[2] Ming [not her real name] was an international student from China. From the beginning she was an enigma. Although her English was quite good, she hardly ever spoke. She walked with her shoulders hunched forward, her face hidden behind her long black hair. She always sought solitude and appeared to be addicted to her devices.

An intelligent young woman, Ming initially signed up only for math and science electives. As a sophomore, however, she was required to take an introductory drawing class. She gradually found herself spending more and more of her free time in the art studio because she was discovering a passion and a talent she did not know she had. Her completed art pieces began to appear on the walls of the school and, very significantly, we began to see her face for the first time. She began to stand taller and to brush aside the hair from her eyes.

As an upperclassman Ming went through a difficult period with her family when she confronted them with her desire to go to art school rather than follow the business/ economics path they had envisioned for her. Her persistence finally won them over and she went off to art school with their blessing.

[3] Arnold [not his own name] arrived as a freshman and almost did not make it. He hid in his mother's car that first day, and kept his entire head buried in a blanket when we tried to coax him out. He eventually settled in and developed a small group of friends. Throughout his years he never really engaged academically, remaining a lackluster student. He was often glued to his computer, fancying himself a techie. He refused to go onstage during class plays, preferring to work the lighting booth instead.

Recently I had the pleasure of re-connecting with Arnold and was amazed at his transformation. He had grown very tall and handsome. More impressively, he had become remarkably outgoing and friendly. He spoke with great enthusiasm about an entrepreneurial undertaking that he is involved in. He has procured a nice plot of land in upstate New York and is growing crops on a large scale. He is making connections with researchers who are experimenting with plants for their various positive uses. He seemed confident, bold, optimistic—a far cry from who he was when I first met him.

Ina Jaehnig, long-time class teacher and high-school humanities teacher, recalls one of her students at the Denver Waldorf School. A student we will call "Ollie" was an early graduate of this school. Ina recalls that Ollie "went to the university in Connecticut, earned his Master's there, then a doctorate in Colorado. He is now a tenured university math professor in Northern Colorado. A pupil in my class from grades 1 to 8, Ollie was a very shy and withdrawn student. The only time he felt comfortable was when he could do magic tricks and juggling. He became so good that parents invited him for birthday parties. He is now married to an energetic wife with two children."

In a similar vein Rebecca Soloway, a Waldorf math teacher who has taught in both East and West Coast Waldorf high schools, writes about Martin [not his real name], "a quiet, shy boy in his early years of high school. He was deeply reluctant to be in the spotlight in any form. He always lobbied to be a stagehand and not an actor on the stage. He dreaded giving any form of presentation to his classmates or, even worse, to the high school as a whole. Nevertheless, he was coaxed into stepping forward, even in small ways, throughout upper elementary and high-school years. By the end of 12th grade, he confidently presented a student speech at graduation. Martin is now working in a field that requires him to make presentations regularly to large groups of people. He feels that he has much to share and enjoys the opportunity to present it to others."

The arts also hold the key to the following story by Colleen Everhart, a founding humanities and drama teacher at the Chicago Waldorf high school. She recalls the case of someone we will call "Dan":

Dan came to our school in 9th grade. He was a quiet, shy boy who often had a long wave of hair covering his face. In our 9th-grade drama class, Dan struggled to learn his lines and blocking for his scene from Our Town His scene partner, a vivacious, outgoing girl, patiently showed him the "ropes" until we decided that they should do their scene sitting on the front edge of the stage. Despite Dan's tremendous stage fright, he managed to get through the final presentation.

In 10th grade, Dan was cast as one of the old men in Lysistrata. With the support and encouragement of the other "old men," Dan loosened up and appeared to actually enjoy himself as they engaged in their slapstick and buffoonery. The following year,

Dan blossomed in the 11th grade monologue class. He wrote a monologue about his difficult transition to a new school. His final presentation was incredibly moving.

In 12th grade, Dan's class decided to do a musical version of The Mouse That Roared. *To my delight, Dan asked to audition, not only for one of the leads, but for a female lead—and asked if he could do it in drag! Dan's musical numbers (yes, he sang and danced in drag) were showstoppers throughout the run. I can't recall the last time I laughed and cried so hard.*

Not only psychological challenges but physical handicaps too, it seems, can be helped by the practice of the arts. John Wulsin, a former humanities teacher and drama coach at the Green Meadow Waldorf School, tells the story of a girl we will name Maria:

Maria was a diligent student who felt her older sister, now a veterinarian, out-scholared her. Maria coped gracefully with scoliosis, a curvature of the spine. She was an outstanding artist. After her college studies, Maria painted large canvasses of skyscapes for years. Daughter of a neuro-surgeon and a well-recognized photographer of primal landscapes, Maria initiated an expedition to Greenland, inspiring mighty, almost wall-sized drawings in pastel chalk, rendering the transitions of melting Arctic worlds.

This modest, formerly shy soul gave one of the most poised, lucid, and moving TED-talks I have ever seen, on science and art in relation to climate change. Not long afterward, she was educating graduate students and professors as an honored speaker at the Harvard School of Design. She has served as artist-in-residence aboard the National Geographic Explorer in Antarctica; she has spoken at Amazon, at Google, and at NASA's Goddard Space Flight Center. Through the marriage of her masterful art and her concern for the science of the climate of the earth, Maria's voice has found the power of a calling.

Then there is the case of a student whom Stephen Sagarin—a high-school teacher at two Waldorf schools and founder of what is now called the Berkshire Waldorf High School in Great Barrington, MA—poignantly calls "The Clam":

William, I'll call him, wasn't interested in anything.

–What do you want to be when you grow up?
–I don't know...

–Any ideas?
–No.

–What about college. Any idea what you want to study?
–No.

–Where you want to go?
–No.

Fascinating, huh? That's how his teachers felt. Like trying to teach a clam.

I can't recall a less motivated student. Bright, talented, but a C student and not interested in doing any better. No hobbies. Coordinated, but no real interest in sports. A reader, but no discernible passion. Other teachers and I shook our heads. Such possibilities going to waste. How to reach someone like this? Dismissive of most literature, dismissive of opinions different from his own, a bit of a know-it-all. A year. A year and a half. Mom was tearing her hair out. Dad was done with him. Teachers rolled their eyes.

And then he signed up for a photography elective. He could have taken it earlier, but, really, we gave other students priority because they were better students, they had earned it. He and another student spent one afternoon a week in our darkroom. At the same time, he was enrolled in a filmmaking class that we instituted this year, for the first time, because our school has grown so large that not every student can participate in the school play.

William enjoyed photography. He loved filmmaking. We closed school early one day for a snowstorm, and William, for the first time, expressed an emotion. He was crestfallen. He would miss photography. So far, so good. A student without apparent interest found an interest. But here's where it gets interesting.

William started making eye contact, even smiling from time to time. He went out of his way to talk to the woman with whom he carpooled to school each morning—earlier, he had sat in silence. His attitude improved, his effort improved, his work improved, his grades improved, his relationships with teachers and schoolmates improved. A tough, experienced teacher commented on his new life. He started to open, like a clam. He went to an established college, and is now in graduate school, studying economics.

Stephen tells another story, this one quite dramatic and even a bit disturbing. We include it here as an example of how the arts can help even in extreme instances of psychological distress in teenagers:

Mike [not his real name] is a large, broad, lantern-jawed young man who looks a bit like a young Elvis Presley, a bit like Marlon Brando. He has inquisitive and wide-set blue-gray eyes, and, offstage, a diffident, even apologetic manner. Mike is nervous as he delivers his graduation speech before an audience of 150. He's not usually so nervous on stage—he's an actor—but this isn't acting. He's himself, speaking from the heart. "This school saved my life," he says.

"I came to this school in 2012 at one of the lowest points of my life. My world seemed to be falling apart around me. But you guys, you turned me around. … I had never had this kind of experience before. The overwhelming welcoming atmosphere of MY school is unprecedented. … I'm terrified of what will happen next in my life. But thank you for making these past two years the best I've ever had."

A year and a half earlier, in December 2011, Mike stood before his 11th grade class at a different school, a small independent (private) school in upstate New York and held the blade of a chef's knife to his own throat. He had smuggled the knife to school from home. He told the class, "I don't plan to hurt anyone other than myself. But can anyone please give me a reason not to kill myself right now?" He was not acting. The teacher and students talked him down. He was taken to a hospital. He was put on anti-depressants and given therapy. He was released, and he found that he had been expelled from school—for obvious if unsentimental reasons. It was January 2012, and he needed to find a new school.

After a lengthy and rigorous admissions process, Mike starts at our school after the Winter Recess in February, and has an immediate, positive effect on the school, as, he says, it had on him. Although he is at our school just less than a year and a half, here is a list of his accomplishments:

Mike starts a popular student elective in improv, one that is still going, three years after his graduation.

He organizes "coffee houses," evening social gatherings in which high-school students can perform for each other. These raise money for foreign travel and for the science program at the school.

He completes an 11th-grade internship in drawing and painting with a local artist and illustrator. Although Mike's primary interest is in acting, he is talented in visual arts, as well.

He writes, casts, directs, and performs in a radio play, "The Adventures of Zap Zimmerman." Our school requires 11th and 12th graders to take three weeks each spring to pursue an independent project or internship, for credit and with a mentor, in an area of interest. Past projects and internships have ranged from work in a law office to furniture making. There are project requirements, but some students, including

Mike, give far more than the required minimum to their work. His play is a space-age comedy-melodrama, imagined during the Cold War. Mike takes sole responsibility for it, including finding a local LP (low power) radio station to host the recording and broadcast. The radio play combines his interests in writing and acting, makes use of his impressive baritone voice, and allows him to draw in friends to assist with production.

He earns lead roles in two plays; Doc Gibbs in Our Town *in 11th grade and Leontes in* A Winter's Tale *in 12th grade. "In working on a play, you get to know people really quickly and really well. I quickly felt accepted and close to most of my classmates," he says. Our school, like many Waldorf schools, includes required drama for all students. While Mike is a student at our school, we produce one all-school play per year, renting a local theater as a venue. Students like Mike, who enjoy theater, audition for larger roles. In remembering his roles at the school, Mike says, "after both my hospitalizations, traumatic times, I found solace in acting. I find peace in being on stage, especially in improv, something that other people would consider a nightmare."*

At the start of his senior year, after only one semester in our school, Mike voluntarily performs a Jim Steinman monologue, "Love, Death, and an American Guitar," in front of more than 100 strangers around a campfire. He and his class and I are on Hermit Island, on the coast of Maine, for a week, camping and studying tide-pool zoology with 12th-grade students and teachers from eight other Waldorf schools. This is an annual trip for the schools, but a one-time experience for the students. I'm nervous for Mike, for our school. What's he getting himself into? The rest of the volunteer performances have all been songs, sung by small groups, some a cappella, most with guitar accompaniment. No one else is performing alone, or acting. How will he react if his risk is not well received? Is he emotionally strong enough to see this through, and, more important, to handle potential failure?

Mike gathers himself and launches in, dark hair flying. Here are the first lines of the monologue:

I remember everything!
I remember every little thing as if it happened only yesterday.
I was barely seventeen, and I once killed a boy with a Fender guitar.
I don't remember if it was a Telecaster or a Stratocaster,
But I do remember that it had a heart of chrome and a voice like a horny angel...

The words are raw and aggressive. Mike, anxious and quiet most of the time, inhabits the role, commits fully, and stalks back and forth in front of the fire. The audience is rapt, and they roar their approval and applause at the end. Mike has taken a risk and triumphed.

In 12th grade, he is elected President of the Student Council. With a friend in the 11th grade, he runs a dramatic campaign—posters show the actor, "Mr. T," saying, "I pity the fool who doesn't vote for Mike and Arthur." And weekly skits in Morning Meeting drum up support. He acknowledges that, for him, campaigning is more fun than leading, and that, perhaps, actors shouldn't really be politicians. He now feels bad for his opponent, a young woman who was a more sincere but less charismatic candidate.

What about our school makes it possible for Mike to pursue these accomplishments, particularly in the context of self-healing through artistic activity? Here's what he has to say: "Classes are very often discussion-based. Students can discuss what they're reading, what they're learning. They can interpret. They can agree or disagree with each other, but not in a personal way." Dialogue and engagement—versus lecture and reception—characterize our general approach to educating teens. Desks in most classrooms are arranged in a square or rectangle, not in rows facing the blackboard. Classes tend to be participatory, lively and, at least part of the time, student-driven. These methods call on students to awaken themselves, to rely on themselves, and to build and pay attention to interactions among each other and with their teachers. While not strictly artistic, we could say that these are characteristics of creative engagement.

"The school is small," Mike continues at his graduation speech:

"This makes it personal, not impersonal. The school is peaceful, warm, and welcoming. I was bullied in public school when I was younger, even though I'm a big guy. And at my other private school, I never felt like I could be myself. This is rare in my experience, but at Waldorf I felt like I could be myself. I was comfortable. I believed in myself. I felt loved and supported. People have to take responsibility for how they act and what they say. The school focuses on developing the healthy individuality of each student. The school emphasizes the arts, which was important to me. And it encourages even those who are not particularly gifted in the arts. At my old school, only the people who were already good at art were honored. And, for me, acting brings freedom, which is a really, really good thing."

Mike is admitted to a prestigious acting school in New York, the only school to which he applies. He finds himself emotionally unprepared. He doesn't feel comfortable in or accepted by the "excited, dramatic, charismatic crowd." He says, "It's like a bad high-school experience, all over again." But, by now, he's off antidepressants, he isn't tempted to harm himself, publicly or otherwise. He does well academically, and says that he is the only student to receive a perfect score in his history of drama class.

He completes his foundation year in acting, then moves to the West Coast, to take classes in improv at a theater owned by a well-known television comedian. Although

Mike enjoys all forms of acting, he says improv is his passion and his strength. He loves entertaining others, "not knowing where we're going" in a sketch, and the support that improv actors have to develop and demonstrate to each other.

The Gift of Gratitude

Much more could be said about the traits that Waldorf graduates typically share, but we close this section with a brief vignette that captures many of the themes articulated in the examples shared above. In a simple story are combined the themes of balancing ideal and practical, the professional and the personal, individual and social consciousness, private modesty and public confidence, and above all the role of the arts in cultivating individual growth and maturity. This vignette comes from Lisa Babinet, math teacher at the Waldorf School of the Peninsula in Northern California:

One of the students in our first graduating class, a Waldorf "lifer," went off to a small liberal arts college, where she took time to pen a note to each of her professors—once the courses were over and the final grades were in, of course. She let them know what she had appreciated most about the class as part of a sincere thank you note of gratitude. This student not only excelled in college, but won an academic award upon graduation. She has been working in a law firm and is contemplating applying to Law School.

For all the stories of struggle and success, there are others, to be sure, that are less felicitous in outcome. Some of these can be found anecdotally in the commentary sections of this survey but, not surprisingly, are largely missing from the circles of students who have stayed in touch with their teachers. The fact remains, that the number of students expressing fundamental dislike or disdain for their Waldorf education is dwarfed by the number who hold their education—as well their teachers— in high regard.

It is also worth mentioning that the notes of idealism and optimism that resound through the stories of these graduates grow no fainter as the students grow older. They are exemplars of what Rudolf Steiner called "achieved," rather than "naïve," idealism, meaning that they have tested the exuberant and externally stimulated idealism of youth in the fires of life's experience. Out of what might have been highly discouraging circumstances, they have discovered for themselves new and self-originating inner strength. In colloquial terms, their hearts may have been broken, yet still they have come to love life all the more as a result of this experience.

X Maintaining Alumni Relationships

In many ways, this study is focused on the life that Waldorf alumni lead after leaving their original school communities and venturing out into the world. While we are very much interested in learning more about the possible impact of their past education on their current lives, we are also interested in the current relationships these alumni may or may not have with their former school and school community. We were able to collect rich information about these relationships through their responses to our survey questions, but we also gained knowledge and insight on the issue by the very activities of pursuing this information. That is to say, the various modes of contacting schools and alumni, and the difficulties therein, along with the various face-to-face interviews with alumni of different generations, contributed to the impressions presented in this penultimate chapter. Our main conclusion is that while the majority of Waldorf alumni greatly cherish their education and appreciate its multifaceted impact on their lives, much more could be done to cultivate a strong alumni relationship with their school. A tradition of alumni relations, often a fixture of other independent schools in North America, appears to be tenuous in the Waldorf movement. It is the role of the schools to maintain a culture of alumni involvement by keeping them informed and engaged, especially if the school is seeking its former students' support in current efforts and needs. Responses from alumni of many different Waldorf schools suggest that infrastructure for creating and maintaining such a culture is still in need of development.

KEEPING IN TOUCH

Waldorf alumni, it is clear from survey responses, feel significantly connected to their former schools. As reported in previous chapters, alumni who graduated from high school more than 10 years ago report that they have positive feelings about their school (82%), that it has contributed to who they are (83%), that they are proud of their affiliation with the school (70%), and that they will recommend the school to others (87%). Among those who graduated more recently (after 2010), close to 70% say they would welcome email updates from their school, half are interested in keeping contact through social networking websites and services, and about 43% express their commitment to maintaining the relationship by visiting alumni events.

Keeping up with former classmates is the primary way in which alumni maintain a relationship with their school community. This is especially the case for the recently graduated, college-age alumni, 89% of whom say they do this. Otherwise, they connect through the various social networking media and sites (56.3%), which they clearly prefer to reading print alum publications such as newsletters and magazines (36.5%). Close to half of alumni, or 43.9%, keep in touch with their former teachers, and 24%-27% of respondents say they attend school fairs, festivals, plays, and class reunions. Fewer than 6% of college-age respondents say they contribute to the school's annual fund.

A comparison with older alumni, the post-college group (see table below), shows a slight decrease in keeping in touch with former classmates, and somewhat larger decreases in keeping in touch with faculty or attending regular school events such as fairs, festivals, and plays. Far fewer of these alumni maintain contact with their former schools through a sibling or other family member who is currently a student there. On the other hand, older alumni are now more likely to attend a class reunion and almost three times more likely to make a contribution to the school's annual fund than younger Waldorf graduates.

The effects of time, it seems, take their toll on maintaining such long-term relationship with one's former school, while the advancement into an established profession and greater economic stability would explain the increase in financial contributions to the school. Another difference noted by this comparison is that the younger generation of Waldorf alumni is more comfortable with online communication—the social networking contact—than with print in the form of newsletters and magazines.

Table 10.1: Staying in touch with former school community

	Waldorf College-Age Alumni	Waldorf Post-College Alumni
Keep in touch with former classmates	89%	85%
Use social networking (Facebook, LinkedIn, etc.)	56.3%	50.4%
Read alum publications (newsletters, magazines, e-newsletters, etc.)	36.5%	50.2%
Keep in touch with faculty	43.9%	35%
Stay connected through family members now attending the school	27%	12.5%
Attend school fairs (harvest fair, etc.)	27.6%	21.3%
Attend reunions	26.7%	31.8%
Attend school festivals	26.4%	15.5%
Attend school plays	24.5%	11.4%
Attend school athletic events	14.4%	5.5%
Contribute to the school's annual fund	5.7%	15.6%

Comparing Waldorf and NAIS Alumni

A second comparison, this time of both age groups with their two peer groups of contemporary alumni of other American independent schools, supports the generational differences reflected by the figures above but also discloses something about the Waldorf alumni culture.

First, we note (see Table 10.2 below) that there is a similarity across the board among all four alumni groups wherein the personal contact with former classmates is, by far, the number one mode of keeping contact with one's former school community. Second, we note similarities in the generational trend, marked by a decrease in older alumni's efforts to maintain their connection with the school either through personal contact with former classmates and faculty or through attending school events, and an increase in attending class and school reunions. We also note a media gap between the two generations, wherein the younger alumni are more in tune with online communication than with print. Among the college-aged, 56.3% of Waldorf and 61.6% of NAIS alumni say they use social networking to maintain their contact with their former school, while only 50.4% (Waldorf) and 40.6% (NAIS) say so in the post-college cohorts. The older generation clearly prefers print publications as suggested by those who say they read alumni magazines and newsletters: 50.2% of Waldorf and

76.2% of NAIS post-college alumni, in contrast to 36.5% and 50.7% of their respective college-aged cohorts.

We learn something specific about what appears to be a change in the Waldorf-school culture when we look closely at the comparative figures for attending school athletic events. The numbers are low among Waldorf alumni in comparison to those who attend other school events, such as festivals, fairs, and plays, and the generational gap between the 14.4% of college-age Waldorf alumni who attend athletic events and the 5.5% older Waldorf alumni who say they do so appears to be in step with other decreases in involvement as time goes by. However, when we look at this element in all four groups, we discover that the very low attendance of the Waldorf post-college alumni (5.5%) is quite the exception in relation to all three other groups, who are more or less aligned between 14.4% and 16.4%. This suggests that the social-cultural value of the athletic event has risen in the Waldorf community, and it is now considered as important as in the NAIS schools, which have a long tradition—something most Waldorf schools don't have—of valuing athletic achievement as a marker of community identity.

Table 10.2: How Waldorf and NAIS alumni connect with their high school

	Waldorf College-Age Alumni	Waldorf Post-College Alumni	NAIS College-Age Alumni	NAIS Post-College Alumni
Keep in touch with former classmates	89%	85%	91.2%	80%
Use social networking (Facebook, LinkedIn, etc.)	56.3%	50.4%	61.6%	40.6%
Read alum publications (magazines, e-newsletter, etc.)	36.5%	50.2%	50.7%	76.2%
Keep in touch with faculty	43.9%	35%	47.1%	31.8%
Stay connected through family members now attending the school	27%	12.5%	24.7%	13.6%
Attend reunions	26.7%	31.8%	26.5%	45.4%
Attend school festivals (or other events)	26.4%	15.5%	—	24.2%
Attend school athletic events	14.4%	5.5%	16.4%	15.9%
Contribute to the school's annual fund	5.7%	15.6%	19.5%	33.1%

Financial Contributions

The clearest statistical difference between the Waldorf and NAIS groups concerns alumni philanthropy. A third of longtime graduates from NAIS schools say they contribute to their school's annual fund, while only half of that portion—15.6%— among longtime Waldorf alumni say the same. And while it is understandable that recent, college-aged graduates are not in a position to make financial contributions, which explains to a certain extent why only 5.7% of recent Waldorf alumni say they contribute to their school's annual fund, we note that more than three times as many NAIS alumni, 19.5%, of the same age are already making monetary gifts to their former school.

Given the general gratitude and fondness to their school expressed by most Waldorf graduates participating in the survey, it does not seem that the dramatically lower number of Waldorf alumni making contributions to their school is explained by lack of appreciation or unwillingness to donate. And while dozens of alumni write that they currently have absolutely no financial capacity to make any donations, it seems that there are additional grounds for the difference between NAIS and Waldorf alumni giving. These appear to include an established culture of alumni giving and a systematic cultivation by NAIS schools through regular outreach and ongoing communication, a practice that appears to be the norm in other independent schools in a way that it is not so widespread in Waldorf schools.

Several sets of responses collected in the survey support this impression. Most clearly, when asked when they were last asked to give money to their school, a quarter of the Waldorf alumni said they could not recall, while 14% believed they had never been asked. And while 54% said they had been asked to make a donation within the past year, the number was 76% among NAIS post-college alumni, only 2.2% of whom believed they had never been asked for money.

Furthermore, it is not that Waldorf alumni are averse to making monetary contributions, or that none of them is able to afford doing so (though many respondents confess to the latter), but rather that some appear simply to be uninformed of their school's needs and the destination of their potential gifts. One alum writes, "I have not been asked to donate, and honestly am not sure what the process is for my Waldorf school." A second adds, "I continually have asked where I can help and am almost NEVER gotten back to (now on three different development directors), so I assume money is not an issue!" While a third opines, "It is difficult to justify giving to something that already has so much, and charges so much, when others are far more needy."

The last comment not only shows the kind of impression alumni can have about their school when not presented with clear information, but also demonstrates the social and moral sensitivities expressed by many Waldorf alumni. "School should be free for everyone," another alum writes, adding, "I hope to make positive change to the public school system." Similarly, another respondent states, "I'm more likely to donate to the underserved public schools of my hometown than I am to a Waldorf school I attended."

That such perspectives can prevent willing alumni from financially supporting their schools is also indicated by other data collected. For example, we know that alumni *do* give money to other causes: a majority of nearly 60% of post-college alumni say they regularly donate money to non-profit organizations or charities, and 25% say they do make donations to other schools. Still, their philanthropic habits are not exercised in relation to their Waldorf school.

Specifically, 28% of post-college alumni say flat out that their school is *not* a giving priority, and more than half, or 52%, say that it is not currently a giving priority but it might be in the future. At present, though, fewer than 20% of alumni say it is one of their top giving priorities. The numbers, we should note, are not dramatically different from those of NAIS alumni, 24% of whom say their school is not a giving priority and 49% say it is not *currently* a giving priority, though 27% do say their high school *is* a top giving priority. Still, the self-reported reality does show a considerable difference, as reported above, with 33.1% of NAIS post-college alumni saying they have made financial contributions to their school, while only 15.6% of Waldorf alumni—less than half—say the same.

The Information Gap

An indication that this modest level of giving is caused by insufficient communication between school and alumni is supported by the fact that only a quarter of alumni say they are "very well" or "well" informed about where their philanthropic gifts go, while three-quarters of them say it is "important" or even "very important" that they know how their contributions are used. Based on survey responses (see Table 10.3 below), we know now that the majority of Waldorf alumni would like their gifts to support students with financial needs, with a second priority of attracting and retaining the best faculty, followed by making Waldorf education affordable for Waldorf alumni who are not able to pay full tuition. We do not know whether their former schools are aware of these priorities.

Table 10.3: Top five priorities for allocating donations (post-college Waldorf alumni)

1. Creating opportunities for students with financial need (64.9%)
2. Attracting and retaining the best faculty (61.2%)
3. Making school financially accessible to those who are Waldorf-educated and yet are not able to afford Waldorf school education for their children (40.5%)
4. Improving academics (24.5%)
5. Assisting students to be college-ready when they graduate (24.5%)

NAIS alumni, on the other hand, seem to have better communication with their former schools. In contrast to Waldorf alumni, 50% of NAIS respondents feel "very well" or "well" informed about the use of their gifts and 68% say the same in regards to their school's fundraising priorities in general. The top priorities for NAIS alumni in the use of their gifts are nearly identical to the Waldorf ones, only in a different order of importance—seeing the retention of the best faculty as more important than supporting students with financial needs, which comes in second place. Assisting students to be college-ready by graduation is third on the NAIS alumni list and improving the level of academics is fourth.

Some Waldorf alumni are explicit in their comments about the relationship between their financial contributions and their school communication efforts. One writes, "The alumni outreach has not overwhelmed me. I might be more enticed to give in terms of volunteering if the opportunities were better communicated." Another suggests that it is the responsibility of the school to maintain a relationship with its former students: "I feel like the school could have done a better job staying in touch and creating alum networks." And a third combines these views in a detailed comment:

> *The school is not very effective in maintaining a relationship with me, therefore giving to the school does not make it on my radar. I would give what I can (as I do with my college), if I was asked, and if I was kept informed of developments, values and such.*

These opinions are supported by a decisive figure: a majority of respondents, ranging between 51% and 81%, write "not applicable" next to 12 out of 14 alumni services they were asked to evaluate. This suggests that these alumni services—including job boards, online auctions, volunteer opportunities at the school, and alumni lectures at the school or online—are either not offered by the schools or they are not offered in a way that the alumni are aware of them. The only services that receive some recognition are publications, about which 22% say they are satisfied with the online alumni newsletters and publications, and 19% say they are satisfied with print publications. While still quite modest, the most positive response to any given alumni service is to the online community, about which 25% of respondents say they are "somewhat satisfied," which is the middle point between "very satisfied" and "very dissatisfied."

In short, while alumni tend to maintain personal contacts with former classmates and teachers, they appear to expect that the school will take charge of maintaining a community-wide school–alumni relationship. Being adequately informed about changes and needs in the current school community appears to be key in alumni's attitudes toward supporting their school.

MANAGING ALUMNI RELATIONS IN WALDORF HIGH SCHOOLS

In turning to the schools themselves to establish a clearer picture of alumni relations practices, we found some explanations for alumni dissatisfaction.

Of the 39 schools surveyed, only one reported having a full-time person dedicated to alumni work. The other 38 schools indicated that the task of building and developing relationships with their graduates was shared by staff responsible for other administrative or development tasks. No school indicated a well-developed alumni program, yet several successes were repeatedly mentioned, such as regularly scheduled festivals and fairs well-attended by alumni. Special events such as 10- or 20-year reunions are also well attended by both local and out-of-town alumni.

Major challenges named by the schools included the lack of staff dedicated uniquely to alumni relations and difficulties in keeping alumni contact details current. In addition, schools appeared to rely on recent graduates' ability to self-organize and keep in touch with one another through social media.

In fact, the year-long efforts by the managers of this survey to obtain all the requested information from participating schools offer a good indication of the limited human resources dedicated to alumni issues, even as good will and responsiveness are clearly present. Difficulties included obtaining information already in the schools' possession as well as the schools' efforts and success levels in reaching out to their own alumni with requests to participate in our online survey. While we were able to achieve an acceptable response rate of 10% of the total number of alumni who graduated within our target time period of 1990-2017, much of the effort to reach these alumni was exerted by the survey team through online and personal/professional networks.

The impression that the alumni program infrastructure in Waldorf schools is still developing was uniformly received from schools founded after 2000 as it was from veteran high schools that were founded in the 1950s.

In approaching the schools, we asked about staffing allocation, regularity of communication, and descriptions of successes and challenges in maintaining alumni relations. The responses we received include the following:

Staffing Allocated to Alumni Relations

Alumni Relations Associate (FT)

Alumni Coordinator

Director of alumni affairs is also the Event Coordinator

Part-Time Alumni Relations Coordinator (40%, 20-40 hours/month)

Part-Time Alumni Associate (2-3 hours/week)

Part-Time hourly Assistant

Development Director

Development Director in collaboration with the Public Relations Coordinator

Development Director with support from Marketing and Communications Director

Development Director with assistance of a team of alumni class agents

Development Director + Part-Time Alumni Relations Associate (75% position)

Development Director + Part-Time Development Associate (75%)

Task force led by Development Director with Board member support

Development and Marketing staff (three people)

Development Director and Alumni Relations in addition to an active and engaged Alumni

College Counseling Office and the Development Director

Development Office/Staff

Advancement Office (25%)

Office Manager and Faculty Chair (informal role)

High-School Section Chair

High-School Administration

Faculty member

No paid position; various volunteers

"Alumni relations are being formalized"

In process

Communications and Alumni Events

Weekly bulletin, monthly alumni newsletter; Facebook page

Monthly newsletter, Facebook, special event mailers

Monthly communications; events; reunion weekend each June

Monthly communications by email and Facebook, with more communications around significant alumni events; two events each year

Quarterly newsletter; future plans to link with alumni database/social media platforms

Regular communication for events, i.e., yearly Holiday Dinner and "Meet for Coffee"

Regular communication, every 1-2 months, organized "happy hours" and care packages sent to last year's graduating class

Alumni news 3-4 times a year; publish alumni interviews; hold reunions

Twice-a-year alumni magazine and bi-monthly bulletin

Bi-annual Alumni magazine; invited to all school events, weekly school emails, reunions

Monthly newsletter, moving to online blog, bi-weekly podcast, 10- and 20-year reunions

Communications sent out for special events and fund-raisers

Direct mail, email list, Facebook

Alumni newsletter, event mailings and emails, social media

All newsletters and social media

Annual basketball game and social every December; festivals; ten-year reunions every summer; monthly communication to alumni and families

Cards and letters from teachers; Alumni Café at the fall fair; alumni included in newsletters and annual report mailing

Seasonal newsletters, annual report mailing, annual fund mailings, and other fund-raising activities

Communication for specific events

Contact through social media: Facebook, Instagram, and Snapchat

Email invitations to festivals and fundraising events; social media; alumni report allowing them to keep their own networks up to date

Social media communications and highlights of alum accomplishments

Alumni section of website; Facebook page

Email or Facebook page

Regional reunions, local class reunions, and annual alumni event "Alumni vs. Varsity Ultimate Frisbee game"

Alumni invited to school festivals and events; gathering every June

Sporadic communication

Not much communication

Database management has been the first priority

Successes and Challenges
Challenges

Building alumni work into the overall school budget; finding time for staff to maintain connections to alumni. **Goals**: Active Alumni web page; alumni events

Stay connected with alumni from the first graduating classes. **Positives**: alums do stay connected and attend school events

Staff turnover which does not allow for consistent presence and communication with alumni

Finding/keeping track of accurate contact information

Never enough time to communicate with, cultivate gifts from, or track/survey our alumni

Maintaining accurate data on alums

Lack of adequate staffing

Lack of dedicated focus on alumni work

Finding the right mix of opportunities that drive meaningful engagement with the school

Keeping records and contact info current, finding desirable ways to draw alumni to events, keeping alumni engaged, soliciting funding requests

Successes

Events attended by graduates

Annual reunions

Our first-ever alumni giving campaign

Alumni Becoming Faculty and Staff

As a side note to this picture of challenges and successes in maintaining alumni relations, we should add one significant aspect in the relationship between alumni and Waldorf education. This is the regular return of former students to a Waldorf school community—not necessarily to the school from which they graduated—as faculty or staff. All Waldorf high schools participating in the survey reported having on their roster at least one—and up to 11—Waldorf alumni who had either graduated from the same school or from a different Waldorf school. Only one school did not employ any alumni at the time of the survey, but it had previously employed three.

Positions held by Waldorf alumni include early childhood teacher, class teacher, teacher assistant, special-subject teachers (language, handwork, eurythmy), high-school teachers (humanities, science, math, drama, physical education, practical arts), administrator, school director, front-office personnel, and development officer.

While this phenomenon is not necessarily the result of active efforts on the part of the schools, and could eventually include only a relatively small number of alumni, it is a clear mark of a successful feedback loop, in which a strongly influential Waldorf education brings alumni back into the folds of a Waldorf community as active members.

Conclusions

We conclude this chapter on alumni relations with our impression that for many schools a more robust alumni program will bring Waldorf graduates closer to their former school and to Waldorf education in general. Such efforts could both *take the form of* and *result in* introducing new ideas to the schools, becoming more engaged with the changing times, and increasing enrollment and alumni philanthropy. Enrollment is the cornerstone of development and a well-organized and fully staffed development and alumni outreach program can lead to additional funding for the schools.

We also take note of the fact that personal connections provide the most cohesive force in maintaining lasting and engaged alumni relationships. Former teachers and former classmates are clearly the greatest source of attraction for alumni and therefore the most effective agents for sustained engagement. Waldorf schools would benefit from streamlining and formalizing these personal contacts in order to maintain and enhance meaningful relationships between alumni and their schools.

At a practical level, a fundamental step in setting the infrastructure for alumni relations would be organizing the school's database of alumni and regularly refreshing data files for alumni contacts. These appear to be the starting points in cultivating a relationship with alumni and establishing a dynamic, ongoing culture of alumni engagement fostered by the schools.

XI   Conclusions

We set out in this survey to take a closer look at Waldorf students who graduated from high school during the past quarter century or so—that is, since 1990. Stated most generally, our overarching question asked: *How do these Waldorf alumni fare in life?* More concretely, we wanted to know:

- What have they done since graduating from high school?
- What are they doing now?
- What do they choose to study in college and beyond?
- How well do they feel prepared for the various aspects of college life?
- What kind of professions do they choose?
- How satisfied are they with their lives?
- What is their financial standing?
- What is their perspective on life and on their being in the world?
- How engaged are they with their alma mater?
- How do they perceive Waldorf education's influence on their life choices and on the person they have become?

Of course, the most one can hope to achieve in summarizing the descriptions by thousands of graduates from dozens of schools in the span of a quarter century is a general picture of overarching trends, formed by numbers and categories and fortified by samples of personal narratives and poignant comments.

Our survey responses show a decisive majority of alumni say Waldorf education has "prepared them for life," that it has instilled in them the habits of collaboration, of creative and critical thinking, and of concern for the community as a whole. In this sense, Waldorf education is successful in meeting its goals if we understand these goals to be "educating the whole child," nurturing and guiding children and adolescents in ways that contribute to their maturing into well-balanced, morally sensitive individuals who are able to pursue their own initiatives and self-realize while serving the wider community. We see this success in the professional choices of Waldorf graduates, nearly 40% of whom work in education, health services, or social services; we see it in their self-professed high level of life-satisfaction; and we see this in their own perception of the skills, capacities, and formative experiences gained during their years at the Waldorf school.

We learn that since graduating high school they have pursued new experiences and knowledge through gap year activities of work and travel (for some), undergraduate studies (practically for all), followed by more professional and/or graduate studies (for most), before settling into a profession. They study a large variety of subjects, most of which fall in the three broad fields of arts and humanities, the social and behavioral sciences, and life and physical sciences (presented in order of popularity). Among the most recent graduates of the last decade, however, we note an increase in the number of alumni majoring in the natural sciences and a proportional decrease in those who go for subjects in arts and humanities. Of the many who continued to further their education beyond a bachelor's degree, the largest groups focused on the social and behavioral sciences, on the fine and performing arts, on humanities, and on health and medicine (presented in order of popularity). Their professions are many and varied, but it is clear that the one profession that attracts the greatest number of Waldorf alumni is education, followed by the various health services—from mental therapy to physical surgery—and by a variety of creative professions in the fields of entertainment, art, and design.

We further learn that Waldorf alumni are satisfied with their life—so say 90% of them—in a way that does not necessarily correspond to their income, given that nearly 30% of post-college alumni earn less than $40,000 a year and most of these alumni—bearing in mind they are either still in college or no more than two decades past their undergraduate years—earn less than their parents. As a whole, we learn that the Waldorf alumni are not especially affluent, and about 15% of them name finances as a leading challenge in their lives.

This last point suggests that Waldorf alumni seem to be out of step with a certain leading creed of the American ethos, the one that couples success with affluence. (This is not to say that Waldorf alumni are not entrepreneurial: a good fifth of them are business owners or self-employed.) And yet, they do appear to be in tune with other American ideals, perhaps of the Emersonian kind, such as self-realization, love for nature, and a sense of obligation to community.

It is most clear that Waldorf alumni are fully in tune with their cultural moment, which has seen the rise of progressive ethical expectations that extend equality to all members of society and promote a variety of underserved groups and previously unheard voices. Confidence in the collaborative skills learned in Waldorf school, along with an aversion to competition and self-promotion, seem to serve as the foundation for these graduates' ethical worldview. Their commitment to equality and diversity, while appearing to grow out of the practices and perspectives rehearsed at the Waldorf school, can also sometimes turn into a criticism of the Waldorf community they remember from their time as students. Many alumni say they hesitate to send their own children to a private Waldorf school or donate money to their former school because they are concerned by its perceived lack of ethnic, social, and economic diversity—even though these Waldorf schools are no less diverse than other independent schools—or by a curriculum they see as being too Euro-centric.

Like all things, the current picture of the Waldorf alum sketched out in these pages is best understood in context. The two contextual fields we used to better understand and describe Waldorf alumni in this study are the previous survey of Waldorf alumni, conducted in 2007, and a contemporaneous survey conducted by the American National Association of Independent Schools (NAIS) that polled alumni from independent schools across the country. In fact, we used the NAIS questionnaire as the basis for our own survey to make possible closer comparisons between Waldorf graduates and their contemporary peers from other independent American schools.

Below are short reviews of the main points of comparisons made to these two surveys.

COMPARING CONCLUSIONS:
2007 AND 2017 WALDORF ALUMNI SURVEYS

The period covered by the current survey saw a surge of new Waldorf high schools in North America and therefore in the number of Waldorf high-school graduates. That is to say, while 13 new schools were founded during the 1990s and another 10 in the early 2000s, such initiatives tapered off in the 2010s. In fact, the latter part of the current decade has seen a slight decline in the number of high schools, which went down from 43 to 40; enrollment in these high schools, which peaked at about 3,000 in September 2015, dropped to about 2,750 in September 2018. As of 2018, about one in four AWSNA elementary schools had its own high school, in addition to five stand-alone Waldorf high schools.

Of the 37 schools involved in the previous survey of Waldorf graduates, conducted in 2007, five have since closed. In the meantime, ten new Waldorf schools have since started up, though two of them closed recently. In total, starting in 1942, fifty-five

Waldorf high schools have started up in North America; of this number, 40 schools were extant as of summer 2019.

Accordingly, we have been able to greatly expand the pool of survey respondents since the previous study. The 2007 survey polled 550 Waldorf alumni, from 37 high schools, and spanned a period of 60 years of graduates (1943-2005), whereas the current survey polled 1066 alumni, from 39 schools, spanning the most recent 27 years (1990-2017). In both surveys, roughly half of respondents had attended Waldorf school from kindergarten or first grade through graduation. In addition, both surveys polled alumni in comparable proportions from schools located in the three North American "zones": East Coast, West Coast, and the states that lie in between.

A major difference between the two surveys concerns the questionnaire used to solicit information from alumni. While the previous one was modeled on a German survey of Waldorf graduates, the current is an adaptation of two questionnaires designed by NAIS—one version for college-age students and the other for post-college respondents. In effecting this change, we were able to trim an overabundance of detailed questions used in the earlier survey and make closer comparisons with contemporaries from other independent schools.

Despite these differences, a comparison of results from the two Waldorf surveys shows many similarities in various areas of the Waldorf alum experience, as well as trends of growth or change captured in the first survey and becoming more apparent in the second.

Among the similarities between the two Waldorf surveys, we highlight the following:

About a quarter of respondents reported taking a gap year between high school and college.

Main criticisms of Waldorf high-school offerings focused on insufficiencies in math, science, and computer skills, as well as on instruction in practical life skills.

Eurythmy was singled out most often as a subject "rejected at the time and now viewed differently."

A majority in both surveys said they would recommend Waldorf education to others and would like to send their own children to a Waldorf school, though comments in the current survey often mentioned the high cost of Waldorf education and expressed apprehension about sending children to a private, hence perceived as "privileged," school.

Roughly the same percentages expressed positive, negative, and neutral attitudes towards anthroposophy, with the most common response asking: "What is anthroposophy?!"

Professions: A trend observed in the previous survey is continued in the current, wherein the single most popular profession among Waldorf alumni is education. In addition, according to both surveys, alumni often enter this profession only after having studied other subjects as undergraduates and at times after having explored other personal and professional paths.

Otherwise, both surveys show high popularity of careers in health or medical services, in a variety of social services, and in the performing arts.

A major conclusion of the previous survey is that Waldorf graduates are more likely than not to put the interests or needs of others ahead of their own, and that they place the interests of wider communities ahead of their own self-interest. The same conclusion is reached in the current survey.

Trends of change noted in comparing the two surveys:
In the earlier survey, about 6% did not go on from high school to college; in the latest survey only 2% did not do so.

The previous survey showed a turning point in the mid-1990s, when more Waldorf alumni than in previous years took up science and math as their major fields of study in college. The current survey shows a continuing uptick in alumni majoring in these and other STEM subjects, rising from 17% (for those graduated 1990-2010) to 22% (for those who graduated after 2010).

Conversely, we note a clear trend of *decrease* in the number of alumni majoring in arts and humanities and an *increase* in those who major in the social and behavioral sciences.

COMPARING RESPONSES: WALDORF ALUMNI AND NAIS ALUMNI
In Chapters IV-VI we offered some detailed comparisons between the Waldorf and NAIS alumni responses to similar survey questions. We highlight here the major points of these comparisons.

In comparing responses by the most recent graduates, categorized as "college-age alumni," we notice that:
Both Waldorf and NAIS alumni highly value the small class size and the individualized attention offered by their school setting.

Waldorf alumni are more concerned than NAIS alumni about college costs and the availability of financial assistance when choosing their college.

Waldorf alumni are considerably less concerned about the reputation of the college, its culture, or whether a family member has attended the same school.

More Waldorf alumni (68%) than NAIS alumni (61%) attend their college of first choice.

In choosing a major area of studies, subjects in the arts & humanities prove to be considerably more attractive to Waldorf alumni than to NAIS alumni, making up 28% of the subjects the former major in and only 19% for the latter.

Conversely, business & accounting is a field preferred by more than twice as many NAIS alumni (10.3%) than by Waldorf (4.6%), while almost the same percentages in both groups major in the various sciences, with a slight advantage to Waldorf alumni who major in the social sciences (23.5% vs. 22.6%) and a slighter advantage to NAIS alumni who major in the physical sciences or STEM (23% vs. 22.2%).

Both groups feel very confident about their preparation for college and in their various academic skills, and both feel *least* secure about their technology skills.

Both groups also demonstrate an insecurity about their level of preparation in science and math, though Waldorf alumni are decisively less secure than NAIS alumni in this area.

Waldorf alumni are less inclined to self-evaluate their abilities in comparison to those of their peers, something NAIS alumni seem quite comfortable doing. This asymmetry changes direction when both groups are asked to assess concrete, measurable skills that could be judged by past performance (such as public speaking or collaborative work). Here Waldorf alumni give themselves higher grades than do NAIS alumni. In general, Waldorf alumni appear to be more reserved in evaluating themselves and their schools, whereas NAIS alumni often reach for the highest superlatives.

A most telling difference between the two groups is apparent in their responses to questions that probe more into what kind of *person*, rather than student, their high schools prepared them to become. Across the board, Waldorf alumni's evaluations are considerably higher than NAIS alumni's when assessing their preparation in creativity, open-mindedness, artistic sensitivity, coherence of thought, visual thinking, and empathy for others. While these qualities were introduced to the survey by NAIS researchers, they are arguably at the core of Waldorf education; the high scores offered by Waldorf alumni for their preparation in these areas show that they recognize the broader aims and accomplishments of their Waldorf education.

Comparisons of post-college-aged Waldorf alumni with their NAIS peers extended beyond college to the highest level of education these older alumni had pursued and to their established professions. Similarities and differences in the choices of higher education are encapsulated in Table 11.1 below, reproduced from Chapter V (Table 5.4), showing a comparative ranking, in terms of popularity, of study areas in which alumni obtained their highest degree:

Table 11.1: Waldorf and NAIS ranks of highest Degree

	Waldorf Alumni Ranking	NAIS Alumni Ranking
Social & Behavioral Sciences	1	4
Arts—Fine and Performing	2	8
Humanities	3	2
Health	4	5
Business & Management	5	1
Education	6	6
Life Sciences	7	9
Physical Sciences, Engineering, & Math	8	7
Law & Legal Services	9	3
Computer & Information Sciences	10	10

Concerning their employment, the most popular field for both groups is *education*, though considerably more so for Waldorf alumni (23%) than for NAIS alumni (17.5%). Similarly, the two groups are aligned in their second most popular field of employment, *medicine*, where 10.3% of Waldorf alumni work compared to 9.3% of NAIS. The biggest observable differences in the fields of employment are in law/legal services and in financial services, where approximately twice as many NAIS alumni work, and in the fine or performing arts, where twice as many Waldorf alumni work. And nearly three times as many NAIS alumni work in sales and advertising as Waldorf alumni do.

Other comparisons between the two groups show that NAIS alumni identify the strengths of their high-school education to be in cultivating analytic and systematic modes of thinking, while Waldorf alumni recognize their education's influence in fostering a thought process that is more holistic and creative. And whereas NAIS alumni's responses suggest training in work and study habits that are focused on individual achievement, Waldorf alumni's responses clearly indicate an emphasis on collaboration, team work, and the general elevation of the goals and needs of the group over the needs and desires of the self.

A defining qualitative difference in the way each group members see the influence of their secondary education is apparent in Waldorf alumni's top-ranking the "meaningful perspective on life," which they believe their school has fostered. For NAIS alumni, this aspect is ranked third to last.

A final and quite striking difference between the responses of Waldorf and NAIS graduates concerns their relationship to their alma mater. While most Waldorf alumni hold their school in affectionate regard, they are less likely to support it financially, compared to their peers from other NAIS schools. While this may reflect less affluent family backgrounds or personal financial security among Waldorf graduates, it also highlights the fact—as some Waldorf graduates note in stark language—that, compared to other independent institutions, Waldorf schools are less successful overall in cultivating steady and regular relationships with their graduates.

THE SELF-KNOWING WALDORF ALUM

The two last points of comparison above begin to illustrate what stand out for us as three major conclusions arising from this study. One is that Waldorf alumni, already during their college years, clearly recognize the effects of their education on their own development. The second conclusion concerns the general contours of the Waldorf alum as a person.

First, Waldorf alumni recognize that their education has guided them in cultivating a meaningful outlook and that it is designed to be a "preparation for life" (an expression used in many of the comments) rather than solely an academic preparation. Similarly, they recognize the value of Waldorf's creative and artistic curriculum for non-artistic fields of study and work. They even recognize the value of a limited-technology policy, even as they become tech-savvy in their adult professional lives. Many of them express sentiments—reluctantly at times—of belated appreciation for their education, as we saw captured in the answer by one respondent: "Ugh, fine, Eurythmy has a purpose."

To recognize the value of one's earlier education means to see how it has contributed to one's inner capacities. This, in turn, requires a mature capacity for self-knowledge. In recognizing the various contributions Waldorf education has made to the adults they have become, alumni demonstrate the kind of self-knowing which is the goal of any education worthy of its name and certainly of Waldorf education.

Second, recognition by Waldorf graduates of the collaborative, community-oriented tendencies cultivated in them at school matches up with the kind of professions a majority of them choose. These professions—in the fields of education, health services, and social services—are oriented towards serving and supporting other people and communities with the resources of deep knowledge, advanced skills, and compassion. These aspects coalesce into the social profile of the Waldorf alum as a less competitive, more collaborative individual whose individualism comes about more as self-knowledge and self-realization than as self-interest and self-promotion.

A third conclusion arises from close attention to the kinds of criticism voiced in the survey. We identify three kinds of critical comments included in the pool of free-form responses solicited at various points of the questionnaire: (a) complaints (b) claims of adverse outcomes, and (c) constructive criticism.

What we call "complaints" are typically expressed in a bitter or dismissive voice, speaking for instance of a "fairy tale education" out of touch with reality and insufficient for the "real world." A voice of this kind may invoke a negative school experience in which the respondent felt unseen by teachers or unprotected from peer harassment. A handful of strongly worded complaints speak of poor management of school affairs and either extreme rigidity or extreme leniency in a community perceived to be too tight-knit or too loosely held.

"Claims of adverse outcomes" suggest that the protective intimacy of the Waldorf community precipitated in these critics a culture shock once it was time for them to step out into the world and meet the realities of work, competition, and a more impersonal form of higher education. A comment repeated by several respondents suggested that Waldorf's rich, pluralistic introduction to life and learning led to difficulties in choosing a single path during early adulthood.

Interestingly, the aspects described negatively in these two types of critical comments are often the ones emphasized in appreciative ones as the strongest, most positive elements in one's educational experience. A community experienced by critics as intrusive and overbearing is described by others as warm, intimate, and supportive. The creative and imaginative aspects of the education celebrated by most comments are derided as impractical by a few others. The introduction to multiple perspectives and the training of various capacities through a combination of arts and academics, which are described as empowering and liberating by most alumni, are seen as stunting and overwhelming by those who confess to difficulties in finding their own way.

In short—and this is our third conclusion—we see that the same elements of Waldorf education that count for a majority of alumni as among its greatest assets are the very ones that pose the greatest challenges for a small minority.

Critical comments that are more pointed and constructive suggest that personal or ideological conflicts among faculty should have been kept away from students, that instruction in STEM subjects could have been stronger, that portions of the curriculum should be updated to meet cultural changes, and that many could have used instruction in life's "practical skills."

We conclude this survey, then, with the impression that even with its original inspiration rooted in the early 20th century, American Waldorf education is cultivating a clearly 21st-century generation. Its graduates note the limits imposed on their exposure to electronic technology and screen media while still growing up to become tech-savvy and new-media literate. Their perceived deficits in STEM instruction do not appear to hinder a pursuit of the various sciences, technology, and math in college and in professional careers. Furthermore, alumni often trace their passion for these sciences to the pictorial and conceptual introductions they received in Waldorf school. And while they may describe a challenging transitional period in college during which they have to acquire particular skill sets and subject specializations, many of these same graduates recognize how their Waldorf education prepared them to meet these challenges. In effect, they acknowledge a pedagogical division of labor, so to speak, in which high school prepares the grounds for the expertise developed when it's needed in higher education.

Waldorf alumni, specifically those who graduated from high school during the last 25 years, are clearly citizens of the 21st century in their commitment to social justice, which they identify—as does their generation of educated millennials as a whole—with the term *diversity*. Their expectations of society to embrace equality through diversity appear to arise from the values cultivated by the Waldorf community in which they have been raised. Still, these very same expectations can turn into a criticism of their former schools and communities in cases where the make-up of the community and the cultural emphases of the curriculum do not align with the diversity expected in a 21st-century education.

We leave the final word to an anonymous alum, who describes a view of Waldorf education in the following terms:

> *My opinion of all Waldorf schools is that they should be thought of as leadership training academies, whose purpose is to create a generation of leaders in every sector uniquely educated to see systems, think from a whole-system perspective, and bring personal ethics and strong morality back into their industry of choice.*

Acknowledgements

Four groups deserve special thanks for the envisioning, researching, writing, and production of this wide-reaching survey of a quarter-century of North American Waldorf graduates.

THE TEAM

From first to last, this project was carried by a quartet of dedicated researchers, who between them drafted an outline of the survey, created an online questionnaire, reached out to other organizations, engaged teachers and administrators from some 40 Waldorf high schools, conducted face-to-face interviews, analyzed a mountain of data, and transformed it into a readable narrative and accessible graphs and charts. For the most part, they worked separately from home in far-flung places stretching from the Pacific Northwest to the Atlantic Northeast, though they came together once for an intensive and socially rollicking weekend in Portland, Oregon. Though each member of the team had separate assignments, many tasks were shared and executed in a model of collaboration.

The Team comprised:
DOUGLAS GERWIN
Executive Director of the Research Institute for Waldorf Education (RIWE)

ILAN SAFIT
Editor of RIWE's twice-yearly *Research Bulletin* and primary writer of this Survey

ANDREW STARZYNSKI
Math teacher and primary statistician, data analyst, and designer of the graphs
and accompanying PowerPoint of the Survey

CONNIE STOKES
Overall manager of the Survey, including primary interviewer, contact person with
schools, negotiator with NAIS, convener of online meetings, and generous host of
our weekend session at her home in Portland

To this list should be added:

LIZ BEAVEN
who served as initial manager of the project, drafting the plan of action
before handing on the task to Connie Stokes. Liz also conducting two of the
face-to-face interviews

STEPHANIE RYNAS
AWSNA's Executive Director for Operations & Member Resources, who assisted
the project during its early phases with the organization and presentation of data

THE CONTRIBUTORS
Individual names are too numerous to list, and in any case, many contributed as
anonymous respondents to surveys and requests for written reflections and responses.
These include:

1066 STUDENTS
who filled out the (sometimes lengthy) questionnaires and submitted them
electronically to the Research Institute within the timeframe of the survey

22 ALUMNI
from across the continent and spanning 25 years of Waldorf graduates who agreed
to be interviewed in person. Their names are listed separately in Appendix C

75 WALDORF HIGH-SCHOOL TEACHERS
who agreed to submit reflections and insights on the students they had taught
over the past three decades

THE NATIONAL ASSOCIATION OF INDEPENDENT SCHOOLS (NAIS)
which agreed to share its own survey and data results in order to give us a wider
lens of comparison. Hilary LaMonte, NAIS's Senior Vice-President of Data and
Analysis for School Leadership, provided especially helpful assistance in making
this data available to us in a manageable form

THE PRODUCERS

Once the survey was complete and edited, the task of bringing this document to the wider world fell to Waldorf Publications at the Research Institute including Patrice Maynard, its intrepid Director and tireless coach, who cheered on the project from its inception, secured the funding needed to support it, and oversaw the publication of the data in its various forms.

THE FUNDERS

Though many of the participants cited above acted as volunteers for this project, none of it would have been realized without substantial multi-year grants awarded by the Waldorf Curriculum Fund and the Waldorf Educational Foundation, which generously supported this enterprise from its pre-embryonic envisioning to final birth as a printed publication and online resource.

A final acknowledgement goes to David Mitchell, Co-Director of the Research Institute and managing architect of the first survey of Waldorf alumni some 15 years ago, whose vision and imagination for this work survived his death in 2012 and lives on in the form—and even some of the more thought-provoking questions—of the follow-up survey now completed.

Bibliography

This survey in its entirely, *Into the World, How Waldorf Graduates Fare after High School*, is included in the research gathered and presented on the Research Institute for Waldorf Education's (RIWE's) web site, www.waldorfresearchinstitute.org/ research-on-waldorf-graduates-into-the-world-how-waldorf-graduates-fare-after-high-school/. The PowerPoint, which provides a useful summary for the findings of the survey, can also be found separately in the same place for use in presenting to wider communities. Copies of the printed book of this survey can be purchased at www.waldorfpublications.org.

Readers wishing to delve deeper into the subject of how students fare after graduating from a Waldorf high school may find further material in the following resources, many of which served as the backdrop to our own survey:

RIWE'S SURVEYS OF WALDORF GRADUATES

Faith Baldwin, Douglas Gerwin, & David Mitchell, *Survey of Waldorf Graduates, Phase I* (AWSNA Publications, 2005)

David Mitchell & Douglas Gerwin, *Survey of Waldorf Graduates, Phase II* (AWSNA Publications, 2007)

David Mitchell & Douglas Gerwin, *Survey of Waldorf Graduates, Phase III* (AWSNA Publications, 2008)
"Standing Out Without Standing Alone"

"Summary of German/Swiss Study of Waldorf Graduates"
"Summary of Swedish Waldorf Schools Evaluation Report"
"The Health and Heartiness of Waldorf Graduates"
"The Results of Waldorf Education"

OTHER PUBLISHED RESOURCES

Heiner Barz & Dirk Randoll, *Absolventen von Waldorfschulen: Eine empirische Studie zu Bildung und Lebensgestaltung* (VS Verlag für Sozialwissenschaften, 2007).

Douglas Gerwin, "Waldorf Senior Survey" in RIWE *Research Bulletin*, Vol. XI Number 1.

Christine Hether, "The Moral Reasoning of High-School Seniors from Diverse Educational Settings" in RIWE *Research Bulletin*, Vol. XII Number 1.

Aksel Hugo, "Nurturing Human Growth: A Research Strategy for Waldorf Schools" in RIWE *Research Bulletin*, Vol. XI Number 2.

Peter Lawton, "The Transition Experience of Waldorf Elementary Students Attending Non-Waldorf High Schools" in RIWE *Research Bulletin*, Vol. XXIII Number 2.

Judy Lubin, "What Will Today's Children Need for Financial Success in Tomorrow's Economy?" in RIWE *Research Bulletin*, Vol. XII Number 1.

Jon McAlice, "What Have We Learned? Comparing Studies of German, Swiss, and North American Waldorf School Graduates" in RIWE *Research Bulletin*, Vol. XIII Number 2.

Wanda Ribeiro & Juan Pablo de Jesus Pereira, "Seven Myths of Social Participation of Waldorf Graduates" in RIWE *Research Bulletin*, Vol. XV Number 2.

Rudolf Steiner, "On Spiritual Research" in RIWE *Research Bulletin*, Vol. XII Number 1.

Sebastian Suggate, "Reading Research Supports the Waldorf Approach" in RIWE *Research Bulletin*, Vol. XVI Number 1.

WEBSITES AND VIDEOS

https://www.youtube.com/watch?v=6nXKPu3TerI
https://www.thewaldorfs.waldorf.net
https://www.youtube.com/watch?v=js_8EfdPpp0
https://www.youtube.com/watch?v=SiH-_P097h0
https://www.youtube.com/watch?v=RncVJFga0eA
https://en.wikipedia.org/wiki/Studies_of_Waldorf_education

Appendix A

Demographics of Waldorf High Schools Polled in the Survey

School Name		HS Founded	1st Graduating Class	Total Graduates	Total Grads Since 1990	Percent going from 8th to 9th Grade 2016-2017	Directly to College	Junior or Community College	Gap Year	Other
Academe of the Oaks	HS	2003	2006	153	153	50%	99%	0%	1%	
Austin Waldorf School	K-12	1997	2001	314	314	67%	90%	10%		
Berkshire Waldorf HS	HS	2002	2006	74	74	38%	85%	10%	5%	1%
Chicago Waldorf School	K-12	1994	1995	336	336	48%	90%	5%	5%	
Denver Waldorf School	K-12	1995	1998	209	209	35%	95%	4%	1%	
Emerson Waldorf School	K-12	2002	2006	116	116	30%	90%	3%	4%	3%
Green Meadow Waldorf School	K-12	1972	1976	600	378	85%	90%	5%	5%	
Haleakala Waldorf School	K-12	2013	2016	24	24		90%	5%	5%	
Hartsbrook School	K-12	2002	2006	110	110	54%	90%	5%	5%	
Hawthorne Valley School	K-12	1980	1983	530	432	25%	80%	10%	10%	
High Mowing School	HS	1942	1943	1646	667		79%	3%	12%	
Highland Hall Waldorf School	K-12	1968	1971	896	543	47%	85%	10	5%	
Honolulu Waldorf School	K-12	1994	1998	293	293	60%	60%	30%	10%	
Kimberton Waldorf School	K-12	1964	1967	1123	732	70%	90%	2%	8%	

School Name	HS Founded	1st Graduating Class	Total Graduates	Total Grads Since 1990	Percent going from 8th to 9th Grade 2016-2017	Directly to College	Junior or Community College	Gap Year	Other
Lake Champlain Waldorf School	K-12	2001	2005	155	155	25%	36%	0%	64%	
Maine Coast Waldorf School	K-12	2007	2010	74	74	87%	70%	27	0%	3%
Monadnock Waldorf School	K-12	2010	2013	55	55	42%	80%	0%	20%	
Pasadena Waldorf School	K-12	2012	2016	32	32	46%	90%	5%	3%	2%
Portland Waldorf School	K-12	1999	2003	245	245	30%	90%	5%	5%	
Rudolf Steiner School of Ann Arbor	K-12	1997	2000	354	354	43%	95%	4%	1%	
Rudolf Steiner School NYC	K-12	1955	1959	865	445	81%	95%	1%	4%	
Sacramento Waldorf School	K-12	1974	1978	1106	841	37%	90%	8%	2%	
San Francisco Waldorf School	K-12	1997	2001	493	493	69%	96%	2%	1%	1%
Santa Fe Waldorf School	K-12	2001	2005	111	111	50%	90%	2%	7%	1%
Seattle Waldorf School	K-12	2007	2008	135	135	46%	68%	3%	17%	12%
Hazel Wolf High School	HS	1999	2002							
Shining Mountain Waldorf School	K-12	1991	1996	406	406	61%	85%	5%	8%	2%
Summerfield Waldorf School	K-12	1987	1991	550	550	69%	65%	18%	12%	5%
Tara Performing Arts	HS	1997	2001	177	177		50%	0%	50%	
Toronto Waldorf School	K-12	1975	1979	751	599	82%	75%		25%	
Vancouver Waldorf School	K-12	1981	1984	385	341	43%				

School Name		HS Founded	1st Graduating Class	Total Graduates	Total Grads Since 1990	Percent going from 8th to 9th Grade 2016-2017	Directly to College	Junior or Community College	Gap Year	Other
Waldorf School of Garden City	K-12	1956	1960	1174	557	84%	90%	3%	7%	
Waldorf High School of Massachusetts Bay	HS	1996	2000	227	227		90%	3%	7%	
Waldorf School of Orange County	K-12	2007	2011	71	71	63%	75%	14%	8%	3%
Waldorf School of Peninsula	K-12	2007	2011	96	96	58%	84%	8%	4%	4%
Waldorf School of San Diego	K-12	2008	2012	65	65	52%				
Waldorf School of Saratoga Springs	K-12	1998	2001	188	188	57%				
Washington Waldorf School	K-12	1984	1988	399	381	67%	95%	0%	5%	
Whistler Waldorf School	K-12	2013	2016	7	7	80%	20%	0%	80%	
Youth Initiative High School	HS	1996	1997	195	195		29%	9%	29%	33%
TOTAL				14587	11028					

NOTE

The "other" column is for graduates who did not fit into the previous three categories. Greyed out cells indicate either Not Applicable or Data Not Available. These numbers indicate that there have been a total of 14,587 Waldorf high-school graduates in North America, 11,028 of them since 1990.

Appendix B

Sample List of Colleges Attended by Alumni from 1990-2017

Agnes Scott College

American Academy of Dramatic Arts

American University

American River College

Amherst College

Art Center College of Design

Bard College

Bates College

Berklee College of Music

Beloit College

Bennington College

Binghamton University

Blanche McDonald College

Boston College

Boston University

Bowdon College

Brandeis University

Brigham Young University

Brown University

Butler University

Cabrillo College

Cal Maritime

Cal State Humboldt

Cal State Northridge

California Lutheran University

California Polytechnic University (Cal Poly, SLO)

California State Long Beach

Capilano University

Chaminade University of Honolulu

Chapman University

Clark University

College of the Atlantic

College of William and Mary

Colorado College

Colorado Mesa University

Colorado State

Colorado University of Boulder

Columbia College, Chicago

Columbia University

Connecticut College

Cornell College

Cornish College of the Arts

CSU Chico

CSU Sacramento

Dalhousie University

Dartmouth College

Davidson College

DePaul University

Dickinson College

Dominican University of California

Drew University

Eastern Michigan University

Eckerd College

Elms College

Elon University

Emerson College

Emily Carr University of Art and Design

Emory University

Eugene Lang: The New School

Evergreen College

Fashion Institute of Technology

Folsom Lake College

Georgia College and State University

Georgia State University

Goucher College

Green Mountain College

Guilford College

Hampshire College

Harvard University

Hawaii Pacific University

Hofstra University

Humboldt State University

Indiana University

Iowa State University

Ithaca College

John Jay College of Criminal Justice CUNY

Kalamazoo College

Kennesaw State University

Kenyon College

Kutztown University

Lawrence University

Lesley University

Lewis and Clark College

Long Island Universtiy/CW Post

Loyola Marymount University

Macalester College

Maine College of Art

Madison Area Technical College

McGill University

Michigan State University

Minneapolis College of Art and Design

Monouth University

Montana State

Morehouse College

Mount Holyoke College

Nassau Community College

New York University (NYU)

North Carolina State University

Northeastern University

Northland College

Northwestern University

Nova Scotia

Oberlin College

Occidental College

Oglethorpe University

Oregon State University

Penn State

Portland Community College

Portland State University

Pratt Institute

Prescott College

Princeton University

Purdue University

Queen's University

Quest College

Quest University

Reed College

Rhodes College

Rhode Island School of Design (RISD)

Rochester Institute of Technology

Rollins College

Rutgers University

Ryerson University

San Francisco State University

Santa Clara University

Santa Rosa Junior College

Sarah Lawrence College

Savannnah College of Art and Design

School at the Art Institute of Chicago

School of Visual Arts

Seattle University

Sierra College

Simmons College

Simon Fraser University

Skidmore College

Smith College

Sonoma State University

State University of NY at New Paltz

Stoney Brook University

St Mary's College

St. Mary's College of Maryland

St. John's College

St. Johns University

St. Olaf College

Stanford University

Stevens Institute of Technology

SUNY Adirondack

Texas A&M University-Corpus Christi

Texas A&M University-College Station

Texas A&M University-Galveston

The College of Wooster

Thomas More College

Trent University

UC Berkeley

UC Davis

UC San Diego

UC Santa Barbara

UC Santa Cruz

UNC-Asheville

UNC-Chapel Hill

UNC-Greensboro

UNC-Wilmington

United States Naval Academy

University for Creative Careers (SCAD)

University of Alaska Fairbanks

University of Albany

University of Arizona

University of Bridgeport

University of British Columbia

University of Colorado

University of Denver

University of Georgia

University of Hartford

University of Hawaii at Hilo

University of Illinois at Urbana-Champaign

University of Illinois at Chicago

University of Iowa

University of King's College

University of Maine at Farmington

University of Maryland, College Park

University of Massachusetts, Amherst

University of Massachusetts, Dartmouth

University of Miami

University of Michigan

University of Montana

University of New England

University of New Hampshire

University of Northern Colorado

University of Oregon

University of Portland

University of Puget Sound

University of Redlands

University of St. Andrews, Scotland

University of San Francisco

University of Texas at Austin

University of Texas at Dallas

University of Texas at San Antonio Honors College

University of Toronto

University of Vermont

University of Victoria

University of Washington, Seattle

University of Waterloo

University of Wisconsin-Madison

University of Wisconsin-Milwaukee

University of Wisconsin-Richmond

Ursinus College

Vanderbilt University

Vassar College

Warren Wilson College

Wellesey College

Wells College

Wesleyan University

Westchester University

Western Washington University

Whitman College

Worcester Polytechnic Institute

York University

Appendix C
List of Waldorf Alumni Interviewed Face-to-Face

Dorian Alexis	2017	Emerson Waldorf School, Chapel Hill, NC
Genevieve Angle Soloway	1996	Waldorf School of Garden City, NY
John Beaven	1998	Sacramento Waldorf School, Fair Oaks, CA
Jennifer Dorman Weuker	1995	Waldorf School of Garden City, NY
Carol Di Passero	1990	Highland Hall Waldorf School, Northridge, CA
Nicolai Eddy	2010	Rudolf Steiner of Ann Arbor, Ann Arbor, MI
Grace Evans	2008	Portland Waldorf School, Milwaukee, OR
Emma Hulbert	2017	Emerson Waldorf School, Chapel Hill, NC
Molly Kaplan	2006	Highland Hall Waldorf School, Northridge, CA
Cariel Klein	2011	Hartsbrook School, Hadley, MA
Lucy Latuner	2014	Hartsbrook School, Hadley, MA
Grainne Ortlieb	2014	Highland Hall Waldorf School, Northridge, CA
Helena Ortlieb	2016	Highland Hall Waldorf School, Northridge, CA
Morgan Pepper	2007	Highland Hall Waldorf School, Northridge, CA
Caitlin Ragan	2007	Chicago Waldorf School, Chicago, IL
Dennis Robles	2007	Chicago Waldorf School, Chicago, IL
Kiah Shapiro	2007	Chicago Waldorf School, Chicago, IL
Max Silver	2007	Washington Waldorf School, Bethesda, MD
Gareth Soloway	1999	Waldorf School of Garden City, NY
Peter Starzynski	2000	Chicago Waldorf School, Chicago, IL
John Paul Takacs	2016	Portland Waldorf School, Milwaukie, OR
"Anonymous"		Summerfield Waldorf School, Santa Rosa, CA

Appendix D

AWSNA Survey of Waldorf College-Age Alumni/ae 2018

The National Association of Independent Schools has been asked to conduct an online survey of recent Waldorf graduates on behalf of the Research Institute for Waldorf Education supported by the Association of Waldorf Schools of North America (AWSNA). If you graduated from 12th grade between 1990 and 2017 from an AWSNA member high school in the U.S. or Canada, we are asking you to complete this survey. Your perspective is important. We are interested to know how attending a Waldorf school has affected your life and career.

We estimate this survey should take you approximately 20-30 minutes to complete. Your participation is, of course, strictly voluntary and you may withdraw your participation at any time. You may skip any question you prefer not to answer.

All information collected will be kept confidential and may be used only to inform decisions about education programs and the organizational aspects of Waldorf schools. Your responses will never be connected to your name in the results or future publication. A professional analysis of the overall results of this survey will be circulated internationally as part of a published research project on the results of Waldorf education during the run-up to the worldwide 100th year anniversary of Waldorf education in 2019.

If you have any technical questions, please contact: surveycenterhelp@nais.org .

If you have questions regarding the content, please contact Connie Stokes at cstokes@awsna.org

By clicking NEXT you are verifying that you have read the explanation of the survey, that you are 18 or over and that you agree to be a participant. You also understand that your participation in this survey is strictly voluntary.

Thank you for participating in this survey of Waldorf education from the perspective of its graduates.

Part I: Background

1. From which school did you graduate?

2. What was your year of graduation?

3. While at your school, what type of student were you? (Please select all that apply.)
☐ Day student   ☐ Boarding student   ☐ Other, please specify

4. Which grades did you attend at the school from which you graduated (named above)?
Pre-K   K   1   2   3   4   5   6   7   8   9   10   11   12   Post graduate
Begin
End

5. What was your primary interest while a student at your school?
☐ Academic   ☐ Music and/or arts   ☐ Other, please specify
☐ Athletic   ☐ Extra-curricular

6. After graduating from high school, did you go on directly to college?
☐ Yes   ☐ No

7. Did you take a gap year?
☐ Yes   ☐ No

8. How did you spend this gap year?

9. How long did this gap year last?

☐ Less than one year   ☐ One year   ☐ More than one year

10. What did you do between completing high school and entering college?
(Select all that apply.)

☐ Traveled

☐ Worked in a full-time job

☐ Worked in a part-time job

☐ Undertook paid internship (please provide details below)

☐ Undertook unpaid internship (please provide details below)

☐ Volunteered (please provide details below)

☐ Lived at home

☐ Undertook preparatory course for entering college

☐ Undertook vocational training (please provide details below)

☐ Joined sports or athletic team (please provide details below)

☐ Did something really cool (please provide details below)

☐ Other, please specify

11. Details for any of the selections above that request more description.
(If more than one, please note the response above to which each set of details is referring.)

Part II: Preparation for College
Tell us how well your school prepared you for your college experience.

12. Are you currently attending a college or university?

☐ Yes   ☐ No

13. Overall, how well did your school prepare you for your college/university experience?

☐ Very well   ☐ Somewhat well   ☐ Not well at all
☐ Well   ☐ Not too well

14. How well did your school prepare you in the following basic education skills?

	Very well	Well	Somewhat well	Not too well	Not well at all	Not applicable
Writing	☐	☐	☐	☐	☐	☐
Studying	☐	☐	☐	☐	☐	☐
Conducting research	☐	☐	☐	☐	☐	☐
Interpreting mathematical/ scientific concepts	☐	☐	☐	☐	☐	☐
Using technology	☐	☐	☐	☐	☐	☐

15. How well did your school prepare you in these additional skills?

	Very well	Well	Somewhat well	Not too well	Not well at all	Not applicable
Public speaking	☐	☐	☐	☐	☐	☐
Contributing to class discussions	☐	☐	☐	☐	☐	☐
Taking a leadership role	☐	☐	☐	☐	☐	☐
Working collaboratively on a team	☐	☐	☐	☐	☐	☐
Balancing workload	☐	☐	☐	☐	☐	☐

16. How well did your school prepare you in the following areas?

	Very well	Well	Somewhat well	Not too well	Not well at all	Not applicable
Being creative and innovative	☐	☐	☐	☐	☐	☐
Being open-minded	☐	☐	☐	☐	☐	☐
Empathizing with others	☐	☐	☐	☐	☐	☐
Appreciating and/ or participating in the arts	☐	☐	☐	☐	☐	☐
Practicing sports and/ or exercising regularly	☐	☐	☐	☐	☐	☐
Thinking in whole pictures	☐	☐	☐	☐	☐	☐

17. How well did your school prepare you in the following subjects?

	Very well	Well	Somewhat well	Not too well	Not well at all	Not applicable
English: reading and composition	☐	☐	☐	☐	☐	☐
English: literature	☐	☐	☐	☐	☐	☐
History	☐	☐	☐	☐	☐	☐
Geography	☐	☐	☐	☐	☐	☐
Performing arts	☐	☐	☐	☐	☐	☐
Visual arts	☐	☐	☐	☐	☐	☐

18. What about these additional subjects? How well did your school prepare you in these areas?

	Very well	Well	Somewhat well	Not too well	Not well at all	Not applicable
Science	☐	☐	☐	☐	☐	☐
Health	☐	☐	☐	☐	☐	☐
Physical education	☐	☐	☐	☐	☐	☐
Sports/athletics	☐	☐	☐	☐	☐	☐
World languages (French, Spanish, Mandarin, etc.)	☐	☐	☐	☐	☐	☐
Religion	☐	☐	☐	☐	☐	☐
Math	☐	☐	☐	☐	☐	☐

19. When considering other students at your current college/university classes, how would you rank your abilities in comparison?

	Well above average	Above average	Average	Below average	Well below average
Overall academic ability	☐	☐	☐	☐	☐
Study/organizational skills	☐	☐	☐	☐	☐
Analytical skills	☐	☐	☐	☐	☐
Writing ability	☐	☐	☐	☐	☐
Technology skills	☐	☐	☐	☐	☐

20. What about these additional abilities? How would you rank your abilities in comparison to the other students in your current college/university classes?

	Well above average	Above average	Average	Below average	Well below average
Public speaking ability	☐	☐	☐	☐	☐
Leadership ability	☐	☐	☐	☐	☐
Collaboration/team skills	☐	☐	☐	☐	☐
Self-confidence	☐	☐	☐	☐	☐

21. As you look back on your years at your school, what were the most valuable aspects of your Waldorf school experience? (Rate your top 5, with 1 being the most valuable.)

	1	2	3	4	5
Core academic courses	☐	☐	☐	☐	☐
Elective courses	☐	☐	☐	☐	☐
AP courses	☐	☐	☐	☐	☐
Interaction with teachers	☐	☐	☐	☐	☐
Interaction with staff	☐	☐	☐	☐	☐
Small class sizes	☐	☐	☐	☐	☐
Individualized attention	☐	☐	☐	☐	☐
Participation in athletic teams/sports	☐	☐	☐	☐	☐
Participation in specialized clubs	☐	☐	☐	☐	☐
Foreign exchange while in HS	☐	☐	☐	☐	☐
Service learning	☐	☐	☐	☐	☐
Academic overnight field trips	☐	☐	☐	☐	☐
Culture of your school	☐	☐	☐	☐	☐
Other students at your school	☐	☐	☐	☐	☐
Participation in community service/volunteer activities	☐	☐	☐	☐	☐
Participation in travel abroad programs	☐	☐	☐	☐	☐

22. As you look back on your years at your school, what other courses of study or extracurricular activities could have been offered that would have enhanced your experience or better prepared you for college/university?

Part III: College Selection

23. The institution in which you are currently enrolled is your:
☐ First-choice college/university   ☐ Third-choice college/university
☐ Second-choice college/university   ☐ Other

24. Did someone in your family attend this college/university? (Choose all that apply.)
☐ Mother   ☐ Sibling   ☐ No family member attended
☐ Father   ☐ Other relative   this college/university

25. How satisfied are you that the college/university in which you are currently enrolled is the right match for you?
☐ Very satisfied   ☐ Somewhat satisfied   ☐ Very dissatisfied
☐ Satisfied   ☐ Dissatisfied   ☐ Don't know

26. Why?

27. How important were the following factors in your choice to attend this college/university?

	Very important	Important	Somewhat important	Of little importance	Unimportant	Not applicable
Location of school	☐	☐	☐	☐	☐	☐
Size of school	☐	☐	☐	☐	☐	☐
Academic program	☐	☐	☐	☐	☐	☐
Cost of school	☐	☐	☐	☐	☐	☐
Reputation of school	☐	☐	☐	☐	☐	☐
Financial assistance offered	☐	☐	☐	☐	☐	☐

28. What about these additional factors? How important were they in your college/university choice?

	Very important	Important	Somewhat	Of little importance	Unimportant	Not applicable important
Culture of/social activities at school	☐	☐	☐	☐	☐	☐
High school college counselor recommended it	☐	☐	☐	☐	☐	☐
High school teacher recommended it	☐	☐	☐	☐	☐	☐
Parent/relative attended school	☐	☐	☐	☐	☐	☐
Friends attend school	☐	☐	☐	☐	☐	☐

29. In what ways did the teachers and staff at your school help you in making the decision to attend this particular college/university? (Choose all that apply.)

☐ Faculty/staff member suggested that this particular college/university would be a good match for me.

☐ Faculty/staff suggested that colleges/universities with characteristics like this one would be a good match for me.

☐ Faculty/staff member wrote recommendations to this college/university on my behalf.

☐ Faculty/staff member was actively involved in working with the college admissions staff at this college/university on my behalf.

☐ Faculty/staff member assisted me in putting together entrance materials for this college/university.

☐ Faculty/staff members were not helpful in my college selection process.

☐ Other, please specify

30. How well did your school's college counseling office prepare/assist you in the following areas?

	Very well	Well	Somewhat well	Not too well	Not well at all	Not applicable
Began the college selection process at an appropriate time in high school	☐	☐	☐	☐	☐	☐
Offered a variety of programs to inform me of the college selection process	☐	☐	☐	☐	☐	☐
Provided an available and accessible counselor	☐	☐	☐	☐	☐	☐
Provide an approachable counselor	☐	☐	☐	☐	☐	☐
Provided a counselor with knowledge of the college selection process	☐	☐	☐	☐	☐	☐
Offered assistance in the development of a college list	☐	☐	☐	☐	☐	☐
Kept me aware of the deadlines	☐	☐	☐	☐	☐	☐
Prepared me for the application process	☐	☐	☐	☐	☐	☐
Assisted me with the application process	☐	☐	☐	☐	☐	☐
Assisted me with career counseling	☐	☐	☐	☐	☐	☐
Provided a satisfactory college counseling experience	☐	☐	☐	☐	☐	☐

Part IV: College Experience
Tell us about your academic and extra-curricular pursuits.

31. In what year of study are you currently?
☐ Freshman   ☐ Junior   ☐ Post-graduate
☐ Sophomore   ☐ Senior

32. Do you anticipate continuing studies and receiving a degree from this institution?
☐ Yes   ☐ No   ☐ Don't Know

33. If no, do you plan to:

☐ Transfer to another college/university

☐ Leave to pursue a professional license

☐ Leave and come back to your current institution at a later date

☐ Leave and pursue no further post-secondary education

☐ Other

34. What major are you currently pursuing, or do you expect to pursue? (Choose two if double major.)

☐ Architecture

☐ Anthropology

☐ Biological, Environmental, or Physical Sciences

☐ Business/Accounting

☐ Chemistry

☐ Economics

☐ English/Literature

☐ Education

☐ Engineering

☐ Health-related Fields

☐ History

☐ International Studies

☐ Journalism/Communications

☐ Math

☐ Performing Arts

☐ Philosophy

☐ Political Science

☐ Psychology

☐ Religion

☐ Technology/Computer Programming

☐ Sociology

☐ Visual Arts

☐ World Languages

☐ Undecided

☐ Other

☐ Other, please specify

35. What is your current grade point average?

☐ 4.01 or higher

☐ 3.68 to 4.0

☐ 3.34 to 3.67

☐ 3.01 to 3.33

☐ 2.68 to 3.0

☐ 2.34 to 2.67

☐ 2.01 to 2.33

☐ 1.68 to 2.0

☐ 1.34 to 1.67

☐ 1.33 or below

36. In addition to your academic pursuits, what other extracurricular activities are you involved in? (Choose all that apply.)

☐ Member of an athletic team

☐ Member of an academic team (e.g. debate)

☐ Member of a specialized club, center, or group (e.g. drama)

☐ Member of a music group

☐ Volunteer at school or within the community

☐ Volunteer for a political campaign

☐ A part-time or full-time worker (earn wages)

☐ Self-employed or runs own business

☐ Intern in a field I wish to explore as a career

☐ Other

☐ Other, please specify

Part V: Future Plans
Tell us about your plans for the years ahead.

37. As you look to the future, do you plan to: (choose all that apply.)

☐ Complete studies and receive a degree from the college/university in which you are currently enrolled

☐ Transfer to another college/university, complete studies, and receive a degree

☐ Pursue further study towards a Master's degree, Ph.D., or professional degree, such a J.D. or M.D.

☐ Begin your own business

☐ Pursue a career in the for-profit business world

☐ Pursue a career in the nonprofit social sectors world

☐ Other

☐ Other, please specify

38. As you look to the future, in what profession do you think you will pursue a career?

☐ The arts
☐ Business
☐ Community service/social sector
☐ Education/teaching

☐ Engineering
☐ Journalism/communications
☐ Law
☐ Medicine/dentistry

☐ Science
☐ Technology
☐ Other
☐ Other, please specify

39. Did your experience at your school influence your thinking about a career choice?

☐ Yes   ☐ No

40. Please describe:

Part VI: Connection to School Today
Tell us about your interaction with members of your school community today.

41. In which ways do you stay in touch with your school's community (check all that apply):

☐ Keep in touch with old classmates

☐ Read alum publications (e.g. newsletters, magazine, e-newsletter, etc.)

☐ Attend reunions

☐ Attend other alumni events

☐ Keep in touch with faculty

☐ Keep in touch with staff

☐ Contribute to the school's annual fund

☐ Volunteer in some capacity for the school

☐ Stay connected through family members now attending the school

☐ Use social networking sites (e.g. Facebook, Twitter, LinkedIn, etc.)

☐ Attend school athletic events

☐ Attend school festivals

☐ Attend school assemblies, forums, outreach events

☐ Attend school fairs (e.g. harvest fairs, holiday fairs, May fair, etc.)

☐ Attend school plays

☐ None of the above

42. How well does your school do in keeping you connected/informed as an alum?

☐ Very well   ☐ Somewhat well   ☐ Not well at all

☐ Well   ☐ Not too well

43. What kinds of alum services would you like to see your school offer that it doesn't offer now? Please describe.

44. Of the choices below, in which ways would you like your school to stay connected with you? (Select all that apply.)

☐ Print/magazines/newsletters   ☐ E-mail updates   ☐ Social networking sites

☐ Alum events   ☐ Calls from students ☐ Other, please specify

Part VII: About You

We would like to ask a few questions about how you describe yourself. This information is confidential and will be used for analysis only. You may skip any question you do not wish to answer.

45. Your current gender identity is (please check all that apply):

☐ Male   ☐ Transgender   ☐ Intersex

☐ Female   ☐ Genderqueer/   ☐ Other, please specify
                           gender non-conforming

46. Are you of Hispanic or Latino origin?

☐ Yes   ☐ No

47. Your race is (check all that apply):

☐ White   ☐ American Indian or   ☐ Native Hawaiian or Other
                           Alaska Native   Pacific Islander
☐ Black or African American
                         ☐ Asian

48. Your approximate yearly income, including your spouse or domestic partner before taxes in the most recently completed year was:

☐ Less than $30,000   ☐ $80,000 to $99,999   ☐ $350,000 to $499,999

☐ $30,000 to $39,999   ☐ $100,000 to $149,999   ☐ $500,000 to $749,999

☐ $40,000 to $59,999   ☐ $150,000 to $199,999   ☐ $750,000 to $999,999

☐ $60,000 to $79,999   ☐ $200,000 to $349,999   ☐ $1,000,000 or higher

49. What was your parents' combined income in the most recently completed year?

☐ Less than $30,000
☐ $30,000 to $39,999
☐ $40,000 to $59,999
☐ $60,000 to $79,999

☐ $80,000 to $99,999
☐ $100,000 to $149,999
☐ $150,000 to $199,999
☐ $200,000 to $349,999

☐ $350,000 to $499,999
☐ $500,000 to $749,999
☐ $750,000 to $999,999
☐ $1,000,000 or higher

50. What is the highest degree earned by your mother?

☐ High school
☐ Some college
☐ Associate's degree: occupational, technical or vocational program

☐ Associate's degree: academic program
☐ Bachelor's degree
☐ Master's degree

☐ Professional degree (J.D., M.D., D.V.M., etc.)
☐ Doctoral degree
☐ None of the above

51. What is the highest degree earned by your father?

☐ High school
☐ Some college
☐ Associate's degree: occupational, technical or vocational program

☐ Associate's degree: academic program
☐ Bachelor's degree
☐ Master's degree

☐ Professional degree (J.D., M.D., D.V.M., etc.)
☐ Doctoral degree
☐ None of the above

APPENDIX E

AWSNA Survey of Waldorf Post-College Alumni 2018
Introduction

The National Association of Independent Schools has been asked to conduct an online survey of recent Waldorf graduates on behalf of the Research Institute for Waldorf Education supported by the Association of Waldorf Schools of North America (AWSNA). If you graduated from 12th grade between 1990 and 2017 from an AWSNA member high school in the U.S. or Canada, we are asking you to complete this survey. Your perspective is important. We are interested to know how attending a Waldorf school has affected your life and career.

We estimate this survey should take you approximately 20-30 minutes to complete. Your participation is, of course, strictly voluntary and you may withdraw your participation at any time. You may skip any question you prefer not to answer.

All information collected will be kept confidential and may be used only to inform decisions about education programs and the organizational aspects of Waldorf schools. Your responses will never be connected to your name in the results or future publication. A professional analysis of the overall results of this survey will be circulated internationally as part of a published research project on the results of Waldorf education during the run-up to the worldwide 100th year anniversary of Waldorf education in 2019.

If you have any technical questions, please contact: surveycenterhelp@nais.org.

If you have questions regarding the content, please contact Connie Stokes at cstokes@awsna.org

By clicking NEXT you are verifying that you have read the explanation of the survey, that you are 18 or over and that you agree to be a participant. You also understand that you participation in this survey is strictly voluntary.

Thank you for participating in this survey of Waldorf education from the perspective of its graduates.

Background

1. From which school did you graduate?

2. What was your year of graduation?

3. While at your school, what type of student were you? (Please select all that apply.)
☐ Day student   ☐ Boarding student   ☐ Other, please specify

4. Which grades did you attend at the school from which you graduated (named above)?
Pre-K   K   1   2   3   4   5   6   7   8   9   10   11   12   Post graduate
Begin
End

5. Did you attend other Waldorf school(s) prior to the one from which you graduated?

☐ Yes   ☐ No

6. What was the name of the other Waldorf school that you attended?

7. Which grades did you attend at this Waldorf school?
Pre-K   K   1   2   3   4   5   6   7   8   9   10   11   12   Post graduate
Begin
End

8. Did you study abroad (outside North America) on exchange or foreign study while being a Waldorf high school student?
☐ Yes   ☐ No

9. In which country(ies)?

10. For how long?

11. At a Waldorf high school?
☐ Yes   ☐ No

12. Did you take a gap year between high school and college?
☐ Yes   ☐ No

13. What did you do?

Education

14. What is highest level of education you completed?

☐ High school   ☐ Associate's degree: ☐ Professional degree (J.D.,
☐ Some college   academic program   M.D., D.V.M., etc.)
☐ Associate's degree: ☐ Bachelor's degree   ☐ Doctoral degree
   occupational, technical or ☐ Master's degree   ☐ None of the above
   vocational program

15. Please describe your highest level of education in the space provided:

16. In what subject did you receive your highest degree?

17. Please list the subject in the space provided below.

18. If applicable, in what subject area did you earn your undergraduate degree?

Other, please specify

19. Are you currently pursuing a degree or certificate?

☐ Yes   ☐ No   ☐ Unsure

20. Which of the following are you pursuing? (Please select all that apply.)

☐ Associate's degree: occupational, technical or vocational degree

☐ Associate's degree: academic program

☐ Bachelor's degree

☐ Master's degree in arts and sciences (e.g.,MA, MS, MFA)

☐ Master of Business Administration (MBA)

☐ Other master's degree (e.g., MSW, MSE, MSN, MAT, MPA)

☐ Law degree (JD or LLB)

☐ Medical degree (e.g.,MD, DO, DDS, DVM, PharmD)

☐ PhD

☐ Other doctoral degree (e.g., EdD, PsyD, DBA)

☐ Other certificate

☐ Other degree

21. Please type the name of the certificate below.

22. Please type the name of the degree below.

23. What did you do immediately following graduation?

24. What type of occupation are you currently pursuing?

25. How long have you been in this occupation?

26. Did you seek additional training for your occupation?

☐ Yes   ☐ No

27. Please describe the additional training that you sought:

28. Are you planning to pursue additional education?

☐ Yes   ☐ No   ☐ Unsure

29. Which of the following are you planning to pursue? (Please select all that apply.)

☐ Associate's degree:
occupational, technical
or vocational degree

☐ Associate's degree:
academic program

☐ Bachelor's degree

☐ Master's degree in arts
and sciences (e.g., MA,
MS, MFA)

☐ Master of Business
Administration (MBA)

☐ Other master's degree
(e.g., MSW, MSE, MSN,
MAT, MPA)

☐ Law degree (JD or LLB)

☐ Medical degree (e.g., MD,
DO, DDS, DVM, PharmD)

☐ PhD

☐ Other doctoral degree
(e.g., EdD, PsyD, DBA)

☐ Other certificate

☐ Other degree

30. Please type the name of the certificate below.

31. Please type the name of the degree below.

32. Please rate your level of satisfaction or dissatisfaction with how the Waldorf school from which you graduated prepared you for post-high school education.

☐ Very dissatisfied   ☐ Neutral   ☐ Very satisfied

☐ Dissatisfied   ☐ Satisfied

33. Comments about your level of satisfaction or dissatisfaction:

Employment

34. Please select the choice that mostly closely represents your employment status:

35. If you would like to share the name of the company or organization where you work, please use the space provided.

36. If you would like to share your current job title, please use the space provided.

37. In which sector are you employed? (Please select the answer that most closely matches.)

☐ Self-employed in own business or professional non-group practice

☐ For-profit corporation/ company/group-practice

☐ Government or other public institution or agency, including military

☐ Non-profit organization, institution or NGO (non-governmental organization. E.g. environmental, humanitarian, international, etc.)

☐ Other

38. Please enter the sector in which you are employed.

39. Please select the industry that best describes your employer:

40. Please enter your industry in the space provided:

41. Which of the following best describes your current position?

☐ Entry level
☐ Mid-level

☐ Senior level
☐ Executive level (except chief executive)

☐ Chief executive (e.g. CEO, COO, CFO, GM or principal in a business or other organization)
☐ None of the above

42. Please describe your current position.

43. Whether or not you are currently employed, what is your principal occupation?

44. Please enter your principal occupation in the space provided:

45. About your current professional activities:

	Yes	No
Is your current employer a start-up company?	☐	☐
Are you currently developing a start-up company?	☐	☐
Have you ever started a company?	☐	☐
Are you on a corporate board of directors?	☐	☐
Are you a member of a professional, academic, or business association?	☐	☐

46. Please rate your level of satisfaction or dissatisfaction with how the Waldorf school from which you graduated prepared you for your current career.

☐ Very dissatisfied   ☐ Neutral   ☐ Very satisfied
☐ Dissatisfied   ☐ Satisfied

47. Comments:

Experience of Life

48. What is your general level of satisfaction with your life?

☐ Very Dissatisfied   ☐ Neutral   ☐ Very Satisfied

☐ Dissatisfied   ☐ Satisfied

49. What has been your greatest gift thus far in life?

50. What is your greatest challenge thus far in life?

51. What brings you the greatest joy in life?

52. Which of the following skills are most important to you? (Please choose THREE (3).)

☐ Communication   ☐ Leadership   ☐ Truthfulness

☐ Control   ☐ Problem solving   ☐ Wealth

☐ Ethical Standards   ☐ Reputation   ☐ Other, please specify

☐ Initiative   ☐ Sociability

Civic Engagement

53. About how often do you engage in community service or volunteer work for organizations?

☐ Not at all   ☐ Several times a year   ☐ Daily

☐ Less than once a year   ☐ Monthly

☐ Once or twice a year   ☐ Weekly

54. Please rate our school on civic engagement.

☐ Very poor   ☐ Fair   ☐ Very good

☐ Poor   ☐ Good

Faculty at your Waldorf School

55. Please indicate your level of satisfaction or dissatisfaction with faculty at your school in the following areas:

	Very dissatisfied	Dissatisfied	Neutral	Satisfied	Very satisfied
Level of interest in students	☐	☐	☐	☐	☐
Feedback regarding assignments	☐	☐	☐	☐	☐
Willingness to spend time outside of class to discuss issues of interest	☐	☐	☐	☐	☐
Desire to help students grow in more than just academic areas	☐	☐	☐	☐	☐
Non-classroom Interactions	☐	☐	☐	☐	☐

56. On a scale of 1 to 5, with 1 being not influential and 5 being very influential, rate your non-classroom interactions and your Waldorf school in each of the following areas:

	Not influential at all 1	2	Moderately 3	4	Very influential 5
Your personal growth	☐	☐	☐	☐	☐
Your intellectual growth	☐	☐	☐	☐	☐
Your career goals	☐	☐	☐	☐	☐
Your ethical reasoning	☐	☐	☐	☐	☐

57. On a scale of 1 to 5, with 1 being least active and 5 being most active, how active or inactive were you in extracurricular activities while at the Waldorf school from which you graduated?

1 Least active	2	3	4	5 Most active

58. Please check the box next to each of the following in which you participated while at the Waldorf school from which you graduated (check all that apply):

☐ Academics club (e.g. math, science, debate club, etc.)

☐ Athletics

☐ Honor Society

☐ Language club

☐ Multicultural group

☐ Performing arts/ music electives

☐ Political club

☐ Religious group

☐ Service organizations (e.g. Habitat for Humanity, Red Cross, etc.)

☐ Strategic game clubs (e.g. chess, Odyssey of the Mind, etc.)

☐ Student government

☐ Student publications (e.g. yearbook, school paper, etc.)

☐ Working with faculty on research or special projects

☐ Robotics club

☐ I did not participate in any type of school club or group

☐ Other, please specify

Critical Thinking

59. For each of the areas listed below, please rate how well the Waldorf school from which you graduated prepared you:

	Very well	Well	Somewhat well	Not too well	Not well at all	Not applicable
Reading comprehension	☐	☐	☐	☐	☐	☐
Information literacy	☐	☐	☐	☐	☐	☐
Quantitative literacy/ mathematical skills	☐	☐	☐	☐	☐	☐
Critical thinking	☐	☐	☐	☐	☐	☐
Communication	☐	☐	☐	☐	☐	☐
Collaboration	☐	☐	☐	☐	☐	☐
Creativity	☐	☐	☐	☐	☐	☐

60. For each of the areas listed below, please rate how well the Waldorf school from which you graduated prepared you:

Use system thinking (the ability to analyze how parts of a whole produce overall outcomes)

	Very well	Well	Somewhat well	Not too well	Not well at all	Not applicable
Analyze evidence	☐	☐	☐	☐	☐	☐
Analyze alternative points of view	☐	☐	☐	☐	☐	☐
Synthesize information in an argument	☐	☐	☐	☐	☐	☐
Draw conclusions based on the best analysis	☐	☐	☐	☐	☐	☐
Solve unfamiliar problems	☐	☐	☐	☐	☐	☐
Think in whole pictures	☐	☐	☐	☐	☐	☐

Communication

61. For each of the areas listed below, please rate how well the Waldorf school from which you graduated prepared you:

	Very well	Well	Somewhat well	Not too well	Not well at all	Not applicable
Articulate ideas through oral communication	☐	☐	☐	☐	☐	☐
Articulate ideas through written communication	☐	☐	☐	☐	☐	☐
Communicate ideas through non-verbal communications (body language)	☐	☐	☐	☐	☐	☐
Listen effectively	☐	☐	☐	☐	☐	☐
Use multiple media technologies	☐	☐	☐	☐	☐	☐
Communicate effectively in diverse environments (including multilingual and multicultural)	☐	☐	☐	☐	☐	☐

Collaboration

62. For each of the areas listed below, please rate how well the Waldorf school from which you graduated prepared you:

	Very well	Well	Somewhat well	Not too well	Not well at all	Not applicable
Work respectfully with diverse teams	☐	☐	☐	☐	☐	☐
Exercise flexibility to achieve a common goal	☐	☐	☐	☐	☐	☐
Value individual contributions in teamwork	☐	☐	☐	☐	☐	☐
Assume responsibility in teamwork	☐	☐	☐	☐	☐	☐
Creativity and Innovation	☐	☐	☐	☐	☐	☐

63. For each of the areas listed below, please rate how well the Waldorf school from which you graduated prepared you:

	Very well	Well	Somewhat well	Not too well	Not well at all	Not applicable
Brainstorm	☐	☐	☐	☐	☐	☐
Create new ideas	☐	☐	☐	☐	☐	☐
Evaluate new ideas	☐	☐	☐	☐	☐	☐
Identify a problem	☐	☐	☐	☐	☐	☐
Develop a plan based on new ideas	☐	☐	☐	☐	☐	☐

64. In your estimation, how often do you:

	Never	Rarely	Occasionally	Usually	Almost always
Demonstrate originality in your work	☐	☐	☐	☐	☐
Understand the real-world limits to adopting new ideas	☐	☐	☐	☐	☐
View failure as an opportunity to learn	☐	☐	☐	☐	☐

Influence

65. For each of the areas listed below, please rate how well the Waldorf school from which you graduated contributed to your:

	Very well	Well	Somewhat well	Not too well	Not well at all	Not applicable
Self-confidence	☐	☐	☐	☐	☐	☐
Awareness of your weaknesses	☐	☐	☐	☐	☐	☐
Awareness of your strengths	☐	☐	☐	☐	☐	☐
Development of a meaningful perspective on life	☐	☐	☐	☐	☐	☐
Interest in discussing points of view different from your own	☐	☐	☐	☐	☐	☐
Creative capacities	☐	☐	☐	☐	☐	☐
Spiritual/religious orientation	☐	☐	☐	☐	☐	☐
Practical knowledge (e.g. how to repair a bicycle)	☐	☐	☐	☐	☐	☐
Ability to step into the thoughts and feelings of others	☐	☐	☐	☐	☐	☐
Ability to resolve conflicts with others	☐	☐	☐	☐	☐	☐

66. For each of the areas listed below, please rate how well the Waldorf school from which you graduated prepared you to:

	Very well	Well	Somewhat well	Not too well	Not well at all	Not applicable
Lead	☐	☐	☐	☐	☐	☐
Balance workload	☐	☐	☐	☐	☐	☐
Handle competition	☐	☐	☐	☐	☐	☐
Handle criticism	☐	☐	☐	☐	☐	☐
Resolve conflicts	☐	☐	☐	☐	☐	☐
Express your views and attitudes to others	☐	☐	☐	☐	☐	☐
Work on your own and with others	☐	☐	☐	☐	☐	☐
Know your own capacities and limitations	☐	☐	☐	☐	☐	☐
Be fair and tolerant regarding other people's opinions	☐	☐	☐	☐	☐	☐

67. Please describe any aspects of your Waldorf school experience that you viewed critically at the time you were a student, but that you now see in a different light.

Diversity

68. While at the Waldorf school from which you graduated, how often did you interact with the following people or groups of people?

	Never	Rarely	Occasionally	Usually	Almost always
People of a race or ethnicity other than mine	☐	☐	☐	☐	☐
People from an economic background other than mine	☐	☐	☐	☐	☐
People with religious beliefs other than mine	☐	☐	☐	☐	☐
People with political views other than mine	☐	☐	☐	☐	☐
People from cultures or countries other than mine	☐	☐	☐	☐	☐

69. In your personal and professional life now, how often do you interact with the following people or groups of people?

	Never	Rarely	Occasionally	Usually	Almost always
People of a race or ethnicity other than mine	☐	☐	☐	☐	☐
People from an economic background other than mine	☐	☐	☐	☐	☐
People with religious beliefs other than mine	☐	☐	☐	☐	☐
People with political views other than mine	☐	☐	☐	☐	☐
People from cultures or countries other than mine	☐	☐	☐	☐	☐

School Strengths

70. Choose the top strengths of the Waldorf school from which you graduated (Please select no more than THREE (3)):

- ☐ The core academic program
- ☐ The arts program
- ☐ The extracurricular clubs
- ☐ The faculty
- ☐ The staff
- ☐ The culture of the school
- ☐ The individualized attention students received
- ☐ The school's commitment
- to service
- ☐ School grounds
- ☐ The mission of the school
- ☐ Academic facilities (e.g. library, laboratories, computers, etc.)
- ☐ Diversity
- ☐ Honors/advanced classes
- ☐ School climate
- ☐ The science program
- ☐ The humanities program
- ☐ The math program
- ☐ The IT (or computer studies) program
- ☐ The athletic programs
- ☐ Location
- ☐ Other, please specify

School Areas of Improvement

71. Choose the areas that needed the greatest improvement at the Waldorf school from which you graduated during the time you were enrolled (Please select no more than THREE (3)):

- ☐ The core academic program
- ☐ The arts program
- ☐ The extracurricular clubs
- ☐ The faculty
- ☐ The staff
- ☐ The culture of the school
- ☐ The individualized attention students received
- ☐ The school's commitment
- to service
- ☐ School grounds
- ☐ The mission of the school
- ☐ Academic facilities (e.g. library, laboratories, computers, etc.)
- ☐ Diversity
- ☐ Honors/advanced classes
- ☐ School climate
- ☐ The science program
- ☐ The humanities program
- ☐ The math program
- ☐ The IT (or computer studies) program
- ☐ The athletic programs
- ☐ Location
- ☐ Other, please specify

72. Please use the space provided for any additional comments about your time at the Waldorf school from which you graduated:

Connection to your School

73. How connected to this school's community do you feel?

- ☐ Very disconnected
- ☐ Disconnected
- ☐ Neither connected nor disconnected
- ☐ Connected
- ☐ Very Connected

74. In which ways do you stay in touch with your school's community (check all that apply):

☐ Keep in touch with old classmates

☐ Read alum publications (e.g. newsletters, magazine, e-newsletter, etc.)

☐ Attend reunions

☐ Attend other alumni events

☐ Keep in touch with faculty

☐ Keep in touch with staff

☐ Contribute to the school's annual fund

☐ Volunteer in some capacity for the school

☐ Stay connected through family members now attending the school

☐ Use social networking sites (e.g. Facebook, Twitter, LinkedIn, etc.)

☐ Attend school athletic events

☐ Attend school festivals

☐ Attend school assemblies, forums, outreach events

☐ Attend school fairs (e.g. harvest fairs, holiday fairs, May fair, etc.)

☐ Attend school plays

☐ None of the above

75. Did you make any presentations at school events?

☐ Yes   ☐ No

Alumni/ae Services

76. Please rank the following services for alumni/ae in order of importance to you (with 1 being most important and 14 being least important):

☐ Alumni/ae reunions by graduation year

☐ Multi-year alumni/ae reunions

☐ Alumni/ae online communities

☐ Print publications for alumni/ae

☐ Online publications for alumni/ae

☐ Online auctions

☐ Regional gatherings

☐ Alumni/ae lecture series at the school

☐ Alumni/ae lecture series online

☐ Alumni/ae travel abroad opportunities

☐ Volunteer opportunities at the school

☐ Job board

☐ Internship board

Career advancement opportunities

77. Please indicate your level of satisfaction with the following alumni/ae activities/services at the Waldorf school from which you graduated. (If you have not participated in any of the activities below, or if they are not available to you, please select "not applicable.")

	Very satisfied	Satisfied	Somewhat satisfied	Dissatisfied	Very dissatisfied	Not applicable
Alumni/ae reunions by graduation year	☐	☐	☐	☐	☐	☐
Multi-year alumni/ae reunions	☐	☐	☐	☐	☐	☐
Alumni/ae online communities	☐	☐	☐	☐	☐	☐
Print publications for alumni/ae	☐	☐	☐	☐	☐	☐
Online publications for alumni/ae	☐	☐	☐	☐	☐	☐
Online auctions	☐	☐	☐	☐	☐	☐
Regional gatherings	☐	☐	☐	☐	☐	☐
Alumni/ae lecture series at the school	☐	☐	☐	☐	☐	☐
Alumni/ae lecture series online	☐	☐	☐	☐	☐	☐
Alumni/ae travel abroad opportunities	☐	☐	☐	☐	☐	☐
Volunteer opportunities at the school	☐	☐	☐	☐	☐	☐
Job board	☐	☐	☐	☐	☐	☐
Internship board	☐	☐	☐	☐	☐	☐
Career advancement opportunities	☐	☐	☐	☐	☐	☐

78. Please describe any other alumni/ae services you would like to see your school offer?

Feelings about your School

79. How would you describe your overall feelings about your school today?

☐ Very negative ☐ Neutral ☐ Very positive
☐ Negative ☐ Positive

80. How much do you feel...

	Very Weak	Weak	Neutral	Strong	Very Strong
Pride in your affiliation with the school?	☐	☐	☐	☐	☐
An emotional connection to the school?	☐	☐	☐	☐	☐
That the school is part of who you are?	☐	☐	☐	☐	☐

81. On a scale of 1 to 10, with 1 being DEFINITELY WOULD NOT recommend and 10 being DEFINITELY WOULD recommend, how likely are you to recommend our school to a friend or family member?

1   2   3   4   5   6   7   8   9   10

Supporting your School

82. When was the last time that you were asked (by mail, email, telephone, or in person) to make a financial donation to your school?

☐ Within the past month   ☐ Within the past year   ☐ Never been asked
☐ Within the past few months   ☐ More than a year ago   ☐ Do not recall

83. Please rate how well your school is communicating...

	Very well	Well	Somewhat well	Not too well	Not well at all	Not applicable
Its fundraising priorities	☐	☐	☐	☐	☐	☐
The impacts gifts have on the school	☐	☐	☐	☐	☐	☐
Who the beneficiaries of gifts to the school are	☐	☐	☐	☐	☐	☐
Where gifts are directed	☐	☐	☐	☐	☐	☐
How gifts are used	☐	☐	☐	☐	☐	☐

84. If it were up to you, please rank the top 3 (with 1 being most important) objectives to which you would allocate donated money. (Select your top THREE (3) only. Leave the rest blank.)

___ Attracting and retaining the best faculty

___ Improving academics

___ Assisting students to be college-ready when they graduate

___ Creating opportunities for students with financial need

___ Supporting athletic programs

___ Supporting extracurricular programs

___ Supporting field trip opportunities

___ Improving physical grounds

___ Improving facilities

___ Supporting learning technology

___ Supporting professional development for faculty

___ School strategic plan and direction

___ Endowment

___ Financially accessible to those who are Waldorf-educated and yet are not able to afford Waldorf school education for their children

85. How important or unimportant are each of the following considerations in your decision when asked to make a gift to your school?

	Very important	Important	Somewhat	Of little importance	Unimportant	Not applicable
Knowing how your contributions are used	☐	☐	☐	☐	☐	☐
The school's policies	☐	☐	☐	☐	☐	☐
The professional organization of school administration	☐	☐	☐	☐	☐	☐

86. How important are the following types of giving in affecting your decision to give to your school?

	Very important	Important	Somewhat	Of little importance	Unimportant	Not applicable
Giving to other organizations	☐	☐	☐	☐	☐	☐
Giving to loved ones	☐	☐	☐	☐	☐	☐
Giving to other schools	☐	☐	☐	☐	☐	☐
Giving to other non-profit organizations	☐	☐	☐	☐	☐	☐
Giving to other Waldorf-related organizations	☐	☐	☐	☐	☐	☐

87. Apart from your school, do you give money on a regular basis to any charities or other non-profit organizations?

☐ Yes   ☐ No   ☐ Prefer not to say

88. Apart from your school, do you give money on a regular basis to any other schools?

☐ Yes   ☐ No   ☐ Prefer not to say

89. Which of the following most closely resembles your attitude toward giving to your school?

☐ This school is not a giving priority for me.

☐ This school is not a giving priority for me at this time, but may be in the future.

☐ This school is one of my top giving priorities.

☐ This school is my top giving priority.

90. Please provide any additional comments regarding giving to your school:

About You

We would like to ask a few questions about how you describe yourself. This information is confidential and will be used for analysis only. You may skip any question you do not wish to answer.

91. Your current gender identity is (please check all that apply):

☐ Male   ☐ Transgender   ☐ Intersex
☐ Female   ☐ Genderqueer/gender   ☐ Other, please specify
                             non-conforming

92. Are you of Hispanic or Latino origin?

☐ Yes   ☐ No

93. Your race is (check all that apply):

☐ White   ☐ Asian
☐ Black or African American   ☐ Native Hawaiian or Other Pacific Islander
☐ American Indian or Alaska Native

94. Your approximate yearly income, including your spouse or domestic partner before taxes in the most recently completed year was:

☐ Less than $30,000   ☐ $80,000 to $99,999   ☐ $350,000 to $499,999
☐ $30,000 to $39,999   ☐ $100,000 to $149,999   ☐ $500,000 to $749,999
☐ $40,000 to $59,999   ☐ $150,000 to $199,999   ☐ $750,000 to $999,999
☐ $60,000 to $79,999   ☐ $200,000 to $349,999   ☐ $1,000,000 or higher

95. What was your parents' combined income in the most recently completed year?

☐ Less than $30,000   ☐ $80,000 to $99,999   ☐ $350,000 to $499,999
☐ $30,000 to $39,999   ☐ $100,000 to $149,999   ☐ $500,000 to $749,999
☐ $40,000 to $59,999   ☐ $150,000 to $199,999   ☐ $750,000 to $999,999
☐ $60,000 to $79,999   ☐ $200,000 to $349,999   ☐ $1,000,000 or higher

96. What is the highest degree earned by your mother?

☐ High school   ☐ Associate's degree: ☐ Professional degree (J.D.,
☐ Some college   academic program   M.D., D.V.M., etc.)
☐ Associate's degree: ☐ Bachelor's degree   ☐ Doctoral degree
   occupational, technical or ☐ Master's degree   ☐ None of the above
   vocational program

97. What is the highest degree earned by your father?

☐ High school
☐ Some college
☐ Associate's degree: occupational, technical or vocational program

☐ Associate's degree: academic program
☐ Bachelor's degree
☐ Master's degree

☐ Professional degree (J.D., M.D., D.V.M., etc.)
☐ Doctoral degree
☐ None of the above

98. Do you have children?

☐ Yes   ☐ No

99. Do you plan on having children?

☐ Yes   ☐ No

100. Do you plan on sending your children to a Waldorf school?

☐ Yes   ☐ No

101. Why?

102. If you have children, have aspects of your own Waldorf education influenced how you are raising your children?

☐ Yes   ☐ No

103. Please describe how your Waldorf education influences how you are raising your children:

104. What is your relationship to Anthroposophy?

Printed in the USA
CPSIA information can be obtained
at www.ICGtesting.com
LVHW021146100124
768622LV00011B/811